Murder Most Foul

and other great crime stories

from the world press

Murder Most Foul

and other great crime stories

from the world press

Edited by Rob Warden

and Martha Groves

SWALLOW PRESS

OHIO UNIVERSITY PRESS

Chicago   Athens, Ohio   London

First Printing

Published by
The Ohio University Press

Library of Congress Cataloging in Publication Data
Main entry under title:

Murder most foul, and other great crime stories
  from the world press.

    1. Crime and criminals—Case studies. 2. Murder—
Case studies. I. Warden, Rob. II. Groves, Martha.
HV6025.M797   364.1'09   78-51586
ISBN 0—8040—0796—9

Dedication

*To the memory of Clem Lane, Damon Runyon,
Meyer Berger and their tradition.*

Contents

Contents

The Fleece

The Heist

The Getaway

Mass Murder

Kidnap

Old West

Assassination

Introduction

Crime is a staple of the newspaper business. If newspapers exploit it, one can hardly blame them. It sells the product. And, like it or not, crime and the game of wits that plays about it are news because they fascinate and affect us all. "Everybody is a potential murderer," said the great Clarence Darrow. "I've never killed anyone, but I frequently get satisfaction reading the obituary notices."

Crime is entertainment first, perhaps, but it is also history. This collection of newspaper crime coverage spans 189 years—from the hanging of William Brodie in Edinburgh in September, 1788, to the murder of diamond broker Pinchos Jaroslawicz in New York in September, 1977. Most of the forty-seven stories we have chosen are historically significant, although significance was not our criterion. We set out merely to find interesting, well-written stories. In retrospect, however, it is not surprising that the most important events have tended to bring out the best in journalists.

We borrowed our book's title from the *Chicago Times* of May 23, 1889. "Murder Most Foul," the newspaper proclaimed in the largest of a half-page-long stack of headlines reporting the fate of Patrick Henry Cronin, America's leading advocate of Irish home rule. "Dr. Cronin Was Assassinated in Cold Blood by Parties Who Are as Yet Unknown." "His Body Is Found in a Lake View Catch Basin and Is Fully Identified by His Friends." "Many Wounds About the Head Bear Silent Witness as to How He Met His Fate."

As we put together the book, it struck us that crime may be either tragic or comic and, at times, some of both. If Adolph Luetgert murders his wife it is a tragedy, but if Bluebeard of France methodically murders a dozen lovesick women it verges on comedy.

1

This collection shows that the tragicomic elements of crime seldom have been wasted on the press. Consider the murder of Albert Snyder by his wife and her boy friend. "The Dumbbell Murder," Damon Runyon called it. "It was so dumb." Or the flippant headline that the *El Paso Daily Times* ran above a story about a fatal gunfight in 1885: "El Paso Indulges in a Little Pistol Practice." And Clem Lane's lead in the *Chicago Daily News* on a story about a 1935 gangland slaying: "This is the story of 'Two-Gun Louie' Alterie, one-time pugilist, one-time policeman, one-time robber, one-time lieutenant of Johnny Torrio and Dion O'Banion, erstwhile rancher and union business agent, and today the subject of a coroner's inquest as to who shot him and why not sooner."

We have seen newspaper writing change from windy, almost poetic style to a terse science of who, what, when, where, why, and how. Previous generations of editors relied on words rather than graphics. Herbert Bayard Swope of the *New York World* wrote of police Lt. Charles Becker: "He is dark in hair and skin. His nose is straight and big, jutting out uncompromisingly over a long upper lip, a mouth like a cut of a knife and a chin that sticks out squarely at the end of a jaw that looks like a granite block. Yes, Becker is strong—his looks do not belie him—but, with all his strength, he has a certain softness that has enabled him to ingratiate himself with his superiors, that has held their confidence when he was gazed at askance by all others, and that has held the belief of some of his friends unto the last, although he now lies, broken and disgraced, shut off from the world, soon to pay the penalty for his deeds, in the most awful manner known to our law." With writing like that, who needed pictures?

—Rob Warden and Martha Groves
Chicago, 1978

Chapter I

TILL DEATH DO US PART

His wife's wedding ring could put noose around Adolph Luetgert's neck

Adolph L. Luetgert, born in Germany in 1845, said he could trace his lineage to the ancient rulers of his native land. He came to the United States in the big rush from Central Europe, landing at New York in 1866 with only three cents, which he spent on a loaf of bread. He worked at odd jobs before coming to Chicago, where he built a fortune making sausage. When his wife disappeared in 1897, he was arrested for murder. This report on his arrest is from the *Chicago Tribune* of May 18 of that year.

Adolph L. Luetgert, president of the A. L. Luetgert Sausage and Packing Company, and worth $25,000, was arrested yesterday on a charge of having murdered Louisa Luetgert, his wife, on Saturday night, May 1.

Should he be hanged, the wedding ring he placed upon the murdered woman's finger eighteen years ago, when he swore to love, honor, and protect her, will be the thing of all things that will put the noose around his neck.

Acid and quicklime all but made away with her frail body, but they left untouched the golden band of wedlock. In its circle are the telltale initials: L. L.

Luetgert was placed in a cell at East Chicago Avenue. No one was allowed to see him, no exception being made in the case of his attorney, who, after being refused an interview, applied for a writ of habeas corpus returnable before Judge Hutchinson at 12:30 P.M. today. Before that time Luetgert in all probability will be in the County Jail, as he will be arraigned before Justice Kersten at 10:30 A.M. on the warrant charging him with murder sworn out by Detective Joe Kinder.

All night policemen guarded Luetgert's cell, he having said he would never be taken alive. It was feared he might attempt suicide.

Though a man of powerful physique and reputed to be "nervy" to desperation, after the arrest was made, Luetgert collapsed and was almost carried into the police station.

The story of the crime, as recited by the police and officials of the state's attorney's office, is replete with details of one of the most diabolical murders ever committed in this or any other section of the country.

Luetgert is charged with having planned the killing a week in advance, and, when all was ready for the deed, with having enticed his wife from the handsome family residence at ten o'clock at night, after which he led her into the adjacent factory and there struck her down.

The story next has her body dumped into a huge vat, into which had been dumped a barrel of quicklime and a large quantity of chemical liquid, the properties of which have not yet been discovered.

The quicklime and the acid failed to eat away entirely the flesh from the bones and otherwise reduce the body.

After a wait of an hour or two, the portions of the remains were raised and placed in a sausage-curing receptacle, around which are steam coils capable of producing a heat of 200 degrees.

Apparently the destruction was not complete enough to satisfy, and what was not wholly removed in the "smoker" was transferred to the boiler furnace in the engine room. Action here was more thorough.

With the acid and the quicklime and the heat of the fire box, there was nothing left of the body when Luetgert went to breakfast at 6:30 the next morning save pieces of human bone found by the police in the cinders and ashes of the furnace and a

4

Adolph L. Luetgert. (Courtesy Chicago Tribune)

quantity of bone sediment discovered in the bottom of the vat into which Mrs. Luetgert's body was thrown after she was strangled or struck down.

But the most damaging evidence is in two rings that have been identified as the property of Mrs. Luetgert. One of these was the wedding ring, the other a plain guard ring of gold. The police have evidence that Mrs. Luetgert wore the rings on the night she left her house and, as they assert, accompanied her husband to the basement of the factory, where the night's work was done.

When the wedding ring was first placed upon her finger in St. John's Lutheran Church, at Ohio and LaSalle, on her wedding day, it was much too large, and another ring was bought by Mrs. Luetgert to keep it from slipping off. Both rings she had worn constantly until the day of her taking off, but of late the flesh on her fingers had puffed sufficiently, owing to her increasing weight, that it was impossible for either of the rings to slip off or be drawn from the finger. They had the appearance of being partially imbedded there, and only fell from the finger into the vat after the quicklime and acid had done their work on the tissues.

The ring has been one factor leading to the arrest; the failure of Luetgert's business was another equally as important. Mrs. Luetgert was killed on May 1. Three days later Luetgert's business was placed in the hands of the sheriff, a custodian taking charge of the establishment. Just as soon as the police began an investigation, Luetgert became anxious to get into the factory. It would seem he was afraid he had not thoroughly cleaned the vat—which was a fact—and that the fire had not entirely consumed what the acid had left.

He was correct, and to the sheriff's possession of the building, which gave the police a chance to sift ashes and examine vats, is due the discoveries that led to yesterday's arrest.

The disappearance of Mrs. Luetgert became the subject of police inquiry on Friday afternoon, May 7, when Captain Schuettler of the Sheffield Avenue station detailed Detectives Qualey and Dean to visit the Luetgert home. These officers could learn nothing of value on that day. Suicide was vaguely hinted at by Mary Simering, a relative of the Luetgerts, who has been a servant in the family for more than a year.

On the next day Captain Schuettler was visited by Luetgert, who said he was unable to account for his wife's absence, unless she had gone to visit relatives or had thrown herself into the river at the nearby Diversey Avenue bridge or into the stagnant depths of one of the clay pits that are numerous in the vicinity, where several brick kilns are located.

Suspicion was first directed toward Luetgert when the police failed to find Mrs. Luetgert's body in the river or clay holes, and after Captain Schuettler had pondered over Luetgert's strange indifference concerning the fate of his wife and his neglect to report her disappearance until after she had been gone one week.

The captain had not forgotten the conduct displayed by Luetgert several months before when one of his Great Danes strayed from its kennel. This fact was reported quickly by Luetgert, and for several days he haunted the police station seeking information concerning the animal. Day after day he was a visitor there and always betrayed the deepest concern.

Captain Schuettler thought this over and wondered why Luetgert should be overcome at the loss of his dog and apparently care very little about the absence of his wife, the mother of his two children—Louis, 12, and Elmer, 5.

Yet the dragging of the river and the clay holes was continued for one week by Sergeant Spengler and three patrolmen.

Meanwhile, the captain had reported his suspicions to Inspector M. J. Schaack at divisional headquarters, with the result that the theory of murder was taken up and worked upon with great secrecy. Luetgert was left to nurse the delusion that the police were not on his track.

Inspector Schaack, Captain Schuettler, and Detectives Qualey and Dean, equipped for effective work, searched the big factory and talked to employees and neighbors in their hunt for clues, while other policemen worked away in the river and clay holes with grappling hooks and pike poles.

Ash heaps were sifted, the officers working industriously by night while Luetgert slept in his big house a few yards away. The ashes and cinders were examined handful after handful, and every nook and corner of the factory raked over.

The day after these discoveries were made, the *Tribune* printed a story telling of them, giving everyone except the coterie of police officials working on the case the first intimation that Mrs. Luetgert's disappearance was in all probability a crime.

Luetgert was furious when he read the story, and sent two men to the *Tribune* office to demand the authority for the statements made. He also felt it incumbent upon him to visit the Sheffield Avenue station, where he told Captain Schuettler he would kill the man who wrote the story. But something in the captain's manner showed that these protestations were not received in the spirit in which they were offered.

The captain asked him if he really meant what he said when he offered a reward of $200 for his wife. He said he did. Then the captain asked him to write out a promise to that effect. He finally did so.

Another idea struck Luetgert. He would swear out a warrant for the arrest of his wife. But he never did, although the police told him it would be a good thing to do.

All this time the police were gathering threads of evidence that finally were woven into a mesh that State's Attorney Deneen considers of unbreakable strength.

Diedrich Becknese, Mrs. Luetgert's brother, who first called police attention to the case, told of quarrels between husband and wife. The night Mrs. Luetgert disappeared, sources said, she was in a cheerful mood and appeared to be thinking of anything other than suicide.

The relatives of the missing woman were located and interviewed.

Wilhelmina Mueller, Mrs. Luetgert's sister, said she never had heard of the alleged threats to commit suicide and informed the police that bitter quarrels between husband and wife were frequent.

The finding of the charred bones was good evidence, but not strong enough to warrant an arrest. Yesterday, however, the vat was examined, and then came the climax. Close to the bottom of the vat is a draining hole, and, after the body had been removed, the murderer evidently turned the hose in and overflowed the receptacle, withdrawing the plug from the hole near the bottom, thinking that the contents would go to the sewer. The mixture thus diluted with water ran off, but enough remained in the bottom of the vat to betray its character. Upon examination the sediment and the rings were found. Two pint bottles of the sediment were secured and will be formally submitted today to a chemist for analysis, and the pieces of joints and skull to an anatomist.

Mrs. Luetgert, who was forty-two, weighed about 115 pounds, and had her body been placed in the bottom of the "smoker," its incineration, save the bones, would have been a matter of but a few minutes. These smokehouses are five in number and are constructed on the furnace idea. They extend to the top story of the factory and are designed to create a terrific smudge or smoke. Coils run around them, making heat sufficient to dry the sausage placed at the top.

The idea of destroying the body in the vat was the first thought of and acted upon. According to the evidence discovered by the police, the vat was prepared for its gruesome task one week before the murder. The factory had been shut down for weeks, and it was found that there was no excuse for the presence of the destructive compound in the vat.

On the night of the killing, Luetgert left his house between 10:15 and 10:30, accompanied by his wife, for the apparent purpose of going to the office. Contrary to habit, Luetgert went into the basement of the factory, and circumstances seem to indicate that he overcame his wife by choking or hitting her, and then threw her into the vat with its quicklime and acid.

No human being could live there five minutes.

It is believed that the vat, which is twelve feet long, three feet wide, and five feet deep, contained two and a half feet of the compound.

It also has been learned that Luetgert turned on the steam around the vat, the boiler having been fired for the occasion.

During this time Luetgert worked behind doors that he had carefully barricaded and that the watchman failed to open when he made his rounds.

The quicklime and the acid did not act speedily enough, and there are indications that Luetgert sat by the vat waiting for the stuff to do its deadly work. Later, the heat was turned into the smokehouse and the remains thrown into it.

The immense heat consumed all but the harder portion of the bones. These include the ends and joints, which were dismembered by the compound in the vat.

What was not destroyed in the smokehouse was transferred to the furnace.

Meantime, the watchman and William Fulbeck, the hostler, growing suspicious that something wrong was going on within the factory, tried the doors, but they had as well tried to push their way through Gibraltar, so strongly barricaded was the man at work inside. They had, it is said, been told by Luetgert to keep out of the building that night.

When the body of Mrs. Luetgert had been run through the vat, the smokehouse, and the furnace, the murderer turned his attention to the vat, into which he turned a stream of water.

At eight the next morning, Luetgert went into his house, washed, and sat down to a breakfast prepared by Mary Simering.

At ten o'clock the absence of the mother was noted by Luetgert's children. They mentioned the fact to the servant.

Luetgert, when spoken to about the matter, told his boys their mother was away on a visit to their aunt, Mrs. Mueller of Cleveland Avenue. The forenoon was spent by Luetgert in playing with his children and dogs, and after dinner he re-entered the factory. One theory is that on this occasion he carried the ashes and cinders away from the furnace.

A short distance from the main ash pile was found a smaller heap. From this, buttons, a piece of bone, and bits of corset steel have been taken by the police. It was upon this pile that Luetgert is supposed to have dumped the ashes and cinders raked from the furnace.

The events of the night before did not seem to have changed Luetgert's course of life. He went about in an indifferent way, probably giving his work of a few hours previously as little thought as he did action about a year ago, when he drove his wife out of the house at the point of a revolver and threatened to kill her.

Up to within a day or two ago, Luetgert carried himself in an arrogant manner, behaving as if it were nobody's business whether he disposed of his wife or not. He lost his nerve on Sunday and made the statement that he never would be taken alive.

Captain Schuettler established a watch over Luetgert two days after the disappearance was reported. While two or three policemen dragged the river, others guarded the front and rear of the Luetgert residence. Wherever its chief occupant went, a detective was on his trail, and yesterday forenoon, when he went out for a drive with his brother, Arnold Luetgert, a detective jumped into a buggy and followed.

A couple of hours later, Luetgert dropped into a saloon near his factory and among those who lined up at the bar to drink with him was one of Captain Schuettler's men detailed to shadow the subject.

Neighbors of the Luetgerts have done little else for two weeks but discuss the mystery, now cleared up. Luetgert has a number of friends among women of his neighborhood, and it is asserted that the police have the names of three or four who are said to have visited him in his office at improper hours of the night. Luetgert has slept there for several years, and it is asserted that the motive for the crime was Mrs. Luetgert's objection to his conduct.

Mary Simering was closely questioned from time to time. Yesterday Arnold Tripp, a lawyer, appeared before Judge Chetlain and asked for the young woman's release on a writ of habeas corpus. The writ was served upon Inspector Schaack, who at once brought the girl into court. She said she was not being held by the police against her will. Judge Chetlain accepted her statement, and she returned to the East Chicago Avenue station. During the afternoon she was questioned by Inspector Schaack, Captain Schuettler, and Assistant State's Attorney McEwen.

The police arrested Luetgert at his handsome residence on Hermitage Avenue, near Diversey, at 1:30 P.M. The Great Danes that have been noticeable about the house and ample grounds since people began getting curious on the subject of Mrs. Luetgert's disappearance sprang to their feet and growled at the two detectives who had come to charge their master with the murder of his wife. They showed their teeth and would have

11

sprung at the intruders, as they have at all other strangers who have come about the place within the last few days, but little five-year-old Elmer, the baby of the woman whose fate the police are trying to unravel, threw his chubby arms around the necks of first one and then another of the big brutes and petted them.

"Be good, Duke," cried the boy to one of the gaunt animals. "You mustn't bark at the gentlemen," and the child quieted the dogs while the detectives walked on up the steps and rang the bell.

Old Mrs. Simering, Mary's mother, came to the door. The two detectives, Qualey and Dean, stepped immediately into the hall. They said they would like to see Luetgert at once. It was very important business and they could not delay a moment. So old Mrs. Simering led them back to the sitting room where Luetgert and his nephew, Fred Miller, were talking.

The sausage manufacturer had complained of feeling ill in the morning, and had stayed close at home all day. When the detectives entered, he was lying on a sofa. Mrs. Feldt, a widow, who is a friend of the family and has been visiting at the Luetgert home since Saturday, followed the detectives in.

"We have come to arrest you, Mr. Luetgert," said Qualey, "on the charge of murdering your wife."

Luetgert's face turned deadly white. He sprang from the sofa.

"Take me if you want," he cried, "but I am innocent. God knows I am innocent."

"Yes," put in Mrs. Feldt. "Of course he is. Mrs. Luetgert told me lots of times that if ever her husband was bankrupt she would go away."

The detectives broke in on Mrs. Feldt's outburst and read their warrant to Luetgert. He had recovered his equanimity and listened quietly enough until they were through. Then he asked if he might go upstairs and change some of his clothing. Permission was granted. He came down in a few minutes, while Mrs. Feldt was describing how many times Mrs. Luetgert had said that she never could remain with her husband if he should lose his money.

"But," went on Mrs. Feldt, "I said: 'Mrs. Luetgert, a woman's place is always by her husband, no matter what happens.' "

Luetgert then appeared and said he was ready to go. He put on his hat and, drawing on a light overcoat, stepped out to the porch with Miller and the detectives.

"Good-bye, Papa," shouted little Elmer. "Good-bye! Bring Mama back with you."

"I think we had better go," said Luetgert hurriedly, and the party went out the gate and around to the front of the factory, where Captain Schuettler was waiting in a buggy to hear from his men. Luetgert was put into the buggy with him and taken to the Sheffield Avenue station, where he was held until Inspector Schaack ordered him brought to East Chicago Avenue, where no one was allowed to talk with him.

Mrs. Feldt stood out at the gate after Luetgert had been taken away. "It was a shame," she told everyone who came along. "It was a shame. Mrs. Luetgert told me herself, right on that porch, time and time again, that she would leave if her husband ever lost his money. But I said 'No'; I said, 'No, Mrs. Luetgert, a woman's place is by her husband, whatever happens to him.' It's all the fault of the English press. It's all their fault. A-stirring up all this trouble for a good man. And look at the trouble she's a-making for her folks. And him such a nice man, too. Why, all the men in the factory thought everything of him. One of them told something to a German paper two years ago that made trouble for Mr. Luetgert, and I went right over to the factory and I said: 'You tell such things again and I'll settle you,' and I had him a-beggin' in no time."

While Mrs. Feldt talked, little Elmer and the Great Danes kept on with their play in the big yard under the newly budded trees. Curious neighbors stood on the sidewalk near the Luetgert residence and stared steadily at the silent house nestled among the bright green of the trees and bushes. Little groups stood in front of the numerous saloons around the factory and looked first at the deserted, gloomy sausage works and then at the residence back of it on Hermitage Avenue. Newsboys with an eye to business swarmed around the neighborhood selling extra editions of the afternoon papers at all the way from two cents to a nickel and sold out in a brief time in spite of the premium on their wares.

Just as soon as the police placed him under arrest, Luetgert told one of his employees to telephone to W. A. Vincent, his lawyer, to whom he made an assignment when his recent financial troubles came to a head, telling him what had happened.

Vincent hurried to the East Chicago Avenue station and asked to see his client. Captain Barcal, who was in charge, refused to grant an interview. Then Vincent asked Inspector Schaack if he might consult with Luetgert. He was told he could not. Vincent insisted that the prisoner had sent for him and demanded that he be allowed to see the prisoner. Schaack, after sending downstairs to see if Luetgert had sent for the lawyer and finding that he had, still refused to let attorney and client confer.

Then Vincent called the inspector's attention to the statutes, which provide that a prisoner can see his attorney in private at any time.

This had no effect, and then Vincent wrote the following letter:
"Chicago, May 17—Dear Sir: I am the attorney for A. L. Luetgert, now confined in this, the Chicago Avenue police station, on a charge of murder. He has stated to Captain Schuettler, who repeated to you in my presence within the last five minutes, that he had sent for me. I have informed you that as his attorney I desire to consult with him about the charge on which he has been arrested. I now request in writing the privilege of consulting my client. —W. A. Vincent."

This also failed to give the lawyer access to Luetgert.

Assistant State's Attorney McEwen, who was in the room at the time, told Inspector Schaack a lawyer had the right to see his client, but the inspector remained obdurate, and Vincent left the station. He immediately proceeded to the courthouse, where he filed a writ of habeas corpus, which is returnable before Judge Hutchinson at 12:30 P.M. today.

The petition declares that Luetgert was arrested and is being detained at the East Chicago Avenue station for the sole purpose of enabling Inspector Schaack to obtain information from him relating to the disappearance of his wife. The prisoner, it is alleged, is being subjected to what is known in police parlance as the "sweating" process to compel him to give information. The attorney goes on to relate how he made application at the station to be permitted to see and converse with Luetgert, and how the application was refused and the inspector gave orders that the prisoner was to see no one. This order, the petition says, will be adhered to until the police have finished their pumping process with the prisoner. It is further alleged that a copy of the warrant on which the prisoner is held has been refused, and that the Constitution has been violated by the refusal to permit him to have the benefit of legal counsel.

"This thing is an outrage," said Vincent. "Leaving the question of the guilt or innocence of Luetgert, of which I know nothing, out of the question, there is no situation or circumstance that justifies the police in refusing to allow a prisoner the right to see his attorney. Schaack had a personal object in refusing to allow me to see Luetgert. I was vice president of the meeting at the North Side Turner Hall, at which his action in the O'Malley case was criticized, and he is trying to whip me over poor Luetgert's shoulders."

Luetgert was tried twice for murdering his wife. The first trial ended with a hung jury. He was convicted at the second trial and sentenced to life in prison. His lawyers contended that Mrs. Luetgert had wandered away, possibly ending up in an asylum for the insane. Shortly after entering the Illinois penitentiary at Joliet, Luetgert died of a heart attack. His wife, of course, never reappeared.

15

The doctor who couldn't explain away the corpse beneath the cellar floor

Hawley Harvey Crippen was born in Coldwater, Michigan in 1862 and received an M.D. degree at Hospital College in Cleveland before moving to England in 1883. In 1910, Inspector Walter Dew, suspicious about the sudden disappearance of Crippen's wife, unearthed what were believed to be the remains of her mutilated body from the clay floor of Crippen's cellar. This story about the case is from the *Times of London* of October 19, 1910.

The trial of Dr. Hawley Harvey Crippen for murder of his wife, Cora Crippen, otherwise Belle Elmore, was opened yesterday at the Old Bailey before the lord chief justice.

As soon as the lord chief justice had taken his seat, the clerk of arraigns called Hawley Harvey Crippen, who immediately appeared in the dock. On being called upon to plead to the indictment, the prisoner replied in clear, firm tones, "Not guilty."

R. D. Muir, in opening the case for the Crown, began by tracing the history of the prisoner and of his wife, whom he married as his second wife in 1892 or 1893, and also the circumstances of their married life at Hilldrop Crescent, down to the end of last year. So far as their friends were concerned, the relations between husband and wife seemed of the best possible kind; they lived together apparently on affectionate terms. The prisoner had not for some four years, however, according to his own statement, cohabited with his wife, but had during three years of that period been carrying on an intrigue with the young woman Ethel Le Neve, who had been in his service as a typist. For three years he had been having immoral relations with her of a clandestine kind, never staying away from home at night, but meeting her in hotels by day. That being so, the prisoner was a strange one.

The prisoner said he provided all the money for the home in which he and his wife were living. If that was so, he was keeping up an establishment for a woman toward whom, according to him, he had no affection at all.

The prisoner and his wife during some years of their married life were putting by money. Between March, 1905 and March, 1909 they had deposited with the Charing Cross Bank various sums amounting to £600. These were deposited, some jointly and some in the name of his wife alone by which she was generally known—Belle Elmore.

In the beginning of the present year, the financial position was not so good. Up to November the prisoner had received a weekly salary of £3 from the business known as Munyon's Remedies, but that salary escaped, and he became their agent in this country on commission. On January 31 his relations with Munyon's Remedies ceased altogether—a remarkable coincidence of date. The prisoner had some other businesses, but it was doubtful whether any of them was profitable. It was quite certain that at the date referred to the prisoner was pressed for money.

The position, therefore, was this: his affections fixed upon Ethel Le Neve, and himself desirous of establishing closer relations with that young woman; the physical presence of his wife an obstacle to those relations; the fact that he had no money another obstacle. If Belle Elmore died, both these obstacles would be removed, because Belle Elmore's money and property would enable him to keep Ethel Le Neve.

That was the state of things on January 31. On that day the prisoner desired that Paul Martinetti and his wife should spend the evening with him and his wife. He pressed the invitation, and it was accepted. Mrs. Crippen was in the best of health and spirits on that evening, and the relations between husband and wife were of the very best. So there were Mr. and Mrs. Martinetti witnesses, if ever they should be required, to the fact that on the early morning of February 1 Mr. and Mrs. Crippen were on their usual affectionate terms, and if Mrs. Crippen should from that moment disappear from the sight of all who knew her, who would suspect the kind, attentive, and affectionate husband of being the cause?

Belle Elmore was a woman who attracted friends—a busy

17

woman, enjoying life for the pleasure it gave her and for the good she could do others. She was described as a bright, vivacious woman, fond of life, fond—perhaps inordinately fond—of dress and jewelry. Her friends said she was a good correspondent; but from the moment Mr. and Mrs. Martinetti left the house in the early morning of February 1, she passed out of the world as completely as if she were dead. She left behind her everything she would have left if she had died—money, jewels, furs, clothes, home, and husband.

The prisoner at once began to convert her property, and on March 12 Ethel Le Neve, who had been seen wearing a brooch and furs belonging to Belle Elmore, went permanently to him at 39 Hilldrop Crescent. Crippen was, therefore, quite certain that his wife would never return, but he did not tell her friends he knew she would never return. He started a campaign of lies to account for her disappearance.

He knew that if his wife did not attend the meeting of the Music Hall Ladies Guild on February 2, inquiries would be made, and so he sent by the hand of Le Neve the two letters to the guild and to Miss May, one of the officials of the guild. Then came the story of his wife's disappearance to America, and the invention of further lies, because a visit to America might be expected to terminate at some time or other, to account for the fact that she was never to return.

On March 23 he told Mrs. Martinetti that he had very bad news, and was momentarily expecting worse. He said that if anything should happen to Belle, he was going to France for a week. Mrs. Martinetti said, "Whatever for?" He said, "Oh, I shall want a change," the truth of that being that at this time he had arranged an Easter trip to Dieppe with Ethel Le Neve. The slate had been wiped clean of Belle Elmore before he started, and from Victoria on the early morning of February 24 he sent a telegram to Mrs. Martinetti saying that Belle died at six the previous night. That nothing should remain to interfere with the rest he was seeking in France, he sent the advertisement to the ERA announcing that Belle Elmore had died in California—no nearer than that. The object of the advertisement was to stop people asking a lot of questions. But Belle Elmore's friends were not prevented from asking a lot of questions, and they got some answers.

They obtained, too, the address of Crippen's son. The ladies wished to send a wreath to their friend's grave in California. They were told that the wreath was no use—she had been cremated, and her ashes were to be brought home; they could have their little ceremony then. On May 18 he solemnly announced that he had the ashes at home.

Then the ladies became still more curious. They wanted to know the name of the ship in which Belle Elmore sailed for America, and Crippen was not at all sure about it. It must have been obvious to Crippen then that his statements with regard to the disappearance of Belle Elmore were being doubted. It was perfectly plain after his interview with Chief Inspector Dew that it was useless to proceed with the stories he had told.

He said to the inspector: "It is untrue what I have told them about her death. So far as I know she is alive." Crippen then made a long statement giving quite a new version of his wife's disappearance. He said that in 1902 or thereabouts he had to visit America, and that while he was away his wife had met Bruce Miller and become attached to him; that upon his return, her manner changed, and that she threatened in outbursts of temper to leave him and go to Miller; and that she had said that when she left him she would pass altogether out of his life, and that he would never hear from her again.

He went on to say that because of a lack of courtesy to Mr. Martinetti at the dinner party on January 31 his wife said that this was the finish of it—that she would go, and that he could do what he thought best to cover up the scandal with the guild and with their friends.

On February 1 he returned from business to find his wife gone, and he sat down to think how he could account for her absence.

Almost while he was in the act of making those statements to gain a few hours' delay from the police officer who was making the inquiries, the prisoner was preparing for flight. The jury had to ask themselves why Crippen left—what it was he had to fear if his statement were true that, as far as he knew, Belle Elmore was alive. If that statement were true, he had nothing to fear. But he fled.

What he fled was found on July 13, when under the brick floor in the cellar of the house in Hilldrop Crescent where Belle Elmore was last seen alive on February 1, the police found human remains.

Whose were the remains? On July 14 they were carefully examined where they lay in the cellar by Mr. Pepper, the eminent surgeon, and by Dr. Marshall, the police surgeon. The remains were headless, limbless, and boneless, and the sex could not be determined, but some curlers with long human hair in them and some feminine undergarments might be said to indicate that the remains were a woman's.

The human hair in curlers was naturally dark brown, but had been bleached lighter. Belle Elmore's hair was a dark brown, and she was in the habit of bleaching it. Those facts were undoubtedly true of a good many other women besides Belle Elmore. The undergarments had been seen by some of Belle Elmore's friends, and they were such as Belle Elmore was in the habit of wearing, but they were also such as many other women would wear.

One piece of flesh has been identified as coming from the lower part of the abdominal wall, and it has upon it an old scar. Belle Elmore was operated upon in that region in 1892 or 1893, and the scar was seen by two persons who would be called.

The place of burial was significant. It was in the house occupied by Crippen and Belle Elmore from September 21, 1905 to February 1, 1910, and by nobody else, and in the house where Belle Elmore was last seen alive.

It was for the jury to say whether they were satisfied that those remains were the remains and could only be the remains of the missing woman, Belle Elmore.

Another question the jury would have to consider was: Who put the remains there? In endeavoring to answer that question, they would ask themselves who but Crippen had the opportunity to put them there, if the surgeon were accurate as to the date of burial—some period between eight months at the longest and four months at the shortest. Belle Elmore disappeared on February 1, five and one-half months before July 13, when the remains were unearthed.

20

The remains were mutilated in a way that indicated the person who did it had some acquaintance with anatomy and some dexterity in dealing with dead bodies. Crippen had a very good degree; he practiced in America, and, according to his own statement, before he took his degree in America he spent some time in London visiting the hospitals. Putting the remains in place and preparing the hole in the cellar would require both considerable time and entire freedom from observation.

The prisoner was not seen again by Inspector Dew until July 31. Counsel narrated the story of the pursuit of Crippen across the Atlantic to Canada and his arrest on board the steamship Montrose, pointing out that Crippen was found with his heavy mustache shaved off and passing under the false name of John Robinson, while his companion, Ethel Le Neve, was found disguised as a boy, with her hair cut and wearing the brown suit purchased on Crippen's orders on July 9 when he was preparing for flight.

When told by the inspector that he would be arrested for the murder of his wife, Crippen at first made no reply, but a little later said, "I am not sorry; the anxiety has been too much." He was searched, and on him were found two cards, one of which claimed their attention. This was the card that he obviously had printed for a disguise. It bore the name John Robinson and a Detroit address. The result of the search was that there was found sewn to his underwear four of Belle Elmore's rings and two of her brooches.

There was a further piece of evidence. How did Belle Elmore, if it was Belle Elmore, meet her death? How did the person whose remains were found in the cellar die? A skilled surgeon could discover no cause of death in the remains. But the viscera were submitted to Dr. Willcox, the senior scientific analyst to the home office. Dr. Willcox found a quantity of hyoscin, sufficient to show that there must have been in the body more than half a grain of hyoscin hydrobromide, the form in which hyoscin was used for medical purposes. The drug was a powerful narcotic poison, not commonly prescribed. The official dose was from one two-hundredth to one one-hundredth of a grain. From a quarter to half a grain was fatal.

Of this drug not commonly known and not commonly used by medical men, Crippen, on January 17, 1910, bought five grains that were delivered to him on January 19. He ordered it from Lewis and Burrows, chemists.

He had to sign the poisons book, and in that he had to state for whom the drug was required and for what purpose. He made false statements in both cases. He said the drug was required for Munyon's, which was untrue, because Munyon's made no preparations in this country. He also said he wanted it for homeopathic purposes, but the drug is not mentioned in the *Homeopathic Pharmacopeia.*

What had become of it? Unless it went into the body of Belle Elmore and unless the remains were those of Belle Elmore, no explanation was forthcoming as to what became of the poison.

The first witness called for the prosecution was Frederick Lown, the owner of 39 Hilldrop Crescent. Lown said Dr. Crippen paid his rent regularly and displayed no sign of agitation or anxiety.

Dr. John Herbert Burroughs, the next witness, said Crippen always seemed to be kind-hearted and courteous to his wife and willing to render her any little service he could. He would describe Mrs. Crippen as a well-dressed woman of smart appearance.

Mrs. Paul Martinetti repeated her account of her association, including the visit to 39 Hilldrop Crescent. The witness said that while Mrs. Crippen was staying at her bungalow up the river she saw her body on one occasion and noticed a mark on the lower part of the stomach. It seemed like the mark of an old cut, about six inches long, running from the lower part of the stomach to the navel.

The witness said Crippen apparently was a kind-hearted man. She and her husband liked both him and his wife. She noticed nothing unusual in Crippen's manner, either at the dinner party on January 31 or on the next day when he called to inquire after Martinetti or any of the subsequent occasions on which she saw him.

Theresa Hunn, of Newport, Rhode Island, said she was Belle Elmore's younger sister. Her sister had a scar on the stomach. She first saw that scar a few months after her sister's marriage. On April 16 of this year she saw a letter that her half-sister and her half-sister's husband received from Dr. Crippen, as follows: "My dear Louisa and Robert, I hardly know how to write to you my terrible loss. The shock to me has been so dreadful that I am hardly able to control myself. My poor Cora has gone. To me the shock has been more dreadful because I did not even see her at the last. A few weeks ago we had news that an old relation of mine in California was dying, and to secure important property for ourselves it was necessary for one of us to go and put the matter in the lawyers' hands at once. As I was very busy, Cora proposed that she should go, and as it would be necessary to be there at once, she would go straight through from here to California without stopping at all, and then return by way of Brooklyn, when she would be able to pay all of you a long visit. Unfortunately, on the way out my poor Cora caught a severe cold, and, not having proper care at once, it settled on her lungs and later developed into pleuropneumonia. She wished not to frighten me at first and said it was a slight matter. Next I heard by cable that she was dangerously ill, and two days later I had the dreadful news that she had passed away. Imagine, if you can, the dreadful shock to me never more to see my Cora alive or hear her voice again. I don't know what I shall do—probably find some business to take me traveling for a few months until I have recovered from the shock. It is so terrible to me to have to write this dreadful news. Please tell all the others of our loss. Love to all. From Doctor."

Bruce Miller, the next witness, said he was a real estate agent living in East Chicago, Indiana. He was formerly engaged in the music-hall profession and came to England in that connection. While in England he made the acquaintance in London of Belle Elmore, meeting her first at some time in December, 1899 and last about the first part of April, 1904. He was now living with his wife and child in Chicago. He said he first met Mrs. Crippen at a house in Torrington Square in London.

Was her husband present when you were introduced to her?—No, he was in America.

Do you know how long it was after you were first introduced to Mrs. Crippen at her house that Dr. Crippen came back?—Sometime in the spring, perhaps April or May.

Did you visit Mrs. Crippen at the house where she was living?
—Very often.

During her husband's absence? —Yes.

Where was she living when you visited her at her house in her husband's absence? —In Guilford Street.

Did you visit her several times a week while her husband was in America? —Three or four times, perhaps.

In the evening? —Sometimes afternoon, sometimes in the evening.

Did you ever tell her you loved her?—I don't know that I ever put it that way.

Then you did love her?—I did not say that I loved her. There was a great deal of friendship. She was a married lady.

You know the difference between friendship and love?—Yes.

Were you more than a friend?—I could not be more than a friend; she was a married lady.

Did you write love letters to her ending, "Love and kisses to brown-eyes"?—I have.

Do you think those are proper letters to write to a married woman?—Under the circumstances, yes.

What circumstances?—Because her husband knew about it.

You do not suggest that he knew at the time you were writing?—I don't know.

You said, "Under the circumstances...because her husband knew about it." You now admit that he knew nothing about it at the time you were writing?—When he came back from America, he knew all about it.

Do you now agree that those were most improper letters to write to her?—I do not think they were under the circumstances.

Were you her lover?—I was not.

Have you ever kissed her?—I have.

Have you ever done anything more than kiss her?—That is all.

Why did you stop at that?—Because I always treated her as a gentleman should.

In defense, Crippen's lawyers called a string of witnesses who described the doctor as "good-hearted," "good-tempered," and "one of the nicest men I ever met." But at the end of his five-day trial, the jury deliberated only half an hour before finding him guilty. Crippen was hanged a few days later.

Carl Wanderer in jail. (Courtesy Chicago Historical Society)

The celebrated case of Carl Wanderer and the "ragged stranger"

Journalist-playwright Ben Hecht wrote this story about the deaths of Ruth Wanderer and the ragged stranger for the *Chicago Daily News* of June 22, 1920.

Carl Wanderer, freshly shaved and his brown suit neatly pressed, stood looking over the back porch of his home at 4732 North Campbell Avenue. His wife, who was murdered last night by a holdup man in the doorway downstairs, lay in their bedroom.

Wanderer looked at his gold watch, and his hand was steady. He smiled blankly at the back porches in front of him and, with his eyes grown cold, repeated, "Well, I got him. I got him anyway."

At two this afternoon there are scheduled two inquests, one over the body of Mrs. Carl Wanderer and the other over the body of the stickup man. Wanderer, standing two feet from the man who had killed his wife, opened fire with his .45.

Last October Wanderer was discharged from service as a first lieutenant. He came back from France with a Croix de Guerre and a DSC [Distinguished Service Cross]. He had for a year been the best pistol shot in his battalion—the 17th machine-gun battalion.

Campbell Avenue is a quiet, snug neighborhood, and in the morning children play under the trees in the backyards. Wanderer, putting his gold watch back into his pocket, went on talking in a quiet, tense voice.

"The first shot blew him across the hallway," he said. "Then I couldn't see him. But I knew where he'd landed, and I let him have three more. I got him but—."

The machine-gunner and owner of a Croix de Guerre stopped talking, and a young husband in a brown suit with eyes reddened

27

from tears finished the sentence. "If I'd only gotten him sooner. Just a nickel's worth sooner."

Later the husband said, "There isn't much to tell. We'd been to a movie, and this man followed us, I suppose. I was going to turn on the light in the vestibule to see the keyhole, when I heard a voice, 'Don't turn on the light.' I reached for my gun. I knew what the fellow was up to. But he got cold feet. He never asked us to put our hands up, but began shooting right off the bat. I was a few seconds late. I don't know why. But I got him. He got what was coming to him."

Outside, neighbors sat on their sunny porch steps and stared at the house at 4732. The street was again quiet and peaceful, as if tragedy had never visited it. A gray hearse motored up in front of the address, and the neighbors discussed the life of the couple as it had been before last night. One of them said, "She told me only yesterday she was going to be a mother, and was so happy."

Through a card found in the clothes of the assailant, he was tentatively identified at the hospital as Edward Masters, who, the police say, is a well-known slugger and gunman. The card bore the name of the John Robinson circus and indicated that he had at one time been an employee of the commissary department of the circus. He also wore a newspaper driver's badge, which bore the number 706.

Capt. Michael Evans of the Bureau of Identification tried to identify the dead slayer of Mrs. Wanderer through fingerprints. He said later, however, that the prints did not correspond with any on record. It is thought that the man was an ex-convict, but that he came here from another city. The manager of the circulation department of a morning paper viewed the man and said that he believed he had formerly been employed on a wagon driven by one of the newspaper's employees.

Five days after the shooting, Harry Romanoff of the *Chicago Herald-Examiner* found a photo of a girl in a drawer in Wanderer's bedroom, along with a torn-up love letter. Pieced together, the letter indicated that Wanderer was having an affair with the girl in the photo, who was only sixteen. The police soon discovered that the ragged stranger's gun had been in Wanderer's possession the day before the shooting, and that the same gun had been used in both killings. Wanderer confessed to the police that he had hired the stanger to kill his wife, and had killed them both himself. Wanderer received twenty-five years for the murder of his wife, and the death penalty for killing the stranger. Hours before his hanging, Hecht visited the condemned man in his cell at Cook County Jail, and obtained a promise that he would read some words that Hecht had composed for the occasion of his parting. Wanderer pocketed the swan song, which was a bawdy denunciation of Hecht's editors at the *Daily News*. When the accused approached the gallows, however, his hands were tied behind his back and his head was quickly fitted in its black hood, so Wanderer went out singing a religious ditty. Said Humorist Alexander Woollcott: "From one of the crowd of reporters watching the execution came the audible comment that Wanderer deserved hanging for his voice alone."

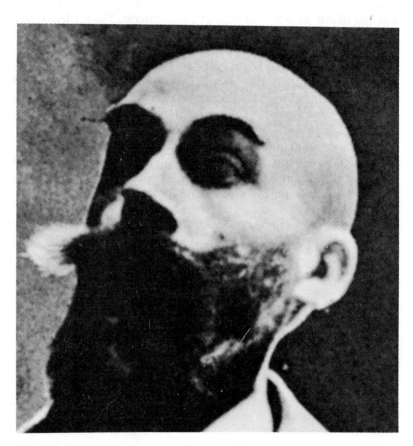

Bluebeard of France

Bluebeard of France and his wife eradicator: the stove at Vernouillet

Women, it is said, went into ecstasies over Henri Désiré Landru, more commonly known as Bluebeard of France. When police seized his records, they learned that Landru had corresponded with 283 women. No one knows how many he murdered. This story from *L'Echo de Paris* of November 7, 1921 describes his methods.

Although the crimes with which Henri Désiré Landru is charged are very numerous, they have all been cut to the same pattern, and the whole list of them therefore grows rather monotonous. This is not so much because Landru is lacking in criminal imagination as because his first crime was so successful that he had no need to change his methods.

This is the scheme he used with his victims—a trap that always worked: By the very simplest means, a newspaper advertisement, for example, he opened communication with some woman who wanted to be married. At the first or second meeting, he would propose marriage, and the unknown of yesterday would become the fiancée or even the mistress of today. A few days of illicit honeymoon, and then the woman would disappear into the stove at Vernouillet or at Gambais. "In that valuable implement over there," Landru said to a witness, "you can burn anything you wish."

The stove is to be seen at the trial among the other pieces of evidence—an old cook stove almost ready for the junk shop. But Landru knew how to use it. Once his fiancée had disappeared, that is to say, once she had been turned into ashes, the murderer would proceed to take inventory. He would get together all her furniture and, if he had not done it already, he would go through her pockets, not forgetting the smallest coins or even little trinkets without any particular value. If he discovered any securities, he would hasten to realize them at the bank, and he would even put aside a few souvenirs, such as false hair, false teeth, an old comb, or a skirt. This turns out to have been highly imprudent because these "souvenirs," discovered in his garages and recognized by the relatives and friends of his victims, have become formidable evidence against him.

He was guilty of one other imprudence, still more serious. Landru is an orderly man, keeping account of everything that he does, receives, or spends. Ah, this mania for records!

No matter with how much certainty the prosecutor pretends to have reconstructed each crime of which Landru is accused, there remains, notwithstanding, a troublesome gap in the evidence. It is known how he snared the birds. That was not very hard. It is known how he caged them for a few days near him. That was easy enough. But what did he do with the bodies?

It is easy enough to reply that he burned them—that is very probable—but what infernal cleverness had he developed in the art of incineration? There is no crematory, no matter how perfect, that can reduce a human body to an impalpable bit of cinder. Certain bones resist the very highest temperatures; and then there are fats in the body that can never be completely destroyed.

Have the experts been set to hunting for traces of fat in the country houses where Landru lived and in the pipe of the stove?

The first woman to disappear, Mme. Cuchet, met Landru in 1914, and in February of that year she told her stepbrother, M. Friedman, and his employer that she was going to marry a man named Diard, whom she adored, and who was nobody else than Landru himself. In April she followed Landru to Chausée, where he was living in a simple room with a garage—for Landru always had an auto. It is even probable that the prospect of being able to make trips in it helped him to lure his victims.

She stayed there until August, receiving frequent visits from her son, André, who was working in Paris. Then war was declared, and Landru disappeared with the balance of a deposit of 5,000 francs that he had at a branch of the Société Générale. But he was forgiven in advance, for Mme. Cuchet loved him, and when he came back to her—he knew that she had a little property—she went with him willingly, taking all her furniture to a villa that she leased at Vernouillet. There, in December, 1914, they took up their life together—but not for a very long time.

The son of Landru's financee, André Cuchet, was just about to go to war with his class, at the beginning of 1915. It was natural that he should go to Vernouillet to spend his last days of liberty with his mother and his future stepfather. On January 27, he wrote to his family that he was glad to be going to the front. That was the end. Nobody ever heard anything more of either the mother or the son. Their family does not appear to have been especially disturbed about it. No doubt, they thought, the son, André, must have gone to the army; and so far as Mme. Cuchet herself was concerned, Landru doubtless would say to the relatives that she had left him. Silence settled over the affair.

On May 27, he went to visit Mme. Laborde-Line, 47, who lived at 47 Rue de Patay. A few days later, they became engaged. His new conquest announced her approaching marriage to her friends and acquaintances. Like the previous victim, she too was a widow, and she seemed overjoyed. She consented to go live at the villa Vernouillet, and the people who lived there used to see her in the garden. She seemed to be at home there, but after June 28 she disappeared. She had "gone to Paris"; and that very same day Landru gathered up her belongings and put them in a storeroom. On July 13 he turned into cash what securities she possessed, and that was the end. Nobody, not even her son, took the trouble to hunt for Mme. Laborde-Line, for Landru inspired confidence in everyone who approached him.

On July 15, two days later, it was the turn of a third widow, Mme. Guillin, 51, who recently had received a legacy of 22,000 francs. A betrothal, a marriage, a trip to Vernouillet—August 22 Landru disposes of Mme. Guillin's jewels as well as a bond and sells her furniture. For Landru is a man who wastes no time.

Who was troubled about this new disappearance? Nobody except Mme. Guillin's concierge, to whom Landru replied with an air of detachment: "She's gone." To prevent any trouble, he took away the furniture, paid some back rent—with her money—and bade farewell to his apartment. Another!

And now it was the turn of Mme. Héon, for whom Landru set up his crematory in a new villa at Gambais. On September 30, an engagement. From that date to December 8, the couple lived in a hotel on the Rue de Budapest. December 8, a trip to Gambais. Landru bought two tickets, a return ticket for himself, a single-trip ticket for her, for he is an economical man, this Landru. It was the last trip that his fourth fiancée, Berthe Héon, ever made; but nobody noticed her disappearance any more than those of the others. The deaths were occurring quickly, but Landru wanted to speed them up.

A lady named Collomb, a stenographer in Paris, left her lover to become Landru's fiancée. Not immediately, but in 1916, soon after the disappearance of Mme. Héon, Landru had taken the name of Fremyet, and posed as an engineer at Montmorency. Invited to go with Fremyet, Mlle. Collomb took along her sister, Mme. Pollet, who spent a delightful day with the two lovers. The table was covered with flowers through the thoughtfulness of Landru. Mme. Pollet formed the very best opinion of her stepbrother and was delighted with the fine marriage that was to be celebrated in May. A man with an auto! But under the date of December 27 you see in Landru's notebook certain figures that lead you to believe that on that day there was no idea either of marriage or betrothal, but that Landru had received 5,067 francs 95 centimes—the exact sum that Mlle. Collomb had drawn from the Comptoir d'Escompte. This money pocketed, the gallant fiancé had taken the poor woman away with him—a single-trip ticket and a return ticket—and the next day he killed her and burned her. This was one of the most successful of Landru's "affairs."

It appears that the next woman, Mlle. Babelay, a young chambermaid of nineteen, did not bring Landru any money. At that age, one isn't very rich, usually, even when one works for a fortune-teller. Like all the others, Mlle. Babelay fell in love with Landru instantly and followed him to Gambais on March 29, 1917. On April 12 you read in the notebook: "Four o'clock." That means that on that day, at that hour, Mlle. Babelay shared the usual fate of Landru's fiancées. The honeymoon before the marriage had lasted a fortnight.

The widow Buisson seems to have adored the man who was to be her assassin. She went into ecstasies over him. "My place in life is low enough," she wrote to him. "I love my son well, but I love you more." In another letter she apologized for having only 13,000 francs in savings; but for Landru that was a windfall. This affair dragged out over two years. Is it because she thought herself disdained or likely to lose her beloved that she was so slow in turning over her little savings to his use? At length, in August, 1917, she drew her money from the Crédit Lyonnais and entrusted it to Landru, telling him to invest it as he wished. She went to live at Gambais, where her sister, Mme. Lacoste, visited her. Landru and the two women went to Paris on August 17, and two days later Landru brought Mme. Buisson back. That was the end. Nobody ever saw her again.

No one knows exactly how he killed her, but, according to the notebook, her murder must have taken place at a quarter past ten in the morning of September 1, and that very day her assassin started for Paris to court another fiancée, Mlle. Segret, while he was selling the wardrobe of Mme. Buisson.

Landru never lost any time, but he spared Mlle. Segret. Why? Was it because she had no money, and he did not want to "draw a blank" again, as he had with Mlle. Babelay? Or, as has been suggested, did he really fall in love with Mlle. Segret? That would be the most extraordinary thing in the whole catalog of crimes so coldly and pitilessly carried out. Whatever the truth may be, Mlle. Segret is still alive and is to publish her memoirs; but she must have goose flesh sometimes when she thinks of the danger that she incurred.

Even while he was getting ready to murder Mme. Buisson, and while he was courting Mlle. Segret, Landru was carrying on two other intrigues, one with Mme. Jaume and the other with Mme. Pascal. The murder of Mme. Jaume is perhaps the most original of them all. Married, but separated from her husband, Mme. Jaume was never willing to get a divorce, for her deep religious feeling forbade it. Landru was able to do away with this objection. On October 5, 1917, Mme. Jaume left the workshop where she was employed, telling her comrades that she was soon to be divorced and that she would be married as soon as possible afterward. Landru went to Mass with her, knelt beside her, and pretended to mingle his prayers with hers. Whereupon Mme. Jaume, highly edified and completely conquered, agreed to everything.

Landru did the honors. A single-trip ticket to Gambais, as usual, for her, and return ticket for him—and he jotted down in his notebook under October 26, "three o'clock." That was the epitaph of Mme. Jaume. Then, still in the notebook: "Lyanes business. 827 francs," and then, "274 francs"—found in the pockets of the victim. Mme. Jaume lived in the Rue des Lyanes, and that very evening he went back to Paris, entered her home, broke into the money box, and sold 1,500 francs' worth of property.

Had he any idea at that time that his game might become dangerous? Was he afraid that someone might in the end be disturbed over the disappearance of his last victim? At any rate, he spread the report among Mme. Jaume's acquaintances that she had gone to America, and nobody asked him how or why. This devil of a man understood to the very bottom the art of lying and getting himself believed. Will he still have it when he is before the jury? Perhaps that will be more difficult.

"Young in appearance, dressmaker and milliner"—such is the characterization that Landru gives to Mme. Pascal. A merry business! Mme. Pascal managed a dressmaker's shop. Engagement, promise of marriage, trip to Gambais on April 5, 1917, with the fatal one-way ticket. Then, on the same day, the inscription in the notebook: "five-fifteen p.m." Mme. Pascal's life was over.

Five days later her belongings had been liquidated—all the more easily because, at Landru's suggestion, she already had sold the shop. This liquidation is the most picturesque of them all. It would have been easy enough to sell furniture alone, but he turned everything into money: "umbrella 5 francs, false teeth 15 francs," and he jots down in his notebook balance of account: "Pascal incidentals, 6 francs 25 centimes." This was the money found in the purse of the victim, to whom he literally left nothing but the hair on her head before he burned her up.

But the widow Pascal had brought something that was of no value to Landru: her cat, of which she was especially fond. Landru killed it and buried it in the garden where its skeleton was recovered.

Till Death Do Us Part

The tenth and last, Mme. Marchadier, was still more indiscreet. She arrived at Gambais with three dogs; but Landru did not spare them. They were buried beside Mme. Pascal's cat, and, on January 13, Mme. Marchadier disappeared forever.

Landru turned up in Paris the next day. He had acquired an expert mastery over the art of killing his victims and making away with their bodies, and he was no less expeditious as a businessman. To go with him and marry him, Mme. Marchadier had sold her apartment at 330 Rue Saint-Jacques and part of her furniture. Landru got hold of the product of these sales. And it was time! On the very day of the crime, he was compelled to borrow twelve francs from the shoemaker at Gambais, but on the 15th he paid 950 francs of debts.

Such is the long series of crimes for which Landru will have to stand trail at Versailles. This trial, as has been said, inspires reflection, but it would have been better to write "surprise." How is it that all these disappearances did not cause any feeling in the locality where they took place? Not one of these ten women lived alone. They all announced their approaching marriages to a rich engineer who had an auto and a country house. People congratulated and envied them. Then they disappeared suddenly, and nobody ever thought of them again.

"She is happy," people must have said about every one of them. Who knows whether people do not still talk about these women, and express surprise at their forgetfulness and ingratitude toward former friends? Landru could keep on, for he never let a breath of suspicion escape where he went.

But the pitcher goes too often to the well.

Among the women who disappeared, we have mentioned Mme. Buisson, and we have said that while she was at Gambais, she entertained her sister, Mme. Lacoste, in August, 1917. When Mme. Lacoste did not hear of the marriage of Mme. Buisson and Fremyet—the name which Landru had assumed to make love to her sister—she felt some anxiety, which she confided to the *procureur* of the Republic (public prosecutor). She had heard, moreover, about another fiancée of Landru, Mlle. Collomb, who had disappeared under identical conditions. She devoted herself to unceasing investigation.

After that the inquiry began. A lucky chance brought it speedily to a successful conclusion. Mme. Lacoste had addressed her complaint to the *procureur* in February, 1919. In April a friend of Mme. Buisson found herself face to face with the pretended engineer, Fremyet. Working on the information that she furnished, the police arrested him at his home, 76 Rue de Rochechouart, where he was known by the name of Guillet. His identity was quickly established, and from engineer he descended in the social scale to a mere fugitive from justice, six times condemned for swindling, and banished from France. Why had he not been sent to Guiana? How had he been able to live quietly at Paris, Vernouillet, and Gambais, never even concealing himself, although he was at least eligible for military duty during the war? So many mysteries the more, added to the disappearance of his fiancées, which, perhaps, will be brought to light by justice.

Seldom have misdeeds so cruel and methodical been brought to trial. Yet Landru has become a kind of comic personage. Comic songs are sung about him. He is represented on the stage, and for all we know some impresario already has asked for rights to a possible American tour if Landru should be acquitted.

Landru was convicted of murder and guillotined. In 1923, his stove was sold at auction for 4,200 francs.

Albert Snyder murder: a "perfect crime" that was unspeakably dumb

Damon Runyon, often acclaimed as the greatest newspaperman of all time, covered the sensational Ruth Snyder-Henry Judd Gray murder trial for International News Service. This Runyon story appeared in many newspapers on April 27, 1927.

A chilly-looking blond with frosty eyes and one of those marble, you-bet-you-will chins, and an inert, scare-drunk fellow that you couldn't miss among any hundred men as a dead set-up for a blond, or the shell game, or maybe a gold brick.

Mrs. Ruth Snyder and Henry Judd Gray are on trial in the huge weatherbeaten old courthouse of Queens County in Long Island City, just across the river from the roar of New York, for what might be called, for want of a better name, The Dumbbell Murder. It was so dumb.

They are charged with the slaughter four weeks ago of Albert Snyder, art editor of the magazine *Motor Boating*, the blond's husband and father of her nine-year-old daughter, under circumstances that for sheer stupidity and brutality seldom have been equalled in the history of crime.

It was stupid beyond imagination, and so brutal that the thought of it probably makes many a peaceful, home-loving Long Islander of the Albert Snyder-type shiver in his pajamas as he prepares for bed.

They killed Snyder as he slumbered, so they both admitted in confessions—Mrs. Snyder has since repudiated hers—first whacking him on the head with a sash weight, then giving him a few whiffs of chloroform, and finally tightening a strand of picture wire around his throat so he wouldn't revive.

This matter disposed of, they went into an adjoining room and

39

*Photographer Tom Howard strapped a small camera to his leg
to get this picture of Ruth Snyder in the electric chair on
January 12, 1928. (Courtesy Chicago Historical Society)*

had a few drinks of very bad whiskey used by some Long Islanders and talked things over. They thought they had committed "the perfect crime," whatever that may be. It was probably the most imperfect crime on record. It was cruel, atrocious, and unspeakably dumb.

They were red-hot lovers then, these two, but they are strangers now.

Mrs. Snyder, the woman who has been called a Jezebel, a lineal descendant of the Borgia outfit, and a lot of other names, came in for the morning session of court stepping along briskly in her patent-leather pumps, with little short steps.

She is not bad-looking. I have seen much worse. She is thirty-three and looks just about that, though you cannot tell much about blonds. She has a good figure, slim and trim, with narrow shoulders. She is of medium height, and I thought she carried her clothes off rather smartly. She wore a black dress and a black silk coat with a collar of black fur. Some of the girl reporters said it was dyed ermine; others pronounced it rabbit.

They made derogatory remarks about her hat. It was a tight-fitting thing called, I believe, a beret. Wisps of her straw-colored hair straggled out from under it. Mrs. Snyder wears her hair bobbed, the back of the bobbing rather ragged. She is of the Scandinavian type. Her parents are Norwegian and Swedish.

Her eyes are blue-green and as chilly-looking as an ice cream cone. If all that Henry Judd Gray says of her actions the night of the murder is true, her veins carry ice water. Gray says he dropped the sash weight after slugging the sleeping Snyder with it once, and that Mrs. Snyder picked it up and finished the job.

Gray, a spindly fellow in physical build, entered the courtroom with quick, jerky little steps behind an officer, and sat down between his attorneys, Samuel L. Miller and William L. Millard. His back was to Mrs. Snyder, who sat about ten feet away. Her eyes were on a level with the back of his narrow head.

Gray was neatly dressed in a dark suit, with a white starched collar and subdued tie. He has always been a bit on the dressy side, it is said. He wears big, horn-rimmed spectacles, and his eyes have a startled expression. You couldn't find a meeker, milder-looking fellow in seven states, this man who is charged

41

with one of the most horrible crimes in history.

He occasionally conferred with his attorneys as the examination of the talesmen was going forward, but not often. He sat in one position almost the entire day, half slumped down in his chair, a melancholy-looking figure for a fellow who once thought of "the perfect crime."

Mrs. Snyder and Gray have been "hollering copper" on each other lately, as the boys say. That is, they have been telling. Gray's defense goes back to old Mr. Adam, that the woman beguiled him, while Mrs. Snyder says he is a "jackal," and a lot of other things besides that, and claims that he is hiding behind her skirts.

Some say Mrs. Ruth Snyder "wept silently" in court yesterday. It may be so. I could detect no sparkle of tears against the white marble mask, but it is conceivable that even the very gods were weeping silently as a gruff voice slowly recited the blond woman's own story of the murder of her husband by herself and Henry Judd Gray.

Let no one infer she is altogether without tenderness of heart, for when they were jotting down the confession that was read in the courtroom in Long Island City, Peter M. Daly, an assistant district attorney, asked her:

"Mrs. Snyder, why did you kill your husband?"

He wanted to know.

"Don't put it that way," she said, according to his testimony yesterday. "It sounds so cruel."

"Well, that is what you did, isn't it?" he asked in some surprise.

"Yes," he claims she answered, "but I don't like that term."

A not astonishing distaste, you must admit.

"Well, why did you kill him?" persisted the curious Daly.

"To get rid of him," she answered simply, according to Daly's testimony; and indeed that seems to have been her main idea throughout, if all the evidence the state has so far developed is true.

She afterwards repudiated the confession that was presented yesterday, with her attorneys trying to bring out from the state's witnesses that she was sick and confused when she told her bloody yarn five weeks ago.

The woman, in her incongruous widow's weeds, sat listening intently to the reading of her original confession to the jury, possibly the most horrible tale that ever fell from human lips, the tale of a crime unutterably brutal and cold-blooded and unspeakably dumb.

Her mouth opened occasionally as if framing words, and once she said, not quite distinctly, an unconscious utterance, which may have been a denial of some utterance by the lawyer or perhaps an assurance to her soul that she was not alive and awake.

Right back to old Father Adam, the original and perhaps the loudest "squawker" among mankind against women, went Henry Judd Gray in telling how and why he lent his hand to the butchery of Albert Snyder.

She—she—she—she—she—she—she—she. That was the burden of the bloody song of the little corset salesman as read out in the packed courtroom in Long Island City yesterday.

She—she—she—she—she—she. 'Twas an echo from across the ages and an old familiar echo, at that. It was the same old "Squawk" of Brother Man whenever and wherever he is in a jam, that was first framed in the words:

"She gave me of the tree, and I did eat."

It has been put in various forms since then, as Henry Judd Gray, for one notable instance close at hand, put it in the form of eleven long, typewritten pages that were read yesterday, but in any form and in any language it remains a "squawk."

"She played me pretty hard."..."She said, 'You're going to do it, aren't you?' " ... "She kissed me." ... She did this....She did that....Always she—she—she—she—she ran the confession of Henry Judd.

And "she"—the woman accused—how did she take this most gruesome squawk?

Well, on the whole, better than you might expect.

You must remember it was the first time she had ever heard the confession of the man who once called her "Momsie." She probably had an inkling of it, but not its exact terms.

For a few minutes her greenish-blue eyes roared with such fury that I would not have been surprised to see her leap up, grab the window sash weight that lay among the exhibits on the district attorney's table, and perform the same offices on the shrinking Gray that he says she performed on her sleeping husband.

She "belabored him," Gray's confession reads, and I half-expected her to belabor Gray.

Her thin lips curled to a distinct snarl at some passages in the statement. I thought of a wildcat and a female cat, at that, on a leash. Once or twice she smiled, but it was a smile of insensate rage, not amusement. She once emitted a push of breath in a loud "phew," as you have perhaps done yourself over some tall tale.

The marble mask was contorted by her emotions for a time; she often shook her head in silent denial of the astounding charges of Gray, then finally she settled back calmly, watchful, attentive, and with an expression of unutterable contempt as the story of she—she—she—she ran along.

Contempt for Henry Judd, no doubt. True, she herself squawked on Henry Judd, at about the same time Henry Judd was squawking on her, but it is a woman's inalienable right to squawk.

As for Henry Judd, I still doubt he will last it out. He reminds me of a slowly collapsing lump of tallow. He sat huddled up to his baggy clothes, his eyes on the floor, his chin in hand, while the confession was being read. He seems to be folding up inch by inch every day.

He acts as if he is only semiconscious. If he was a fighter and came back to his corner in his present condition, they would give him smelling salts.

The man is a wreck, a strange contrast to the alert blond at the table behind him.

The room was packed with women yesterday, well-dressed richly befurred women from Park Avenue and from Broadway, and others not so well-dressed from Long Island City, and the small towns farther down the island. There were giggling young schoolgirls and staid-looking matrons, and, my friends, what do you think? Their sympathy is for Henry Judd Gray!

I made a point of listening to their opinions as they packed the hallways and jammed the elevators of the old courthouse yesterday and canvassed some of them personally, and they are all sorry for Gray. Perhaps it is his forlorn-looking aspect as he sits inert, numb, never raising his head, a sad spectacle of a man who admits he took part in one of the most atrocious murders in history.

There is no sympathy for Mrs. Snyder among the women and very little among the men. They all say something drastic ought to be done to her.

If you are asking a medium-boiled reporter of murder trials, I couldn't condemn a woman to death no matter what she had done, and I say this with all due consideration of the future hazards to long-suffering man from sash weights that any lesser verdict than murder in the first degree in the Snyder-Gray case may produce.

It is all very well for the rest of us to say what *ought* to be done to the blond throwback to the jungle cat that they call Mrs. Ruth Brown Snyder, but when you get in the jury room and start thinking about going home to tell the neighbors that you have voted to burn a woman—even a blond woman—I imagine the situation has a different aspect. The most astonishing verdict that could be rendered in this case, of course, would be first degree for the woman and something else for the man. I doubt that result. I am inclined to think that the verdict, whatever it may be, will run against both alike—death or life imprisonment.

Henry Judd Gray said he expects to go to the chair, and adds that he is not afraid of death, an enviable frame of mind, indeed. He says that since he told his story to the world from the witness stand, he has found tranquility, though his tale may also have condemned his blond partner in blood. But perhaps that's the very reason Henry Judd finds tranquility.

He sat in his cell in the county jail in Long Island yesterday, and read from one of the Epistles of John.

"Marvel not, my brethren, if the world hate you. We know that we have passed death unto life, because we love the brethren. He that loveth not his brother abideth in death. Whosoever hateth his brother is a murderer: and ye know that no murderer hath eternal life abiding in him."

A thought for the second Sunday after Pentecost.

In another cell, the blond woman was very mad at everybody

45

because she couldn't get a marcel for her bobbed locks, one hair of which was once stronger with Henry Judd Gray than the Atlantic cable.

The jury deliberated ninety-eight minutes before condemning Mrs. Snyder and Gray to die in the electric chair. Before his execution, Gray received a letter of forgiveness from his wife, who had shunned him after his arrest. He then announced: "I am ready to go. I have nothing to fear." Mrs. Snyder, saying God had forgiven her, died with a prayer on her lips.

"I wanted to put the fear into her against being an adulteress"

"Do not shout. Do what I tell you. Or else you will die," Dr. Geza deKaplany wrote in Hungarian on a prescription blank. The message was intended for his wife of five weeks, a model and one of San Francisco's most photographed beauties. She did shout. And she did die. This story by Carolyn Anspacher, from the *San Francisco Chronicle* of August 30, 1962, tells how.

© 1962 by the Chronicle Publishing Co. Reprinted by permission.

A beautiful twenty-five-year-old Hungarian refugee, who fled torture by the Communists in 1956, lay near death yesterday in Santa Clara General Hospital, mutilated almost beyond recognition by her physician-bridegroom of five weeks.

Victim of the coldly professional assault was Hajna Piller deKaplany. She was described by Hollywood impresario Barry Ashton as "very, very beautiful—with the purest, whitest skin I have ever seen."

Her assailant was the man she married on July 21 in Our Lady of the Wayside Church in Portola Valley, Dr. Geza deKaplany, 36, former Hungarian freedom fighter and now an anesthesiologist.

The physician, descendant of a notable Hungarian family, shrugged nonchalantly as San Jose police charged him with attempted murder.

"She's not going to die," he said indifferently. "I wanted to take her beauty away. I wanted to put the fear into her against being an adulteress."

Police said the doctor told them a "gossiping old woman" informed him in San Francisco earlier in the day that his beautiful

47

young wife had a boy friend. But Mrs. deKaplany herself denied she had been unfaithful or even had thought of another man.

Doctors at Santa Clara General Hospital, however, are not nearly so sanguine about Mrs. deKaplany's future as was her husband.

They say she has a "bare chance" to live. And, if she does live, her sight may be lost and the glowing beauty that made her one of San Francisco's top fashion models, and an arresting showgirl in several Hollywood and local nightclub productions, will be gone forever.

Doctors attending her said the extent of Mrs. deKaplany's disfigurement cannot yet be determined. They emphasized the extreme gravity of acid burns and said there is also the danger Mrs. deKaplany may be stricken with uremic poisoning.

According to Bart Collins, chief of detectives, this is what happened to Mrs. deKaplany, daughter of Mrs. Ilona Piller, of 56 Cervantes Boulevard, and the late Gyorgy Piller, world-noted as a fencing master:

Tuesday evening Mrs. deKaplany returned from San Francisco to her new and very elegant apartment at 1125 Ranchero Way, San Jose, after visiting with her mother and inquiring about resuming her modelling career.

Her bridegroom, wearing Bermuda shorts and sandals, had been pacing the patio, waiting for her. When she arrived, they went into the house.

Mrs. deKaplany managed to gasp the rest of the story to police and doctors.

She said her husband had an interlude of lovemaking almost immediately upon her return home. Then, inexplicably, she said, he pulled the shades throughout the house, turned up the radio, returned to the bedroom, and struck her repeatedly.

Then he bound her hands, one to each twin bed, and went to work after donning a pair of rubber surgical gloves.

Almost out of her mind with agony, Mrs. deKaplany managed to tell officers that her husband hit her in the face and slashed her with a butcher knife before he began applying the various acids—nitric, sulfuric, and hydrochloric— to her body with surgical gauze.

A neighbor, Frank Hernandez, reported he rang the deKaplany doorbell about 8:30 or 9:00 P.M. The doctor, wearing only a pair of undershorts, came to the door and seemed "distant and bewildered" and, when Hernandez invited him and his wife over for a drink, Dr. deKaplany replied:

"No—go 'way, go 'way!"

Mrs. deKaplany's screams were heard—and ignored—for nearly an hour by apartment-house neighbors. Finally, however, police received an anonymous phone call at 10:20 P.M. that "someone was being murdered."

Three minutes later patrolman Robert Moir arrived at the honeymoon apartment, rang the doorbell, and was admitted by Dr. deKaplany.

"She's in there," the physician said calmly and retired to the kitchen, where he took several stiff drinks of sour-mash whiskey.

Returning to the bedroom, he watched indifferently as ambulance attendants cut Mrs. deKaplany's bonds and applied emergency treatment.

At the hospital Mrs. deKaplany asked for and received last rites of the Roman Catholic Church.

Police were trying to determine what caused Dr. deKaplany's aberration.

After their marriage, the deKaplanys honeymooned in Hawaii and established their first home in the Ranchero Way apartment.

Neighbors said the young bride spent most of her days sunning herself beside the apartment-house swimming pool attired in shocking pink or green bikinis or one-piece swimsuits.

A few women said Mrs. deKaplany was "quiet and reserved" when other women were around but "bright and talkative" when the husbands were present.

But another tenant described Mrs. deKaplany as a "beautiful, beautiful creature," utterly devoted to her husband, proud of his profession, and eager to become a good housewife.

"She said she very much wanted children," the neighbor said.

The physician, on the other hand, was usually described as "sullen and introverted."

Before her marriage, the beautiful Hajna worked for a time in the accounting department of a swank San Francisco women's shop and then began a career in modelling. She appeared here and in Hollywood in two productions, the second only four months ago. In the first she was a brunette and in the second a blond.

Perhaps because of her faltering English, she kept "very much to herself." She was "exceedingly ambitious" and "strictly a nice girl—very ladylike," co-workers said.

Dr. deKaplany, a member of one of Hungary's oldest and most respected families, received his medical degree from the University of Szeged in 1951.

He fled Hungary in 1956 after having been wounded during the uprisings and took refuge first in Denmark and then in England, where he wrote a book, *A Doctor in Revolt*.

He came to the United States in 1957.

He interned at Milwaukee Hospital, in that city, and then General Hospital, remaining there until 1960. He spent a year as an instructor in the Yale Medical School and came to San Francisco in 1961. Here, he was chief medical resident at Franklin Hospital until just before his marriage.

Early this month he applied for admission to the Santa Clara County Medical Association and applied for the post of anesthesiologist at Doctor's Hospital there.

At the moment he was being booked for attempted murder, he was "under consideration" for the post.

Mrs. deKaplany and her parents likewise were refugees from Communist Hungary. Her father, coach of Hungary's 1956 Olympic fencing team, defected during the Melbourne Games and came to San Francisco, where he founded the Pannonia Athletic Club. The fencers he trained here won the U.S. National Championships for three consecutive years.

Regarded as the world's greatest fencing master, Piller was himself a gold medal winner in both team and individual saber competitions at the 1932 Olympics. He also twice won the world's individual saber championships.

Piller died in September, 1960 after a long illness.

Mrs. deKaplany's mother, summoned to her daughter's bedside, collapsed at the hospital.

Hajna deKaplany died thirty-three days after the Anspacher

story appeared. Dr. deKaplany was convicted of murder and sentenced to life in prison, escaping the death penalty because the jury believed he was insane. "I broke mentally, morally, and physically," the doctor said after the trial. "I was very sick that day." In 1976 he was paroled; he is now practicing medicine in Taiwan.

Chapter II

GRISLY TALES

Burke smothered his victim, then sold the corpse for dissection

This report was published December 27, 1828 in the *Scotsman* of Edinburgh at the end of the trial of William Burke and Helen MacDougal for the murder of Mary Docherty.

Mary Docherty, of middle age, and in good health, came to Edinburgh in October last, in search of her son. She saw him, had her lodgings paid for by him for a day or two, and seems, after thus satisfying the yearnings of natural affection, to have decided to return to Glasgow; but, as she and her son were both poor, this was to be done by means of begging.

On the morning before Halloween, she was asking charity in a grocer's shop in a western suburb of the town. There she was seen by William Burke, an Irishman too, who represented to this unsuspecting creature that his mother was a Docherty—a relation—and on this ground he offered her breakfast, and afterwards other meals, with a night's lodging. She was also supplied liberally with whiskey; and Burke; a woman, Helen MacDougal, with whom he lived as his wife; William Hare and his wife, a young Carter, and other men and women spent the earlier part of the evening as a merrymaking, with liquor, dance, and song. The stranger-guest acted the part of the musician, while the rest were fully aware that she was doomed—as they spoke of her among themselves freely as being "a shot for the doctors," which means a person intended to be murdered and sold for dissection.

Accordingly, in the later part of the evening, after a real or pretended scuffle betwixt Burke and Hare, during which their victim endeavored to separate them, the poor, deluded wretch was pushed over, and Burke, in presence of the parties before named, threw himself upon her, and extinguished life speedily by throttling or strangulation.

The deed was perpetrated in the most deliberate and scientific manner by Burke, who took from ten to fifteen minutes to make sure of his work, Hare sitting coolly by, and the two women, on hearing the first suffocating screech, running out into the passage, either from an instinctive horror of blood or, what is not less probable, from a design to prevent anyone from entering till the murder was completed. When it was so, the body was immediately stripped naked and, being doubled up, was thrust under some straw that lay on the ground at the foot of an open bed.

Hugh Alston, a grocer, heard quarrelling in Burke's betwixt 11:00 and 12:00, and about 12:00 David Paterson, the keeper of Dr. Knox's museum, accompanied Burke to his house, where, pointing to the straw, Burke said he had got something, by which Paterson understood a dead body for the doctor.

This was in the presence of two men and two women; and, being so immediately after the murder, it is a circumstance of very great importance. It authorizes many painful inferences.

Paterson sent for Burke next morning; and between 12:00 and 2:00 he saw Burke and Hare with Dr. Knox and Dr. Jones, one of his assistants. It was then arranged that the body should be delivered in the evening—that of Mary Docherty, which had been doubled up and compressed into an old tea chest. The porter, John MacCulloch, carried it from Burke's for five shillings, having assisted in the stuffing and packing.

The body was received on Saturday evening, and £ 5, part of the price, then paid; but no examination took place on reception, such as ought to be done in every case in which the medical man desires to satisfy his own mind that there are no indications of violent death on the bodies received by him.

On Sunday morning the box, still roped in the state in which it had been received, was opened in presence of an officer of police, when the body was found "apparently fresh and never interred, the appearance indicating strangulation or suffocation from pressure." [Editors' note: A lodger at Burke's, James Gray, had alerted police to the crime.]

We need not pursue these horrid details further. The true features of the case cannot be misunderstood. A trade in blood had been carried on with a deliberation, an openness, and with the knowledge and concurrence of numbers, which shocks belief and outrages all the feelings of our nature. No one, certainly, would have believed previously that brutalized criminality, depravity, and callousness could have existed on Earth in such a connected chain, to be worked for such terrible purposes.

And, while we would go far, insofar as the press is concerned, in making allowances for professional zeal, both in teachers and students, we must avow and assert, as we do solemnly, that for the future no consideration or motive will justify any teacher of anatomy, surgery, or medicine in paying money for a body without knowing whose it is, and being satisfied that nothing, with a view to dissection, has been done by any human being to abridge or destroy life.

The (medical) profession in general enjoy that reputation and are known to be actuated by such humane and honorable feelings as to place them far beyond the reach of suspicion; but it is manifest that, if after what has happened, a teacher or professor were to give money for a body, without inquiry and proof of natural death, he might not only be accessory to murder but, when education and cultivation of mind is taken into account, would be even worse than the wretch, debased by vice and corrupted by his money, who should have perpetrated the deed. There is not, as we conceive, any means of evading this conclusion.

We would say a word or two for the poor Irish; for it is impossible not to perceive that the circumstance of Burke and Hare being Irishmen will strengthen the Scottish prejudices against the natives of the Emerald Isle.

It is not to be denied, perhaps, that, as there is more ignorance, degradation, and misery in Ireland than in Scotland, the Irish are likely to fall more easily into the habit of committing crime. The population of that country is less elevated above the brute in point of condition; the moral feelings, consequently, less educated, and conscience less active; but we should remember that in yielding to the fiercer passions ourselves we only make matters worse. We would excite that which we would allay.

The Irish are, perhaps, more easily softened by kindness than any other people; and it is by good offices, not by blows or persecution, that they are to be reformed. In their present lamentable state we see nothing but the genuine results of a long course of misgovernment and of the recklessness which brings human beings into the world without the slightest consideration whether their parents shall be able to raise them at all above the level of the brutes.

An all-male jury deliberated fifty minutes after a two-day trial and found William Burke guilty and Helen MacDougal not guilty of the murder of Mary Docherty. Burke was executed in Edinburgh on January 28, 1829.

A brutal murder
by Jack the Ripper
terrorizes the East End

More than a dozen murders were committed in the
east of London in 1888, but probably only five of
those were the work of "Jack the Ripper." The
savage killer's second victim was Annie Chapman, a
destitute widow also known as "Dark Annie" and
"Annie Siffey." This report on her death is from the
Times of London of September 10, 1888.

Whitechapel and the whole of the east of London have again
been thrown into a state of intense excitement by the discovery
early on Saturday morning of the body of a woman who had
been murdered in a similar way to Mary Ann Nichols at Buck's
Row on Friday week. In fact, the similarity of the two cases is
startling, as the victim of the outrage had her head almost severed
from her body, and was completely disembowelled.

This latest crime, however, even surpasses the others in
ferocity. The scene of the murder, which makes the fourth in the
same neighborhood within the past few weeks, is at the back of
the house, 29 Hanbury Street, Spitalfields. This street runs from
Commercial to Baker's Row, the end of which is close to Buck's
Row. The house, which is rented by Emilia Richardson, is let out
to various lodgers, all of the poorer class. In consequence, the
front door is open both day and night, so that no difficulty would
be experienced by anyone in gaining admission to the back portion
of the premises.

Shortly before six o'clock on Saturday morning, John Davis,
who lives with his wife at the top portion of No. 29, and is a porter
engaged in Spitalfields Market, went down into the backyard,
where a horrible sight presented itself to him. Lying close up
against the wall, with her head touching the other side wall, was
the body of a woman. Davis could see that her throat was severed

in a terrible manner and that she had other wounds of a nature too shocking to be described.

The deceased was lying flat on her back with her clothes disarranged. Without nearer approaching the body, but telling his wife what he had seen, Davis ran to the Commercial Street police station, a short distance away, and gave information to Inspector Chandler, H Division, who was in charge of the station at the time. That officer, having dispatched a constable for Dr. Baxter Phillips, Spital Square, the divisional surgeon, repaired to the house, accompanied by several other policemen. The body was still in the same position, and there were large clots of blood all around it.

It is evident that the murderer thought he had completely cut off the head, as a handkerchief was found wrapped around the neck, as though to hold it together. There were spots and stains of blood on the wall. One or more rings seem to have been torn from the middle finger of the left hand.

After being inspected by Dr. Phillips and his assistant, the remains were removed by ambulance to the mortuary in Old Montagu Street. By this time the news had spread quickly that another diabolical murder had been committed, and when the police came out of the house with the body, a large crowd, consisting of some hundreds of persons, had assembled. The excitement became very great, and loud were the expressions of terror heard on all sides.

At the mortuary the doctors made a more minute examination of the body, after which the clothes were taken off. The deceased was laid in the same small shell in which Mary Ann Nichols was placed.

Detective Sergeant Thicke, Sergeant Leach, and other detective officers were soon on the spot, while a telegram was sent to Inspector Abberline, at Scotland Yard, apprising him of what had happened. It will be recollected that this officer assisted in the inquiry concerning the murder in Buck's Row.

A minute search being made of the yard, a portion of an envelope, stained with blood, was found. It had the crest of the Sussex Regiment on it, and the date London, August 20, but the address portion, with the exception of one letter, "M," was torn off. In addition, two pills were also picked up.

Inquiries were quickly set on foot with a view to having the woman identified, and persons of both sexes were taken out of the neighboring common lodging houses, which abound in this district, to the mortuary. One of these, Timothy Donovan, the deputy of a common lodging house, 35 Dorset Street, recognized the body as that of a woman known by the name of Annie Siffey.

He had seen her in the kitchen of the lodging house as late as half past one or two o'clock that morning. He knew her as an unfortunate and that she generally frequented Stratford for a living. He asked her for her lodging money, when she said, "I have not got it. I am weak and ill, and have been in the infirmary." Donovan told her that she knew the rules, and she went out to get some money.

Although there are various statements that she was seen with a man in a public house at five o'clock, the police have no authentic information respecting that point. Donovan did not turn the woman out of the lodging house; he simply did his duty by telling her that she knew the rules of the establishment—that the price of lodging had to be paid beforehand. At that time she was wearing three brass rings.

Other inquiries soon established that the woman's real name was Annie Chapman, and that she was known by the name of "Dark Annie." She was the widow of a pensioner, and had lived formerly at Windsor.

Some few years since she separated from her husband, who made her a weekly allowance of ten shillings. At his death she had to do the best she could for a living.

It is also known that formerly she lived with a sievemaker in the neighborhood, and on account of that got the nickname of "Siffey."

Only on Monday last she had a quarrel with another woman of her acquaintance, and during a fight and struggle got severely mauled and kicked.

On Saturday afternoon Dr. Phillips and his assistant made a most exhaustive post-mortem examination, lasting upwards of two hours. Although, of course, the exact details have not been made public, it is known that Dr. Phillips was unable to find any trace of alcohol in the stomach of the deceased, thus disproving many reports that when the woman was last seen alive she was the worse for drink.

The deceased was a little over five feet in height, and of fair complexion, with blue eyes and dark brown wavy hair. A singular coincidence about the corpse was that there were two front teeth missing, as in the case of Mary Ann Nichols. On the right side of the head was a large bruise, showing that the deceased woman must have been dealt a heavy blow at that spot. There were also other bruises about the face, and finger marks were discernible. The latter indicate that the murderer must first have grasped his victim by the throat, probably in order to prevent her crying out.

The police believe that the murder has been committed by the same person who perpetrated the three previous ones in the district, and that only one person is concerned in it. This person, whoever he might be, is doubtless laboring under some terrible form of insanity, as each of the crimes has been of a most fiendish character, and it is feared that unless he can speedily be captured more outrages of a similar class will be committed.

During the whole of Saturday and yesterday a large crowd congregated in front of the house in Hanbury Street, and the neighbors on either side did much business by making a small charge to persons who were willing to pay it to view from windows the yard in which the murder was committed. On Saturday a rumor got about that the murderer had been caught, but the only ground for such a statement was that a blind man had been arrested in Spitalfields Market on a warrant to answer a charge of stabbing. Later in the day this man was charged at the Worship Street police court, and sentenced to three months' hard labor.

Great complaints are made concerning the inadequate police protection at the East End, and this want is even admitted by the local police authorities themselves, but they are unable to alter the existing state of affairs.

Outrages and acts of lawlessness daily occur in broad daylight in the principal thoroughfares of the East End, and the offenders are seldom brought to justice, owing to the inability of the police to properly cover the whole of the ground within their jurisdiction. During Saturday and yesterday, several persons were detained at the various police stations in the district, but were liberated after proper inquiries had been made; and up to the present time the police have no clue to the murderer, and lament that they have no good ground to work upon.

The identity of "Jack the Ripper" is one of the greatest mysteries of all time. Suspects have ranged from Prince Albert Victor, Duke of Clarence, a known sex deviate, to Dr. Thomas Neill Cream, whose dying words, when he was hanged in 1892 for poisoning London prostitutes, were: "I am Jack the Ripper." In addition to the deaths of Mary Ann Nichols and Annie Chapman, the Ripper was blamed for the subsequent murders of Elizabeth Stride, Catherine Eddowes, and Mary Jane Kelly.

William George Heirens during a re-enactment of the Degnan kidnapping.

Chicago's Jekyll-Hyde case: Bill Heirens the student, George Murman the killer

When University of Chicago sophomore William George Heirens was arrested for the murder of six-year-old Suzanne Degnan, the big Chicago dailies rushed to judgment about his guilt and portrayed him as Dr. Jekyll (hair combed) and Mr. Hyde (hair mussed). This story about the case was written by Elgar Brown and appeared in the *Chicago Herald-American* of July 16, 1946.

William Heirens, the seventeen-year-old crime riddle, was positively identified by an eyewitness today as the man seen walking a block from the James E. Degnan home on the night little Suzanne Degnan was murdered.

The time was 1:00 A.M. on the clear, cold morning of last January 7, and Heirens was carrying something in a brown bag or sack, according to the witness, George Subgrunski, 24, who was a GI at the time.

This was the initial break in the case placing Heirens in the vicinity of the Degnan atrocity, and it came as the dual-personality boy was joining authorities in a chorused denial of detailed, unofficial reports he had admitted slaying Suzanne, Frances Brown, and Josephine Ross.

Experts were pointing out, however, that the vivid word picture of the three crimes may have been given under the influence of truth serum, in which event the university student would not remember his admissions.

Subgrunski, who was discharged from the Army only two days after this nocturnal encounter on Kenmore Avenue near the Degnan home, leveled the finger of identification at Heirens as the sullen boy appeared in court for arraignment on twenty-nine burglary and assault charges.

State's Atty. William J. Tuohy announced immediately he planned to place the Degnan and Brown murder charges before the grand jury with a view of indicting Heirens. As to the Ross case, he added, more evidence is needed.

Said young Subgrunski, after staring long and hard at the suspect shuffling in and out of the jam-packed courtroom:

"Early on the morning of January 7, I took a girl friend to her home at 6159 Kenmore. My car was parked on the east side of the street when I saw a young man carrying a brown bag or sack walk across from the west side to the east side, turning south.

"He passed about five feet in front of my car. I had the headlights turned on. My curiosity was aroused. I drove ahead and overtook him about thirty-five feet from the intersection. I didn't stop, though I had a hunch to ask him what he was carrying.

"I am positive the man was Heirens, whom I saw in the courtroom today."

Almost immediately thereafter Subgrunski went to Camp Grant, where he was discharged on January 9. While in the camp, he said, he read newspaper accounts of the Degnan kidnap-slaying and contacted Chicago police, telling them what he had seen that night in the Degnan neighborhood.

Not until today, he added, had he been called on to attempt any identification. Heirens is reported to have admitted an amazing story of split personality—that he had two identities—Heirens the student and George Murman the killer.

As Murman, he killed for thrill. When he resumed the identity of Heirens after the crimes, he felt that he bore no responsibility for his acts. He seemed able to divorce his two egos completely.

If the alleged admissions were under truth serum, which was administered at one stage of the questioning, they will have no standing in court. All efforts to persuade the boy to make a formal confession have failed.

So long as the suspect persists in denying the crime, authorities hope to convict him on fingerprint evidence.

Prints identified as Heirens' were found on the Degnan ransom note and in the apartment of the slain Wave, Frances Brown.

Also there is the possibility of handwriting evidence and other circumstantial data.

The University of Chicago first-year student was in the role of his normal personality, William George Heirens, when he attended a movie the night of last January 6 with his roommate, Joseph Costello, and an unidentified girl.

Leaving his companions at midnight on the South Side, the boy assumed the role of George Murman, a mythical, swashbuckling character he had conjured up when he was thirteen years old.

He boarded an elevated train and rode directly to the Thorndale station, where he got off. He knew this station was nearest the home of James E. Degnan at 5943 Kenmore.

On the previous night's foray, pursuing his extracurricular career as a fire-escape plunderer of homes, he had looted Harry Gold's apartment at 5959 Kenmore.

He had glanced from the Gold window and seen little Suzanne undressing in her room. He determined then and there to kill her. His keen eyes noted a ladder in the yard of Margaret Perry's day nursery at 6033 Winthrop.

He craftily fitted this ladder into his crazy plan. Beyond slaying the innocent youngster and slashing her body, he did not think. He had cooked up no scheme for disposing of the body or for benefiting by his terrible misdeed.

Emerging from the el in the early hours of January 7, young Heirens went straight to the Perry yard, seized the ladder, carried it to the Degnan home, and set it against the second-floor window of Suzanne's room.

He placed a handkerchief gag in the sleeping victim's mouth and carried her silently down the ladder. At this point the girl awakened and made some muffled cries. The university student, in his mind's eye now the ruthless George Murman, calmly laid her on the ground and strangled her with his bare hands.

He stared a moment at the inert figure on the ground. This was the way George Murman took care of his victims! Then he carried Suzanne's body to the basement of a building at 5901 Winthrop.

He busied himself with gruesome tasks until nearly daylight. He had fared northward armed with a gun and a hunting knife. Now he drew forth the knife and dissected the tiny body.

65

When the pieces were ready for disposal he made use again of earlier knowledge. He knew this neighborhood; he had worked as a delivery boy for a nearby liquor store several years before; he had once lived in the 1200 block of Loyola Avenue.

Carrying one bundle at a time, Heirens plodded through the district he knew so well, distributing pieces of the girl's body in various sewer openings. He believed they would be washed away and no evidence would remain.

During this macabre procedure there were perilous moments for several janitors walking to their work. Heirens saw them coming and drew his gun, ready and apparently willing to shoot them dead. Instead, they turned off his course, and he quietly resumed his operations.

After the body was disposed of, Heirens considered his next move. He returned to the apartment basement where he had dissected the body. He thought of writing a ransom note to confuse the police.

He was not excited. Twice previously he had committed murder, and nothing had happened. He drew a pad of paper from his pocket and tore away the bottom sheet.

He tore the sheet in half lengthwise. With what he considered extreme craftiness, he smeared grease on the paper to "destroy" the fingerprints. (It was these prints that first linked the boy with the Degnan crime.)

He wrote the ransom note and carried it back to the Degnan home, where the ladder still stood against the window. He climbed to the top, tossed the note inside, and walked away.

Riding back to the Midway on the el, he went to his dormitory room, destroyed his blood-stained overcoat, and went to breakfast. He resumed his normal role of William George Heirens. He missed his first class for no other reason than that it was "unimportant." But he went to two later classes that morning, and his appearance and actions were normal.

Less than a month before the Degnan girl was slain, Heirens—again play-acting his favorite outlaw—had been prowling on the North Side in typical fashion. The date was December 10, 1945.

Swinging with the agility of a monkey, he clambered onto a fire escape and reached the sixth floor of the Pine Crest Hotel at 3941 Pine Grove. He entered an apartment shared by Miss Brown, recently discharged from the Waves, and a girl friend. His sole aim was burglary.

As he entered the living room, Miss Brown, clad in pajamas, entered from the bathroom. Reasoning that George Murman would act swiftly in such an emergency, Heirens drew his gun and fired.

The bullet felled Miss Brown but did not kill her. Heirens, alarmed at the gun's explosion in the quiet of the night, hastily retreated to the fire escape and crouched, waiting.

When there was no reaction through the silent building, he then ventured inside again. He stooped over Miss Brown and discovered she was breathing. He went to the kitchen, seized a long bread knife, returned, and twice thrust the eight-inch blade into his unconscious victim's neck.

He lugged the bleeding, lifeless body to the bathroom, stripped off the pajamas, and carefully washed off the blood. He swathed the head in towels. He draped the body in a grotesque position over the edge of the tub, face downward.

He methodically ransacked the apartment. Then, seized suddenly with a desire that seemed paramount in the makeup of George Murman—an impelling urge to do something daring—he snatched up a lipstick. Removing one picture from the wall, he scribbled across this wall in large letters:

"For heaven's sake, catch me before I kill more. I cannot control myself."

The modern Jekyll-Hyde's first venture into homicide—insofar as the present available record is complete—occurred on June 3, 1945, when the boy was indulging his alter ego's passion for prowling on fire escapes and peering into windows.

He looked into the apartment of Mrs. Ross, a twice-divorced widow, at 4108 Kenmore. He saw a purse. His acquisitive instinct was aroused. He saw the purse as a challenge. He did not consider its value. He needed no money, seldom sold any loot. He merely wished to show "Murman's" ability to get away with burglary.

Mrs. Ross, alone in the apartment, was aroused when Heirens

leaped through the window. He coolly drew his hunting knife and stabbed her to death. Then he performed some very peculiar acts motivated by the urge to be "daring and different."

He pasted adhesive tape over one of the neck wounds, though fully aware the victim was beyond human help. He stripped off her nightgown and left the body nude on the bed. He seized a nearby red dress and tied it tightly around the neck, seemingly in an attempt to stanch the stream of blood.

As a last, strange gesture before fleeing, he dropped the blood-stained night clothing into the bathtub. He took the purse and departed via window and fire escape.

In Heirens' memory, the impulse to enact two contrasting roles throughout his life first assailed the boy at age thirteen. He dubbed his alter ego George Murman, his own middle name and a last name that he devised.

As the boy he was born to be, Heirens appeared entirely normal. Associates found him agreeable, thoughtful, smart, easy to get along with. He was studious and at times displayed a deep interest in religion. He denies any unusual sex habits, and his record fails to disclose any sex-tinged crime.

As George Murman, the boy was quite out of this world. He donned the robes of this mythical character always at night. And then he became a personality to be shunned and feared. He prowled, plundered for pleasure. He roamed the city.

One of the circumstances sure to puzzle the alienists is that when he returned to normal as Heirens, the youthful criminal had a vivid memory of the things he had done as George Murman—but apparently no remorse, no feeling of guilt.

Engaged in his nefarious crimes, he felt no fear. Returned to the safety of normal pursuits, he felt no regret.

So far from trying to shield the "Murman" myth from the world, William Heirens actually dragged the figment of his imagination into his own dealing with police after his seizure in a burglary.

Where did he obtain all the loot found in his dormitory room? From George Murman, the broad-shouldered student told questioners. He didn't know where Murman lived or his current whereabouts. But he produced a letter from "Murman, written in

Texas." It read:

"Dear Bill: I feel for you being in jail. Tough luck. You will know better next time. I am on my way to Milwaukee for a month and then to El Paso. Jock has things fixed up in that territory south of there.

"Tom, Sid, Pat, and myself will start the road from there. Once the stuff is on the way, it will be easy. Howey, Johnny, and Carl will be out of the Army soon with a few new ideas.

"I will see you soon. If this doesn't pan out, the gang might be broken up. We are not keeping any of our old plans, so burn what you have. We will burn ours."

The letter, experts said at once, was in William Heirens' writing. Just a little boy who got his dreams of outlawry all mixed up with reality.

After sundry conferences between state and defense lawyers, all bathed in an aura of furtiveness, it had been established today that defense attorneys John and Mal Coghlan and Rolland Towle were "angling" for a deal. They were said to be offering a plea of guilty as bait in the hope of landing a life prison term.

State's Attorney Tuohy has been adamant, it is reported, in his demand for a complete, written legal confession of the Degnan, Brown, and Ross murders in exchange for a sentence of "at least" 199 years.

It was predicted by Criminal Courts Building observers that the dickering would go on, perhaps for several days, before an agreement is reached.

Revelation of the "deal" negotiations explains the unprecedented 2½-hour conference Sunday afternoon among Tuohy, First Asst. State's Atty. Wilbert F. Crowley, and the Coghlans. All principals have supplied no comment and no hints on the nature of this discussion.

The deal story also explains two earlier parleys between opposing counsel, as well as Crowley's secretive conversation yesterday with John Coghlan after the defense lawyer had spent forty-five minutes in his client's cell.

Tuohy and Crowley have simply and persistently denied that they have a confession "at this time." The Coghlans and Towle have been equally persistent in claiming there is no confession.

The term "confession" usually applies in a legal sense to a formal, written statement, whereas Heirens' "split-personality" version is reported to have been an oral recital.

Among those joining yesterday's chorus of denials in the matter of the rumored admissions were Heirens himself and his parents, Mr. and Mrs. George Heirens, who visited their son nearly an hour and brought him magazines and religious tracts.

Mrs. Heirens, visibly upset on her departure from the jail, told reporters William hadn't admitted anything to anybody, but added loyally:

"If he's guilty he'll tell. He's been brought up to tell the truth."

Radio news bulletins are "piped" into the county jail cells, and when young Heirens heard a report of his "admission" last night, he howled for Warden Frank Sain, and repeated his stout denials. The usually grammatical university student caused some puzzlement, however, by shouting to the warden:

"I haven't admitted nothing to nobody."

Defense lawyers' plea for a continuance today was to be based on a need for time to prepare various motions, including one to suppress some of the evidence of burglary on grounds it was seized illegally.

Heirens was convicted of the Degnan murder and sentenced to life in prison.

Dean Corll loved kids, neighbors believed; then police found the corpses

Elmer Wayne Henley, 17, and David Owen Brooks, 18, told Texas police that Dean Arnold Corll offered them $200 for every boy they enticed to his apartment. So they picked up hitchhikers and invited them to paint- and glue-sniffing "parties." "In all, I guess there were between twenty-five and thirty boys killed, and they were buried in three different places," Brooks said. Henley led police to the graves. This story by Ed Deswysen from the *Houston Chronicle* of August 15, 1973 reconstructs Corll's life.

Dean Arnold Corll was born at the happiest of times, on Christmas Eve, 1939, in Fort Wayne, Indiana.

The war building up in Europe then seemed so far away for the baby's parents.

Arnold Corll, a mechanic at a factory, and his wife, Mary, both twenty-three, apparently were delighted with their first child: a healthy, normal boy to all appearances.

"But his parents never were happy," says a relative who doesn't want her name used. "They fought and fussed before they got married, and they fought and fussed right up to the end."

Only the sketchiest of details can be found about Dean Corll's boyhood.

Those closest to him are guarded in their speech now that the horror of unnatural sex, torture, and murder has linked his name to twenty-seven slayings.

The family remained in Fort Wayne until the end of World War II, then their names disappear from the phone book, the city directory, and the courthouse records.

One source in Fort Wayne believes Arnold and Mary Corll

71

Dean Arnold Corll.

ended their marriage about that time, although there's no record there to show it.

"I don't believe in divorce," the relative said, commenting on the breakup. "When people marry and have children, they ought to give up their own lives."

An old-time friend of Arnold Corll in Fort Wayne believes he packed off to "some kind of farming operation in the South."

Mary Corll apparently remarried, because she shows up next with a new name, Mary West. She had custody of her two boys from the first marriage, Dean and his younger brother, Stanley. And she had a daughter, Joyce West, by her second husband.

"Dean was a good boy," the relative says. "But the good ones are so often used by the damnable ones."

The relative says Dean was brought up in the Methodist Church, but he usually limited his churchgoing to special days such as Christmas and Easter.

"Why, I never saw him with a cigarette," she says. "And I never heard him curse."

People thought of him as "good ole Dean," she recalls. "He was almost too good, tried to do favors for people, always tried to make the best of every situation."

Where Dean Arnold Corll lived from the time he left Fort Wayne until he moved with his mother to Vidor, Texas, near Beaumont, in 1954 is not known.

Dean, by then fourteen, enrolled as a freshman at Vidor High School.

Teachers describe him as punctual, neatly dressed, quiet, never a disciplinary problem.

He failed English in his senior year, postponing his graduation until the end of summer school in 1958.

"High school was sort of a struggle for him," the relative says. "He had to work, helping out his mother, and he had odd jobs here and there."

He played trombone in the high school stage band, about the only outside activity he found time for, says a former classmate and fellow musician, who also asked for anonymity.

She recalled that Dean was "a very good musician" and a "nice guy." He dated two girls that she knew of, and there was no suspicion of homosexual tendencies.

"Vidor was so strict in those days, I don't think we even knew what a homosexual was," she says.

"All the acceptable behavior was motivated by the Baptist Church, and you didn't even smoke in Vidor."

A former band instructor remembers Dean only after thumbing through an old yearbook to find his picture.

"He was there in the band, but when you've got a big band, students just don't stand out in your mind unless they are outstanding musicians or unless they are discipline problems," he says. "Dean Corll was neither."

Dean had a "best friend" in high school who still can't believe all they're saying about his old buddy.

"Let me put it this way," he says. "If Dean Corll had knocked on my door last Wednesday night before this story broke, I would have invited him in for a beer."

Dean seemed normal, the friend says. "He liked girls just like the rest of us," he says, recalling that they frequently attended drive-in movies together where they spent most of their time trying to make out with the girls.

He recalls that Dean seemed to be better off financially than most of his classmates. He owned a car.

The boys went camping together on several occasions. "Dean was a good outdoorsman," his friend says. "Sometimes we'd drive down near the Trinity River and pick up pecans."

Dean's mother, Mrs. West, doing her best to keep her children together in Vidor, operated a candy store there and made pralines, which were sold to drugstores and restaurants.

"Dean made up the pralines with the pecans we picked up at the river," his friend says.

Dean remained active in the family's growing candy business after his graduation from high school.

But there was an interruption of two years when he went back to Indiana to care for his recently widowed grandmother. That was in 1960.

"He knew she'd be alone and would need someone to take her to church and places," a relative says. "He got a job up there and stayed with his grandmother for two years, but he always managed to send a little money to his mother down here."

Dean Corll returned home in 1962. His family had moved to Houston.

He lived with his mother, younger brother, and half-sister in a house they rented in the Heights area.

Using the kitchen as their factory, they established Corll Candy Company. Mrs. West was president, Dean vice president, and Stanley secretary-treasurer. Joyce helped with the chores.

Dean was twenty-four when he was drafted by the U.S. Army.

He entered the Army at a reception center in Houston on August 10, 1964 and was assigned to Fort Polk, Louisiana for basic training. From there he went to Fort Benning, Georgia, where he attended the Army's radio-repair school.

He received a permanent assignment as a radio repairman at Fort Hood, Texas.

He had an exemplary record. "Nothing derogatory," an Army spokesman said. "No time lost."

Dean applied for a hardship discharge soon after he arrived at Fort Hood. He asked to be released to help his family.

The Army released him at Fort Hood on June 11, 1965 with an honorable discharge, just ten months after he entered the service.

Dean Corll returned to his family and the candy business.

Shortly, the Corll Candy Company moved to larger quarters at 505 W. 22nd Avenue, directly across the street from Helms Elementary School in the Heights.

Mary West, still president of the company, took her own apartment at 1845 Airport Boulevard.

Dean, who became general manager as well as vice president, rented an apartment on 21st Avenue, just a block away from the business.

Mrs. Fred Hilligiest, who lives at 402 W. 27th, recalls hearing about the candy factory from her children, who attended the elementary school.

"My son, David, would come home all excited, saying the man was giving away candy to the children," she says. "It was the talk of the neighborhood."

But Mrs. Hilligiest says she had a funny feeling about it.

"Then I heard that this man was inviting the children to a back room where he kept a pool table," she says. "I could understand the free candy, maybe, but this sounded a little peculiar to me." She says she forbade her son to visit the candy man.

"I'll never know whether he went back or not," Mrs. Hilligiest says.

Her son, David, 13, disappeared two years ago. The youngster is presumed by authorities to be among the Corll-related victims.

Now, back to Dean Arnold Corll, the pleasant, smiling candy man of the Heights.

He stood 5 feet 11 inches and weighed 190 pounds, mostly muscle. He had closely cropped brown hair, lively brown eyes.

Although his parents were divorced long ago, Dean kept in contact with his father, who settled in Houston about the time the rest of the family was living in Vidor.

Arnold Corll, who had remarried, owned a home in Pasadena, and worked as an electrician at Baylor College of Medicine.

Relatives recall that Dean visited his father two or three times a week, keeping him posted on the activities of the family and business.

About 1968, the Corll Candy Company was dissolved.

Mrs. West and her daughter, Joyce, moved to Colorado. Their address there is unknown.

Stanley took a job as a machine operator in Bellaire.

Dean decided to learn a trade.

He enrolled in an electrician's training program offered by Houston Lighting & Power Company.

And he grew restless. He was to move at least ten times in the next five years, from a one-room efficiency to a town house, from a garden apartment to a bungalow in Pasadena.

In 1969, he struck up a friendship with a fourteen-year-old boy named David Owen Brooks, the son of a paving contractor in the Heights section of northwest Houston.

Brooks said they formed a homosexual alliance, with Corll paying him for his part in acts of sodomy. They shared several apartments from time to time.

Brooks said he was horrified during a visit to Corll's apartment at 3300 Yorktown about three years ago.

Brooks said he walked into the living room, unannounced, and found Corll molesting two boys bound to a three-by-eight-foot board. Corll and the boys were naked.

Brooks said that Corll later told him he killed both boys.

At least twenty-five more victims were to die, perhaps the same way, in the next three years.

Brooks says he helped bury many of the victims, but he denies taking part in killing them.

About eighteen months ago, Elmer Wayne Henley, 17, a junior high school dropout from the Heights, joined Corll and Brooks in the macabre venture that would rank as the most massive murder spree in modern U.S. history.

They left tell-tale signs, but no one apparently suspected them until it was too late.

A former apartment manager at Westcott Towers, 904 Westcott, said a maintenance man discovered three or four bullet holes in the door to the apartment shared by Corll and Brooks.

The door was replaced without question.

When Corll and Brooks moved out a month or so later, the manager said a slab of steel was discovered nailed to the inside of the new door.

The alliance began to crack two months ago.

Brooks moved out on Corll. Now eighteen, Brooks married a girl named Bridget Clark, who is pregnant.

And Henley says he couldn't take it much longer. Corll had a blood lust, he says.

At the same time, Corll's father moved to a new house in Houston. Now that his son did not have a roommate to share expenses, he offered to let him use the house in Pasadena.

Early in the morning of August 8, inside the white frame bungalow, the first inkling of the horror broke.

The world listened in disbelief as the tale unfolded.

There were three witnesses—Henley, another young man of twenty, and a fifteen-year-old girl.

Henley said Corll was going mad. "He said he was going to kill us all, but first he was going to have his fun," he said.

Corll had tied up the two youths and the girl while they were in a stupor from inhaling paint fumes.

"I sweet-talked him," Henley says. "I promised I'd torture and

kill them for him if he'd let me go. So he did."
Then Henley pumped five bullets into Corll's chest.
Corll went to his grave two days later.
He received a Christian burial.
And an American flag draped his coffin, a reminder of his service to his country.
The Reverend Robert D. Joiner, pastor of Sunset United Methodist Church in Pasadena, spoke.
"We must now deliver this man unto God's judgment and also His mercy and grace," he said.
"The greatest heroism is just going on and remembering that Christ came to the world to love those whom others despised."

Elmer Wayne Henley was found guilty of six of the murders and sentenced to 594 years in prison. In 1978, Henley's conviction was overturned on a technicality by a Texas appeals court. David Owen Brooks was convicted of one murder and sentenced to life. The Houston Murder record was broken in 1978 by John Wayne Gacy, whose crimes in the Chicago area were remarkably similar to those attributed to Corll, Henley and Brooks.

Chapter III

UNDERWORLD

Lt. Becker issued the order to Rose: "I want Herman Rosenthal croaked"

This story by Herbert Bayard Swope is from the
New York World of October 27, 1912.

"Herman Rosenthal has squealed again."

Through the pallid underworld the sibilant whisper ran. It was
heard in East Side dens; it rang in the opium houses in
Chinatown; it crept up to the semi-pretentious stuss and crap
games of the 14th Street region; and it reached into the more
select circles of uptown gambling where business is always good
and graft is always high.

Rosenthal had squealed once too often.

This time his action was a direct affront to the "System." He
had publicly defied it. He had set it, through its lieutenant, at
naught. He had publicly thrown down the gauntlet, and it was
snatched up to be returned in the form of four bullets crashing into
his head while he stood in the heart of the city under a blaze of
lights that enabled bystanders to follow every move of the four
assassins, who, their job having been done, and well done,
swarmed aboard the gray auto that had brought them to their
work, and fled, secure, as they thought, from successful pursuit
because they were acting under the sheltering hand of police Lt.
Charles Becker, who had issued the order to Jack Rose:

"I want Herman Rosenthal croaked!"

But in his death Herman Rosenthal found a thousand tongues

Lieutenant Charles Becker.

where he had been but one. His murder cried in accusation a thousand-fold stronger than any he could have made. In his death he gave life to the grudge that he had been nursing in his heart.

In this dream of life, which reads so clearly it would seem to be a work of art—an unreal thing rather than a real story lived by real people—three figures loom.

Around them the plot is spun. Without them the action lags. Of them one is dead by murder, one is about to pay the penalty for this crime by death in the electric chair, and the third in fear and trembling awaits his summons—sure it will come—from the friends of those subordinate actors in the tragedy whom he surrendered to the law.

Rosenthal squeals; Becker the police blackmailer and Rose, his creature, enter upon the stage at the rise of the curtain and are never once away from it until the final fall.

And behind this trio hangs the vast, impalpable spectacle, the System in whose labyrinthian maze men are killed, others are robbed, and women are made slaves—each a sacrifice to the greater glory of the System.

Becker was of the System, by the System, and for the System. He lived and had his being through the grace he found in its eyes. And shining by reflection stood Rose, who had long fought against the System and then had changed and fought for it—for it with such a profit that it was not difficult for him to persuade Rosenthal, then his friend, to abandon the habit of a lifetime, and enlist as an ally instead of remaining an enemy.

To these men and their ilk Becker was the System, and the System was Becker. Like Briareus,* he had a hundred arms, and each of them reached into the pocket of whoever was engaged in an occupation that needed quiet and darkness rather than the light of day and the eyes of the public.

He is big in girth and stature. He stands 5 feet 11 and weighs 190 pounds. His shoulders are broad and his chest deep. His eyes are brown and look straight at you, or did look straight at you until the time came when all men looked at him accusingly, and then he averted his glance.

* In Greek mythology, a hundred-handed giant who freed Zeus after the god was bound by the allies of his jealous wife Hera.

He is dark in hair and skin. His nose is straight and big, jutting out uncompromisingly over a long upper lip, a mouth like a cut of a knife and a chin that sticks out squarely at the end of a jaw that looks like a granite block. Yes, Becker is strong—his looks do not belie him—but, with all his strength, he has a certain softness that has enabled him to ingratiate himself with his superiors, that has held their confidence when he was gazed at askance by all others, and that has held the belief of some of his friends unto the last, although he now lies, broken and disgraced, shut off from the world, soon to pay the penalty for his deeds, in the most awful manner known to our law.

Becker is forty-two years old. He joined the police force in 1893. His career has become a troublesome one since then.

His first serious trouble befell him when, in chasing a supposed gang of burglars, he shot and killed an innocent bystander, a youthful plumber's apprentice named John Fay.

And then it was that Becker learned what the System meant. Then he became a neophyte in the order. For, by the operations of the supreme power of the police department—that vast, mysterious, secret organization which numbers among its devotees the lowest probationer and the highest official in velvet and gold braid, inspired by graft and unified by fear—he was protected from blame.

The body of the innocent Fay was identified as John O'Brien, a burglar, and was sent to the morgue under that name. Becker was acclaimed a hero, to which he was not unreceptive and to which he afterwards laid claim, but never without being sharply questioned, although he did succeed in achieving public recognition for his pretense.

Later it was found that the body had been that of Fay. But the truth had been tied up so long, it was lame and halting when released, and so the truth did not hurt Becker; it only hampered him for a little while.

It was only the man's iron nerve that enabled him to ride out his next storm safely. For a time it looked as if the wave of public indignation and outrage would overwhelm him, but he survived. He had arrested a young and attractive woman in the streets and kept her locked up all night. She had protested her innocence. She had begged to be allowed to prove her identity. Becker laughed at her.

In the morning, explanations came, but with them no retribution. It was found that she was all she said she was, the proper wife of a wealthy New Jersey silk merchant. Though the protests were loud and long, again nothing came of them. Becker was fast learning the value of the System. It had been a friend to him so he became a friend of the System.

The System is many-sided. It can be gently kind as well as fiercely protective. It takes care of its own, and its own take care of it. Becker wanted to be a hero. Becker was a good soldier in the System's cause; therefore, Becker a hero should be.

He was presented with a medal of police heroism for rescuing James Butler from a rushing tide at the foot of West 10th Street one July morning. Proudly, Becker wore his medal and the accompanying bronze star on his sleeve for two years. Then came the exposé.

Butler made an affidavit, fully corroborated, that he was an old lifesaver and expert swimmer and that he had jumped into the river at the request of Becker, who promised him five dollars for doing so but never paid the money. Butler swore that the policeman had been almost overcome himself and that he, not Becker, had had to do the rescuing.

But Becker's iron nerve stood all the blows, and he even frowned down the cry of "fake hero."

Then in 1901 came the first rift within Becker's police lute. He fell afoul of Inspector (then Captain) Schmittberger and made some excise raids over his head. If any doubt existed as to Becker's strength of character, it was dispelled then, for, although Schmittberger was strong, Becker never quavered but went ahead—a subordinate fighting the heavy odds that a superior officer could bring to bear on him. Then, Rhinelander Waldo entered the police department as first deputy commissioner under General Bingham, and it was through him that Becker was able to put his foot on the first rung of the ladder that led to promotion, power, and death. Waldo made the good-looking policeman his orderly.

This gave Becker his first taste of detail work. He was quick to realize the possibilities, and quick too in bringing about a condition so he could realize them. From that time on, Becker operated mostly under his own control. Instead of being an automaton, he became a significant unit in the department's organization, and with his increase of power there came a corresponding increment to his strength in the System.

He began to be talked about as a coming man in police circles.

It was appreciated that in him lay the elements of police success—success, that is, of a certain sort, the brand that is stamped with the approval of the System—the elements of Strength and Force and Ruthlessness and Courage and Greed and Cunning: a willingness to take an ability to enforce the will.

It was a splendid training this man had received for the last and greatest post he was to occupy.

On June 22, 1911, Charles Becker, who had been made a lieutenant four years before, was detailed to the command of Special Squad No. 1, known as the "Strong Arm Squad." From then on his history is written in blackmail and murder, in money and blood.

In ten months after his elevation to the most conspicuous position in the New York Police Department, Charles Becker, receiving a salary of $2,250 and supporting himself and his wife in a luxurious manner, rolled up bank deposits approximating $100,000. He abandoned the apartment in which he had been living and built himself a house on six lots in an attractive neighborhood in the Bronx.

He realized that even if his bank accounts escaped attention, he had laid himself vulnerable on the matter of the house and real estate. After his name had become associated with the scandal of the Rosenthal murder, he announced one day through his counsel that he had gone, before consummating the deal, to Waldo and acquainted him with his intention of making the purchase, which, he explained, he was enabled to do through having saved his salary in nineteen years in the police department and the savings of his wife, who for seventeen years had been a schoolteacher.

This pretty story was punctured when the *World* discovered that he had been married to his present wife for only five years; that he had divorced his first wife and was still paying her alimony, the custody of their child having been awarded to her. And, finally, it was learned from Commissioner Waldo himself that Becker had *not* told him of his realty corporation at the time he had made it, but sought to establish an alibi and clear the record for himself by detailing it at a time when his keen sagacity told him that he was to be made the center of the most gigantic police scandal this city has ever known.

At the outset, Becker's Strong Arm Squad was a lusty invention for the checking of rowdyism, and it did its work well, except perhaps when the rowdies were able to pay well to escape harassment, but the work meant nothing to Becker. It brought little or nothing to his bank account. He saw a bigger field for his labor and, slowly but surely, worked toward his goal.

Here enters on the scene Jack Rose, Becker's man Friday.

Jack Rose, the quiet, soft-spoken slave of the magic lamp that Becker held, the rays of which he turned aside from the dark places on payment of so much down and so much per month. Rose, the humble; Rose, the obsequious; Rose, the fawning, who, at last, was to turn and rend the man for whom he had committed blackmail, perjury, and murder.

Rose's real name was Jacob Rosenschwig. He is thirty-seven. He was born in Russian Poland, and he seemed ashamed of it. He explained apologetically that all his friends are Americans, and he is the only member of his own family, with the exception of his mother and father, who is of foreign birth.

Rose might have amounted to something had his earlier life been cast along more pleasant lines. But he was reared on the East Side just at the time that that melon of the city had discovered that America was indeed an Eldorado—for those who wished to make it so.

Money was to be had for the asking—if the asking was hard enough. Money could be got in so many ways and by such easy methods that it seemed an unnecessary waste of effort to work for it. For example, if the harsher avenues were to be avoided, there was gambling. It seemed one could always do pretty well at gambling. If you won, you had lots of money, and, if you lost, why, the problem was simple; all you had to do was go out and borrow some money and start over again.

Rose was of this type. The gambling fever was deep in his blood. He would rather gamble than eat—and he often did. Rose has the elements of a good mind. He has good imagination, a retentive memory, a well-defined mental alertness, and the commendable habit of improving himself by those with whom he comes in contact.

In appearance Rose is one man in ten thousand. You need see him only once never to forget him.

He has not a hair on his body. His face and head are as smooth and bare as a billiard ball, and from his resemblance he gained the sobriquet of "Billiard Ball Jack." His forehead is rather low. His head slopes down to it from the crown. His eyes, deep-set and wide apart, are brown. They are gentle eyes. They do not look like the eyes of a cutthroat and murderer. The nose is broad. His upper lip is short and curls into a ready smile, showing even, white teeth. His chin is as soft and rounded as a woman's. His hands are delightful to look at. They are long and white, with slender, tapering fingers—quite the hand that you would expect to see on so expert a card player as this man is.

Gambler, theatrical man, racehorse man, bookmaker, card player, businessman, baseball manager, prizefight promoter, grafter, blackmail collector, and murderer—to all these trades Jack Rose has owed allegiance, and in each he was a failure save in the last, and then success came only because a stronger will than his dominated him and he became a puppet.

Among Rose's friends was "Bridgie" Weber, an opium-den proprietor, stuss-room owner, gambler, and, through this friendship, murderer. Weber has been big in the public eye lately, but he is not of original importance; his situations were supplied him, his lines were given him to speak by those two principals, Becker and Rose, and, indirectly, by the third, Herman Rosenthal.

This same characterization applies to Harry Vallon, a subordinate of Weber, who dwelt in Weber's shadow and found sustenance there. What Weber didn't want, Vallon took, and the arrangement worked very well.

And there is another on Rose's list of intimates who, had he been on terms of greater intimacy with the bald-headed one, might have caused a different story to be written and might have made Becker a martyr today instead of a doomed man.

This is the introduction to Sam Schepps, the dapper little East Side dude. His eyes blinked brightly through big glasses, and with his head cocked to one side, he looks at times like a bird—a wise old bird, to be sure. For Sammy Schepps always prided himself on his worldly wisdom.

Down in the underworld, on the fringes of which his life has been lived, they call his type "wisecracking kids," a sort who think they are able to cope with any contingency that may arise—that they are downright "smart" and always just a trifle smarter than the "other fellow"; the kind who have always pitying contempt for "boobs" and "suckers."

Schepps got his living in a quasi-legitimate manner. He is a portrait enlarger and a seller of frames. He is very kind-hearted in his vocation, never hesitating to sell for twenty-five dollars a frame that probably cost him all of sixty cents, taking care, however, to tie up his purchaser in advance so there will be no repentance of the bargain.

Rosenthal need not be described. He is dead. Those men who killed him have been described, and the reasons for the killing and the way they killed him shall now be told.

The murder tore a corner of the underworld and brought to view the rats, the wolves, the preyers, and the preyed upon scurrying away from the light that they so fear. Many are still in their holes, waiting in fear and trembling the hand of the law that plucked up their companions and held them in judgment.

But sordid and mean, gloomy and dark as the tale may be, there is a brighter side to it, for in the storm that followed the crime has come already a cleaning up. The murder of Herman Rosenthal is a boomerang. He has struck back at the System that slew him with a blow that promises to utterly destroy it.

Herman Rosenthal was slain by four gunmen. Behind the gunmen was the brains and money of Jack Rose and his pal. Behind them was the dominance and will of Charles Becker, and he in turn was actuated by an impulse from the very heart of the System itself. So Rosenthal's was a System murder. He was shot down by the System acting through the will of Becker, the brain of Rose, and the hands of the gunmen.

Once the dead man was a chum of Rose and was Becker's "best pal," so denominated by the policeman himself.

It was their common interest in gambling that had brought the three together. Rose was running a poolroom and gambling house when he met Becker through being raided by him. Thereafter, under the tutelage of Rose, spurred on by his own inclination, Becker's interests became even deeper in gambling, because he saw in it a short-cut to wealth, not by playing the game, but by making the game pay him.

Rose has told the story of how he met Becker. He has told it well.

"In August, 1911," said Jack Rose, "I was the part owner of a gambling house at 155 2nd Avenue. It was raided by Lieutenant Becker and his Strong Arm Squad. The next morning at the Essex Market Police Court, at 1st Street and 2nd Avenue, I introduced myself to Becker, of whom I had heard but of whom I knew little, and I asked him if it was a fact that he still had two unserved warrants for men who had been working at my place. He said he had. This was an old trick of police grafters. They swear out more warrants than they need at the time of the raid and hold up those they do not as clubs for blackmailing purposes. They can execute the warrants at any time and on almost anyone they please, provided some association with the gambling house can be shown.

"Becker said he had. I then promised to produce certain men who were named in the warrants. I did this and the warrants were served on the street in front of the court.

"Becker made it out that it was a favor he was doing me in serving the warrants then and there because he gave me to know that he understood the fact that by getting rid of the warrants he was shut off from making another raid on the place unless he got new evidence, and this gave me a chance to go back to the old stand and resume operations.

"I could see from this that Becker would 'listen to reason,' as the saying goes, and we grew quite chummy while these negotiations were going on. So much so in fact that I asked him what disposition could be made of the case against me. Becker, looking around to see that nobody was nearby, said: 'Jack, they tell me you are all right. Now, I'm all right too, and I will always do business with a good fellow. I'll tell you what I'll do for you. With $200 cash I will guarantee you to have the case thrown out, but you must instruct your attorney to waive examination, and I'll take care of it downtown before the grand jury.' I did this, and it turned out all right."

This auspicious beginning was followed by a second meeting, at Becker's request, on the next Saturday, when Becker had Rose call for him at 145th Street and Broadway, near where the policeman lived. They drove to a well-known road house, where Becker confided to Rose that he felt that he had at last "arrived" in the police department. Under the loosening influences of a few drinks, he gave his friend, who, however, had not been known to him for a long time, the information that he proposed starting out on a long line of raids by way of showing what he hoped would be called "splendid police activity," after which he thought the "pickings" ought to be good and safe. In other words, he proposed first establishing a good name for himself as an earnest, incorruptible policeman and then proceeding to grab all the money he could get his hands on.

"Jack," said the magnificent Becker to the pale and esthetic-looking Rose, "you know those gamblers better than anybody else in town. I know a plan that will make money for both of us and without any danger to either of us.

"You get up a list of places where they're making money, and we'll make 'em come over and come over big every month. All you have to do is say you're working for me. If they come across, all right—if they don't, they'll hear from me in the shape of a raid."

The proposition sounded good to Rose. He was broke. He had been getting some hard knocks. He demurred at being stool pigeon in the way of supplying evidence. That was against his canon of ethics. But there was no violation of his code in being a graft collector. That, according to the morals of the underworld, was perfectly proper.

At the time, Herman Rosenthal was running a gambling house on 45th Street. Rosenthal was always a hustler. He was a money-maker. He had been president of the Hesper Club, a one-time well-known social and political organization on the East Side. It used to give annual balls that were really organized forms of blackmail, in which gamblers, keepers of questionable resorts, women of the street, confidence men, and other forms of parasitic life—the consumers who were never producers—paid tribute by the purchase of tickets, each according to his ability.

The Hesper Club received its death blow when Deputy Police Comr. Clem Driscoll raided it. The underworld refused to believe it. It could not credit the news. What dire fate was in store—what condign punishment awaited the one who had the temerity to desecrate and blaspheme that Holy of Holies, the Hesper Club?

And Rosenthal the loose-tongued, Rosenthal the babbler, was freest in his predictions. All his life there had been a break of luck in his favor. He always seemed to have a faculty for saying a great deal and then seeing much of it come true. This time he promised that Driscoll was to be beheaded and that the Hesper Club in all its glory would reign again.

So Rosenthal, in spite of his unpopularity, which was largely because of the fact that he often talked too much about things that he ought not to talk about at all, was credited with certain powers both in and out of the department.

He had watched Becker's rise closely. Rosenthal described himself as not being a "lover of cops." But he saw in Becker a chance to help himself and at the same time help Becker. As the arrangement seemed reciprocal to Becker, it was not difficult for them to strike up a friendship after their first meeting at a ball Thanksgiving Eve, 1911.

They had met casually before, but always with enmity. This time they got on a better footing with each other and reached an understanding, which became more thorough in subsequent meetings between then and New Year's Eve, when, with their families, they met at the Elks' Club, on 43rd Street, at the annual ball.

That New Year's Eve Becker's heart welled over. He was filled with the milk of human kindness—and champagne. He put his arms around Herman Rosenthal's neck and said, "Herman, don't you worry; everything is all right from now on. I'll go the route for you, Herman." And with that he turned to Mrs. Rosenthal and repeated his assurance of friendship to her. Then he called over three of his men who were present—policemen White, Foy, Steinhart—and, with his arm still on Rosenthal's shoulder, said: "Boys, this is my best pal. Do anything he wants you to do. I'll go the route for him."

Rosenthal was not doing very well in his gambling house. He had suffered some heavy losses and his cash drawer was getting light. So he suggested to Becker that the policeman purchase half interest in his gambling house for $5,000. This was rather a new idea for Becker, but he saw possibilities in it.

The $5,000 end of the proposition, however, was one that did not appeal strongly to him. It was a great deal of money, he thought, to have tied up, and so he dickered with Rosenthal, finally agreeing to lend him $1,500.

At the same time Becker asked Rosenthal to admit Rose into partnership, saying that the bald-headed collector was not only a good business-getter, but also would represent Becker's interests. Rosenthal was compelled to give Becker a twenty per cent interest in the house in return for the $1,500 and to give Rose a supplemental fifteen per cent; but this worked no injustice upon the gambler, for Rose brought much patronage to the house.

Rosenthal soon repented of his bargain. He figured that he had sold the interest too cheaply. He began to talk, and the talk began to spread and took the form of gossip that reached the commissioner of police through anonymous letters. These communications complained that Becker was Rosenthal's partner and Rose was Becker's collector. These are the ones that were turned over by Waldo to the careful investigative processes of his then favorite.

Like little drops of water, one friction succeeded another between Rosenthal and Becker. Becker made a raid on a crap game during which his press agent, one Charles Plitt, Jr., shot and killed a Negro named Waverly Carter. At the time, Becker's money was pretty well tied up, so he told Rose to tell Rosenthal that he would like to get $500 for the purposes of Plitt's defense.

Rosenthal's refusal to give Becker the money caused the relations between the two to buckle, if not break. Becker had been telling Rosenthal how he had been under the necessity of "stalling" Waldo, and the two used to have many a laugh over the misplaced confidence of the commissioner in his subordinate, but the pressure at headquarters had become heavy, and so Rose was sent to Rosenthal by Becker to request the gambler to "stand" for a fake raid. Rosenthal refused.

"I am not going to let him make a fool of me," Rosenthal declared vehemently. "This trouble down at headquarters is just an excuse to go after me because I refuse to give him the $500. Now, you go and tell him there is only one way he can raid me and that is to get the evidence against my place, and he can't do that because I am not letting in anybody that I don't know well. I'm certainly not going to let a copper or anybody that looks like a copper inside the door."

Rose brought the answer to Becker. Becker's fierce eyes narrowed. His swarthy cheeks grew red.

Rosenthal's own words best tell the next chapter:

"On April 15 Becker called and told me to go and see a certain party at half past ten that night. He said I would find the man at Pabst's, at 59th Street and 8th Avenue. When I reached Pabst's, there was nobody there to meet me. I suspected something was wrong, and I was afraid I was being jobbed. So I hurried back to my house. I found the windows smashed, the door broken into, and the patrol wagon waiting outside."

When he entered his house, he met his wife. She gave him this message from Becker: "Tell Herman that it's all right and not to worry. Tell him I was sorry to have to do this, but I had to do it to save myself, and I am willing to stand the cost. Tell him we are even now—then he can go down to my lawyers and get the mortgage and that instead of owing me $1,500, he doesn't owe me a cent. Tell him I will see him tomorrow."

Two men had been arrested during Becker's raid, one being Mrs. Rosenthal's nephew, although the warrant on which execution was made was plainly intended for another. Rosenthal, bitter against Becker, nevertheless followed the advice he received from the policeman and had his nephew and the other man waive examination in the hope that when the case reached the grand jury, it would be thrown out as Becker had promised.

When Rosenthal found that indictments had been voted against his nephew and the other man, he realized he had been betrayed by Becker.

He got in touch with Becker by phone. He wanted to know what the failure to have the cases thrown out meant. Becker made short shrift of him.

"Aw, you talk too much," he said, "and so far as I am concerned you can go straight to ----." Rosenthal knew that war had been declared.

Rosenthal, baffled at every turn, his money gone, his friends deserting him, his house not his own because of the police guard there, resolved to fight back in any way he could. He had squealed before; he would squeal again.

He intimated to the *World* reporter that he had a real story to tell, but that not a paper in the city would dare print it.

He was asked to tell his story to the *World,* and he did so. It was reduced to an affidavit, which he signed. When Herman Rosenthal signed the affidavit, he signed his own death warrant.

Thirty-six hours after it appeared, Rosenthal was assassinated.

Although he had been brave enough in his reply to Rosenthal on the phone, Becker was too wise a man not to worry. He knew Rosenthal was dangerous, and he set himself a task of covering his enemy's every move. He conferred frequently with Rose, and, when it seemed as if Rosenthal was beginning to make headway, the two talked of how to stop him.

Late in June, Becker phoned for Rose to hurry to the Union Square Hotel, where the two were in the habit of meeting almost daily, either there or at Luchow's. Becker was disturbed. He said:

"This ---- Rosenthal is going farther than I ever thought he would. He is trying to prove I was his partner. He is peddling the story to the newspaper. He is getting really dangerous. He must be stopped.

"I want to have a serious talk with you. I want you to do me a favor. I want you to go after this fellow Jack Zelig down in the Tombs [the city's prison]. We framed him on a charge of carrying a gun, and I know that your name has been associated with the job because you are a friend of mine. I'll tell you how you can square yourself with Zelig and his friends and at the same time get them to pull off this job for us.

"You go down and see Zelig in the Tombs and give him $100 and tell him that if he wants to save himself you will get him out and then he is to send his gang after Rosenthal."

"What do you mean," asked Rose, "get them to beat him up?"

"No," answered Becker scornfully. "I don't want him beaten up; I want him croaked, murdered, his throat cut, dynamited, anything that will take him off the Earth."

And, as if realizing that the abruptness of his proposition had startled Rose, and fearing that a sufficient cause had not been presented to enlist the collector's sympathy in the undertaking, Becker went on, laying his hand on Rose's shoulder: "Why, Jack, you haven't any idea the kind of man that Rosenthal is. I would be ashamed to tell you the things he has said about you and your wife and children."

The shot struck home. Rose's dormant willingness was vitalized into life. He agreed that something ought to be done, but he wasn't sure at all about the method suggested by Becker—murder. He temporized but Becker would have none of it.

So Rose arranged the $10,000 bail bond for Zelig.

Rose knew four of Zelig's men who traveled together—Frank Muller, alias "Whitey Lewis"; Harry Horowitz, alias "Gyp the Blood"; Louis Rosenberg, alias "Lefty Louie"; and Frank Ciroficci, alias "Dago Frank." All were mankillers, if not in deed, then in spirit, and two of them had real notches on their guns. They knew he came from Zelig and that he had been responsible for getting Zelig out on bail to await trial on a second offense charge of carrying concealed weapons, which, if substantiated, meant imprisonment for fourteen years. They knew, too, that Rose, through Becker, could, if he wished, have the charge vitiated; so they felt grateful for what he had done for their chief and eager to oblige him so that he would do more.

Certainly they would do the job, and glad to do it. But Rose had no stomach for the murder, and he sought to fight it off. Becker gave him no rest. Three times between the date of Rose's conversation with the gunmen and the murder, Becker came to him with reproaches that the job had not yet been done.

"Now," he said, "I want some action or it will be worse for

everybody. This fellow is getting so dangerous that there is no telling what may happen. Go after him anywhere. Kill him anyplace you find him. Break into his house if you have to. I'll take care of everybody that's in it. Not a thing will happen."

Becker's words were powerful. Rose and his errand-runner, Sammy Schepps, drove up to the Southern Boulevard apartment house where Dago Frank and Lefty Louie and their wives had been living and told them to be ready for action that night.

Three of them—Lefty Louie, Gyp the Blood, and Dago Frank—were stationed in front of the Garden Restaurant at 50th Street and 7th Avenue, where Rosenthal and his wife, accompanied by Jack Sullivan, had been trailed. It was 3:00 A.M. They were ready to do their work, but either through fancy or some real cause, Jack Rose's nerve failed him, and he came up on the run from his position a block away to inform the gunmen that they were being shadowed by Burns detectives working for District Attorney Whitman, and that if an attack were made upon Rosenthal there would be no opportunity for a getaway.

"The next day," Rose swore on the witness stand, "I met Becker and he asked me what was the matter with the Rosenthal job. He wanted to know why it had not been pulled off at the Garden Restaurant as planned. I told him about the detectives and he said:

" 'Tell them there isn't anything to be scared of. They don't need to be frightened off by any detective. Why, you tell them they can go right up and shoot Rosenthal in front of any policeman, and they'll be all right. I tell you there won't be any trouble about it at all.' "

That Monday night there had been a heavy feeling about Mrs. Rosenthal's heart, and she sought to dissuade her husband from leaving her. "Don't go out, Herman," she said. "I am dreadfully worried about you. Everybody tells me you're in great danger. So stay home with me."

He was a marked man. Everyone in the neighborhood knew him, and everyone expected that those he attacked would square matters with him. He passed a group of gamblers who had just walked up from the Hotel Knickerbocker, and they stopped and told him he had been the sole topic of conversation and that if he was a wise man he would go home.

With a cheery "Good night," Rosenthal went on. It was then about one o'clock. He entered the restaurant.

Rosenthal talked, as he always did, of his grievances. So filled was he with this subject that he had become a nuisance to his friends. Twice he left his table, once to go into the hallway to speak to a friend and the other time to go to the side door to purchase some newspapers, which had just appeared on the street, it being then about a quarter till two.

He returned to his table, threw down the newspapers, and said in a tone of pride: "That's what the newspapers think of me. Look at that!" And he showed his companions how his story had been given a prominent portion of the front page.

Then, refusing another drink and saying he had promised his wife to be home early, he made a bundle of newspapers, threw a dollar on the table to pay an eight-cent check, and started out. Some of those present think that just at this time a stranger approached him and said, "Herman, somebody wants to see you outside."

Rosenthal passed through the opening formed by the folded-back circular door, and, as his foot touched the pavement, four shots rang out. Four men had been standing on the sidewalk facing the cafe door. As Rosenthal emerged, they acted in unison. The right arms of three of them snapped up, and the left arm of one. As the pistols spoke, Rosenthal toppled forward and fell without a groan.

As he was falling, the left-handed man pulled his trigger again and sent a bullet crashing into the top of the victim's head. The impact was so powerful that the body turned half around and fell on its side. The head was back, and the eyes stared straight up at the brilliant lights, the brows set in an expression of bewilderment and the mouth parted in a fearful grin. There was a jagged hole in the left cheek, and the dropping jaw and relaxed muscles that let the joints twist horribly showed that medical assistance was unnecessary, and on the crown of the head was the great jagged wound made by the last bullet.

Before the body had settled down, the four men ran to a gray car standing on the other side of the street in the shadow of the

George M. Cohan Theater, pointing east, clambered aboard, and fled.

Seven policemen were within 500 feet of the murder, yet the killers made their flight in safety.

"They've murdered Herman Rosenthal!"

This time it was no whisper that spread through the underworld. It was a cry that staggered the city. It ran the length of Broadway and flashed through the East Side, stirring the community as it has never been stirred before, for never had a crime of violence given such direct defiance to law and order.

The news pulled District Attorney Whitman out of bed and brought him posthaste to the West 47th Street Station. It was his presence there that saved the city from the disgrace of an unpunished crime, for it was he who saw that the police records had finally written into them the real number of the auto, instead of the incorrect numbers, seven of which had been supplied.

Whitman did more than see that the number of the auto was recorded. He met a man in the station house he looked at curiously. It was police Lt. Charles Becker. How he came there is best told by Rose.

"I was still at Weber's," said Rose, "when word came in that Rosenthal had been shot. It made me feel sick. I lay down on the couch for a few minutes, and then Weber suggested I phone Becker. It was five till three when I got him. I said, 'Hello there. Did you hear the news?' 'Yes,' he replied, 'I congratulate you.' 'How did you get it so soon?' I asked. 'Oh,' said Becker, 'I got it from a newspaperman.' I said. 'Charlie, that is awful,' and he told me not to be foolish and not to worry, that no harm could come to anyone. He asked me where I was and I told him at Weber's, and he said he would be down right away."

Rose and Weber waited for Becker west of the poker club entrance. It took some time for Becker to arrive, and when he came, the three adjourned to a nearby doorway, where they talked it over.

Rose asked Becker if he had seen Rosenthal's body. "Sure," he quoted Becker as saying. "I went into the back room and had a look at him. If Whitman had not been there, I would have cut his tongue out and hung it up somewhere as a warning to other squealers."

At 7:00 the next morning in the sleeping room of the baths, within arm's length of one another, sat Jack Rose, Bridgie Weber, Harry Vallon, Sam Schepps, and ever-present Jack Sullivan and Sam Paul, whose appearance and reappearance in the case eventually caused his arrest, although he was later discharged.

From the baths, Rose went to his home at 110th Street. He waited there until he got a phone message from Schepps saying that the gunmen had been contacted and that they would wait for him at 50th Street and 8th Avenue. Then Rose went down to Weber's poker room, got a thousand dollars from Weber, and, accompanied by Schepps, went to the meeting place where he says he gave the money to Lefty Louie and Dago Frank, and with it the thanks of Lieutenant Becker. Then Rose went to the home of Harry Pollok, a well-known sporting promoter, where he went to bed.

The next morning Pollok went to police headquarters to tell Becker where Rose was. Becker responded: "All right; that's a good place for him. Tell him to stay there." And that night he called Rose and said: "Everything's all right. Don't worry. There are only about 200 policemen looking for you. Don't get excited. Everything will be taken care of. Just lay low and stay where you are."

It was during this conversation that Becker arranged to have his lawyer call upon Rose that night and get from him an affidavit about the $1,500 that had been put up for a partnership in Rosenthal's place. Indirectly, the visit paid Rose by Becker's lawyer became Becker's undoing. The fact that at such a time Becker should think only of himself and should insist that perjury be done to protect his good name, when far more serious danger was present, planted the seed of suspicion in Rose's mind. The next morning he gave himself up at police headquarters.

Then Weber was   arrested, and with him Sam Paul. The night of July 23, Harry Vallon sauntered into police headquarters and, jauntily disclosing his identity, joined the others in the Tombs.

On July 29, Jack Rose, Harry Vallon, and Bridgie Weber confessed full details of the plot. The grand jury was summoned to a night session and heard their stories. With the consent of the grand jury, District Attorney Whitman gave these three men a promise of immunity from prosecution if it were found that their stories were true, and it was shown that they had not fired any of the shots at the body of Rosenthal.

The grand jury voted a true bill accusing Becker of the murder of Herman Rosenthal.

A few minutes before midnight, he was arraigned before Judge Mulqueen, pleaded not guilty, and was remanded to the Tombs.

A new sensation blazed its way into the case when two days before the trial opened "Big Jack" Zelig, the hunter of men, who had lived all his life by preying, became the hunted, and was shot down on a 2nd Avenue streetcar by "Red Phil" Davidson. Although Zelig's death was pronounced a blow for the prosecution, no disclosure warranted the report that his murder had any connection with the Rosenthal-Becker affair.

The trial, presided over by Justice John W. Goff, which began on October 7 and ended so dramatically one minute before midnight Thursday, October 24, was marked by a jury of unusual quality, the members of which gave to the evidence an absorbed and undivided attention. Witnesses were kept to the point. Counsel were cut short in gratuitous remarks. It was an exhibition of how a criminal trial should be conducted, and it was finished in a briefer period than has been devoted to any other great criminal case in this city.

Never did a witness produce the impression that followed the narrative of Jack Rose. Even the opposing lawyers, bitterly hostile to him, were forced to admit his unusual power. After him came the two confessed accomplices—Weber and Vallon—and then followed the evidence of Schepps, which was complete and convincing.

In many ways the defense was handicapped. Seemingly, they lacked a direct or continuous policy. Their plan was vague, and they professed themselves as being unable to secure the attendance of several of their witnesses.

From the first to the last, Mrs. Becker, the plucky and devoted wife of the defendant, attended every session. It was against the prisoner's wish, because he feared that her constant attendance would have an evil effect upon her in an event that she is looking forward to—she expects soon to become a mother.

It was at 10:30 last Thursday morning that Justice John W. Goff began a four-hour charge to the jury. The jury retired to begin their deliberations at 4:20 in the afternoon. It was at 11:50 that night when they sent word that they had found a verdict.

The Criminal Courts Building became charged with excitement. The news was flashed that the final climax was to be written into this drama of blood.

It was uttered thrillingly when Becker, standing at the bar, his face aflame, was told to look upon the jury, and the jury commanded to look upon him. Then came the set phrase:

"Gentlemen of the jury, how do you find, guilty or not guilty?"

And low but clear came the answer from Harold B. Skinner, the foreman, the answer that meant all to the defendant:

"Guilty of murder in the first degree."

Becker was electrocuted at Sing Sing on July 7, 1915. His wife placed a plaque on his grave declaring: "Charles Becker, Murdered July 7, 1915, by Gov. Whitman."

Six red streams from six heads mark Valentine's Day on North Clark Street

This exclusive account from the scene of the infamous St. Valentine's Day Massacre is from the *Chicago Daily News* of February 14, 1929.

It's too much to tell. You go into the door marked "S-M-C Cartage Company." You see a bunch of big men talking with restrained excitement in the cigarette smoke. You go through another door back of the front office. You go between two closely parked trucks in the garage.

Then you almost stumble over the head of the first man, with a clean gray felt hat still placed at the precise angle of gangster toughness.

The dull yellow light of a lamp—daytime shows dark rivulets of blood heading down to the drain that was meant for the water from washed cars. There are six of the red streams from six heads. The bodies—four of them well-dressed in civilian clothes, two of them with their legs crossed as they whirled to fall.

It's too much, so you crowd on past the roadster with bullet holes in it to the big truck behind.

You look at the truck. It is something to look at because the men were fixing it. It's jacked up, with one wheel off. You look, and the big man called "Commissioner" looks, and a crowd gathers, and then it gets too much for the police dog you had failed to notice lying under the truck, tied to it by a cheap yellow rope.

It gets too much for the big brown and gray police dog and he goes crazy. He barks, he howls, he snarls, showing wicked white teeth in bright red gums.

The crowd backs away. The dog yowls once more and subsides.

Your thoughts snap with a crack back to the circle of yellow lamplight where six things that were men are sprawled.

101

Scarface Al Capone.
(Photo by Jim Fujita/Courtesy Chicago Historical Society)

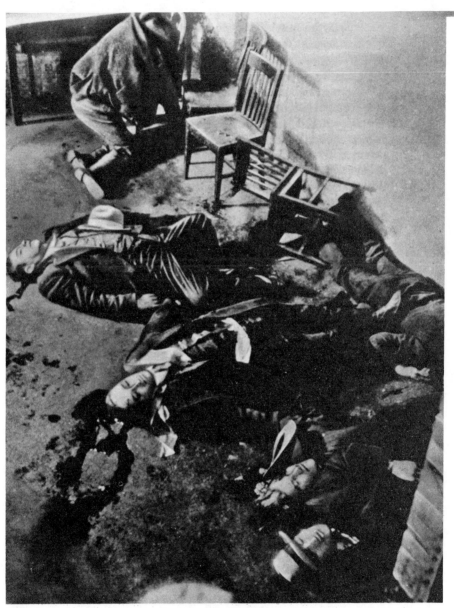

The scene of the St. Valentine's Day Massacre.

103

It's still too much. You push out into the fresh air.

You find that traffic was quiet in front of 2122 North Clark at 10:30 this morning. A streetcar rattled down the narrow way left by parked cars. Across from the high garage, two windows of one of those old-fashioned graystone apartment houses were open. Two women were exchanging gossip despite the cold.

A blue and black sedan stopped in front of the garage. The women exchanged their curiosities about it and then went back to gossip.

They jumped as a muffled roar reached them. The blue and black car sped away and turned the corner.

Out of nowhere the crowd came pouring in from the rooming houses, the little stores, the autos, the streetcars. They set up a hum. A policeman arrived — another. A police siren sounded — the clang of a patrol wagon.

The two women ran down and joined the buzzing in the street.

By this time people from the big apartment hotels on Lincoln Park West, half a block away, had heard and had come. The crowd was a cross-section. Gold Coast and Clark Street merged in the gathering.

"What is it? Who were they? What did they do? Were they in the know? Double-crossers. Them guys had the pull and pulled it too strong...."

Inside six pairs of lips failed to answer.

The victims were members of the Bugs Moran gang, which had been at war with Al Capone's gang for control of North Side speak-easies. It is presumed Capone ordered the massacre, which effectively destroyed the Moran gang. No formal charges ever were brought in connection with the carnage.

John Dillinger meets death—two slugs in the heart, one in the head

John Dillinger was born August 8, 1903 in Indianapolis, and dabbled in petty crime before settling on a permanent career as a bank robber in his thirtieth year. The FBI claims to have killed Dillinger on July 22, 1934 in the manner described by Jack Lait in this International News Service dispatch that appeared the next day in many newspapers.

John Dillinger, ace bad man of the world, got his last night—two slugs through his heart and one through his head. He was tough and he was shrewd, but he wasn't as tough and shrewd as the Federals, who never close a case until the end. It took twenty-seven of them to end Dillinger's career, and their strength came out of his weakness—a woman.

Dillinger was put on the spot by a tip to the local bureau of the Department of Justice. It was a feminine voice that Melvin H. Purvis, head of the Chicago office, heard. He had waited long for it.

It was Sunday, but Uncle Sam doesn't observe any NRA [National Recovery Administration, a New Deal agency that regulated hours of work in industry] and works seven days a week.

The voice told him that Dillinger would be at a little third-run movie house on Lincoln, the Biograph, last night—that he went there every night, and usually got there about 7:30 P.M. It was almost 7:30 then. Purvis sent out a call for all men within reach and hustled all men on hand with him. They waited more than an hour. They knew from the informer that Dillinger must come out, turn left, turn again into a dark alley where he parked his Ford-8 coupe.

Purvis himself stood at the main exit. He had men on foot and

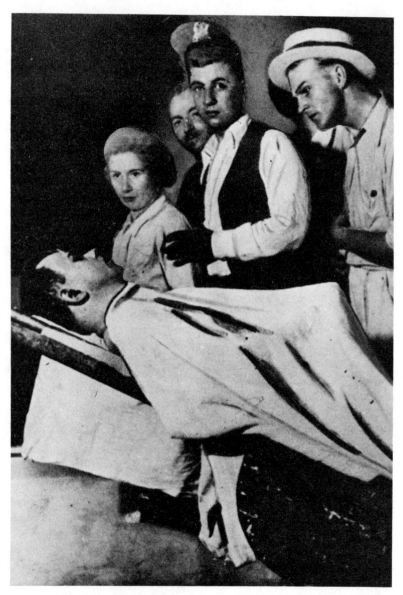

The public views the body said to be that of John Dillinger.
(Courtesy Chicago Sun-Times)

in parked, inconspicuous cars strung on both sides of the alley. He was to give the signal. He had ascertained about when the feature film, "Manhattan Melodrama," would end. Tensely eyeing his wristwatch he stood. Finally the crowd came streaming out. Purvis had seen Dillinger when he was brought through from Arizona to Crown Point, Indiana, and his heart pounded as he saw again the face that has been studied by countless millions on the front pages of the world.

Purvis gave the signal. Dillinger did not see him. Public Enemy Number 1 lit a cigarette, strolled a few feet to the alley with the mass of middle-class citizens going in that direction, then wheeled left.

A Federal man, revolver in hand, stepped from behind a telegraph pole at the mouth of the passage. "Hello, John," he said, almost whispered, his voice husky with the intensity of the classic melodrama. Dillinger went with lightning right hand for his gun, a .38 Colt automatic. He drew it from his trousers pocket.

But, from behind, another government agent pressed the muzzle of his service revolver against Dillinger's back and fired twice. Both bullets went through the bandit's heart.

He staggered, his weapon clattered to the asphalt paving, and as he went, three more shots flashed. One bullet hit the back of his head, downward, as he was falling, and came out under his eye.

Police cleared the way for the police car, which was there in a few minutes. The police were there not because they were in on the capture, but because the sight of so many mysterious men around the theater had scared the manager into thinking he was about to be stuck up, and he had called the nearest station.

When the detectives came on the run, Purvis intercepted them and told them what was up. They called headquarters and more police came, but with instructions to stand by and take orders from Purvis.

Dillinger's body was rushed to Alexian Brothers' Hospital in a patrol wagon. There were no surgeons in it. But the policeman knew he was dead, and at the entrance of the hospital, where a kindly priest in a long cassock had come to the door to see who might be in need of help, the driver was ordered to the morgue.

I was in a taxi that caught up with the police car at the hospital, and we followed across town to the old morgue. No one bothered us, though we went fifty miles an hour.

There was no crowd then. We pulled in. Strong arms carried the limp, light form of the man who had been feared by a great government through that grim door of many minor tragedies. It lay on a rubber stretcher.

In the basement, the receiving ward of the last public hospice of the doomed, they stripped the fearsome remains.

What showed up, nude and pink, still warm, was the body of what seemed a boy, the features as though at rest and only an ugly, bleeding hole under the left eye, such as a boy might have gotten in a street fight. His arms were bruised from the fall and the bumping in the wagon.

But under the heart were two little black, bleeding holes, clean and fresh. These could not have been anything but what they were. That part of John Dillinger did not look as though it was a boy's hurt—it was the fatal finish of a cold-blooded killer and not half of what he had given Officer O'Malley in East Chicago, Indiana in the bank robbery when he cut the policeman almost in half with a machine gun.

The marks of the garters were still on the skin of his sturdy calves, the only part of him that looked like any part of a strong man. His arms were slender, even emaciated. But his legs were powerful-looking. His feet were neat and almost womanish, after the white socks and dudish white shoes had been taken from them.

His clothes were shabby with still an attempt at smartness. The white shirt was cheap, the gray flannel trousers and the uninitialed belt buckle were basement-counter merchandise, his maroon-and-white print tie might have cost half a dollar.

In his pockets were $7.70 and a few keys and a watch in which was the picture of a pretty female.

Two women bystanders were caught in the line of fire and wounded slightly as the Federal men blazed away. They were Miss Etta Natalsky, 45, and Miss Theresa Paulus, 29, both residents of the neighborhood.

Miss Natalsky was taken to Columbus Memorial Hospital with a wound in the leg and Miss Paulus to Grant Hospital, but her wound, also in the leg, was found to be only superficial.

The notorious desperado had resorted to facial surgery to disguise himself, and it was only by his piercing eyes—described by crime experts as "the eyes of a born killer"—that he was recognized.

In addition to the facial alterations, his hair was dyed jet black from its natural sandy shade, and he wore gold-rimmed glasses.

Identification of the fallen man was confirmed on the spot by Purvis. Later, at the morgue, an attempt was made to identify the body from fingerprints, but the tips of the fingers had been scarred, as if with acid.

A recent wound in the chest, which had just healed, was revealed in the morgue examination. It was believed this was a memento of a recent bank robbery.

Dr. Charles D. Parker, coroner's physician, remarked on the alteration in the slain man's features. Scars on each of Dillinger's cheeks had been smoothed out by facial surgery. Purvis, after closely examining the changed features, said:

"His nose, which originally was pronounced 'pug,' had been made nearly straight. His hair had been dyed recently."

Souvenir hunters among the excited crowds that swarmed to the scene of the shooting frantically dipped newspapers and handkerchiefs in the patch of blood left on the pavement.

Traffic became so jammed that streetcars were re-routed, police lines established, and all traffic finally blocked from the area.

Unsatiated by their morbid milling around the death spot, the crowds a little later rushed to the morgue to view the body. Denied admittance, they battled police and shouted and yelled to get inside. More than 2,000 at one time were struggling to force the doors.

I have indisputable proof that the Bureau had information that Dillinger had been here for at least three days. It was the first definite location of the hunted murderer since the affray in the Little Bohemia (Wisconsin) lodge.

"We didn't have time to get him then, but we had time enough this time," Purvis said.

Evidently Purvis not only had enough time, but used it with the traditional efficiency of his department. There always has been open rancor between the Chicago police and the Federals, who have several times done the police out of rewards. The Federals are not permitted to accept rewards.

But the East Chicago force—Dillinger had slaughtered three of their outfit in two raids, and the "coincidence" of their presence "when the tip came in" is obvious.

That Dillinger suspected nothing is proven by nothing so much as that the safety catch on his magazine gun was set. It was a new, high-type weapon, so powerful that its slugs would penetrate the bulletproof vests of the sort that Dillinger himself had worn in other spots. The number had been filed off. Close examination indicated it had never been fired. It was fully loaded, and a clip of extra cartridges was in a pocket.

He had no other possible instrument of offense or defense, this desperado, except a slender penknife on the other end of a thin chain that held his watch.

All his possessions lay on the marble slab beside the rubber stretcher in the basement of the morgue as the interns pawed his still warm face and body as they threw his head to this side and that, slung him over on his face, and dabbed the still wet blood from where the bullets had bitten into him.

I wondered whether, a few brief minutes earlier, they would have had the temerity to treat John Dillinger's flesh so cavalierly.

They pointed to the scar on his shinbone, the one that had been so heavily broadcast as maiming and even killing Dillinger. It was a little bit of a thing and looked more like the result of a stone bruise than a volley from the muzzle of outraged society.

They flopped him over on the slab, quite by a clumsy accident, because the body didn't turn easily within the stretcher, what with its gangly, rubbery legs, and its thin, boneless arms. And as what was left of Dillinger clumped like a clod, face down, upon the slab that had held the clay of hoboes and who knows, a still warm but spent hand knocked off the straw hat that had fallen off his head in the alley and been trampled upon. And a good ten-cent cigar. Strangely intact.

The man who had killed him stood two feet away, smoking a cigar of the same brand. I must not mention his name. Purvis says "keep that a trade secret." With John (Happy Jack)

Hamilton and George (Baby Face) Nelson, Dillinger's lieutenants, still at large, perhaps that is a fair enough precaution.

The Bureau of Identification men were on the job in a jiffy. They proved up the fingerprints, though they had been treated with a biting acid in an effort to obliterate the telltale. But the deltas and cores were unmistakable.

Behind the ears were well-done scars of a face-lifting job by a skillful plastic specialist. A mole on the forehead had been trimmed off rather well. His hair, by rights sandy, had been painted a muddy black with a poor grade of dye.

So had his mustache. The one identifying mark known around the globe as the Dillinger characteristic was there. And even in death he looked just like the Dillinger we all knew from the photographs. Probably the last breath of his ego.

Dillinger was a ladies' man. He didn't want to be picked up and identified by a rube sheriff. But, still, he wanted to whisper to a new sweetie in the confidences of the night:

"Baby, I can trust you—I'm John Dillinger!"

And she would look, and—he was! That mustache!

Having gone to astonishing lengths to change his inconspicuous identifying marks, with the necessary aid and advice of expert medical men, he still had refused to shave off that familiar trademark that every newspaper reader could see with eyes shut.

A scar on his chin had been reopened and smoothed up some, but not very convincingly. The droop at the left corner of his mouth was unmistakably intact. But the most striking facial change was in the tightening of the skin on his chin, almost completely killing his dimple, which was almost as widely known as his mustache.

Gold-rimmed eyeglasses fell off his face as he toppled over. These, one of the most amateurish of elements in disguise, did change his appearance decisively, the officers tell me.

The Federal office, as usual, issued contradictory statements and frankly admitted that certain information would not be given out.

Of the twenty-seven men who worked with Purvis, one was Capt. Tim O'Neill of East Chicago, and four others were O'Neill's men. Purvis said they were there quite by chance, and he had taken them in on the big adventure. A second statement also gave forth that Purvis had seen Dillinger enter as well as leave the theater.

As Dillinger emerged, walking near him were two youngish women, one of them wearing a red dress. Hundreds were leaving the theatre at the time, and almost any number of women naturally would have been near him. But the one with the red dress hurried up the alley, and four Federals made a formation between her and Dillinger before the first shot was fired. It is my theory that she was with Dillinger and that she was the tip-off party or in league with Purvis.

Controversy remains over whether the man shot down at the Biograph actually was Dillinger. Some students of the era contend that the dead man was a cheap crook named Jimmy Lawrence, and that he was set up in an elaborate scheme that allowed Dillinger to disappear and enjoy his accumulated wealth.

"Two-Gun Louie" is taken in the technique he had done so much to perfect

On July 9, 1935, a man who gave his name as "Sullivan" rented a room in a rooming house at 927 Eastwood Terrace in Chicago. Nine days later, after the bullet-riddled corpse of Louie Alterie had been removed from the street below, police discovered that the tenant had departed in such a hurry that he hadn't bothered to pack his automatic rifle and automatic shotgun. These two stories about the event are taken from the *Chicago Daily News* of July 18, 1935. The first was written by Robert J. Casey, the second by Clem Lane.

"Two-Gun Louie" Alterie came out of the shadowy memories of the alky racket this morning long enough to die. He was shot down—in the technique he himself had done so much to perfect—by patient snipers who had placed an automatic shotgun and an automatic rifle in a flat across the street. He died at 10:45, half an hour after the shooting, in the Lake View hospital.

The taking of Alterie, which a few years ago would have been looked upon as a matter of routine procedure in the beer and gun business, was a matter of great surprise to the tenants of apartments adjoining that of the Alteries at 926 Eastwood; to the police who came hastily to gaze upon the messy remains on the sidewalk; to Mrs. Irma Alterie, who narrowly escaped death herself; and presumably to Mr. Alterie, who walked into the ambush with all the carelessness of a novice.

The one-time cannon of Dion O'Banion's North Side mob had been in Chicago for many months since his disappearance from his retreat in exile in Colorado. Prohibition was done, the gangs were dispersed, and there were rumors of love feasts in which ancient enemies had gotten together to laugh over attempts to murder one another.

"Two-Gun" Louie Alterie in 1925.
(Courtesy Chicago Historical Society)

The eminent Alterie, who once went a quarter of the way across a continent to keep away from Alphonse E. Capone, was deluded into thinking that the ways of peace were permanent and that nothing much would happen to him in the city for whose civic reputation he had striven so successfully.

His neighbors knew him as Leland Varain, a pretty name that concealed perfectly the identity of a man who had ceased being a public enemy only through the operation of the statute of limitations.

Mr. and Mrs. Varain had been quiet folk—pleasant-spoken, too. They seemed to be well-to-do, but there was nothing flashy about them. They were the sort from whom one could, on occasion, borrow a cup of sugar or an egg. And Varain had a nice, wholesome smile—he was a regular guy, the men of the apartment house said. Gentle—wouldn't hurt a fly. Good neighbors, the Varains, even if Mr. Varain did have a record of murder many yards long trailing behind him.

So this morning shortly after ten when the Varains passed one of the neighbor women on the stairway, she smiled and they smiled and nothing more untoward seemed in prospect than a trip of these charming people to town. Mr. and Mrs. Varain stepped out to the curb where their auto had been parked on the wrong side of the street.

Louie (Two-Gun) Varain Alterie stepped forward ahead of his wife to unlock the door. And then the patient watchers in the flat across the street opened fire on him. The aim was good. There were a dozen slugs in his head, neck, and right shoulder when the doctors completed their assay at the Lake View hospital.

Conceivably, Two-Gun Louie had some inkling of what had happened to him, for he half turned as he fell. And conceivably his last thought might have been one of admiration for the gunners who, despite their long vacation from such work, had performed so ably. They had rallied round in the old tradition, and Varain Alterie had gone out as he had seen so many others go out. So had died Hymie Weiss, whom Alterie once swore to avenge. So had died Sam Genna.

Mrs. Alterie ran screaming from the scene back into the hotel. Sympathetic neighbors looked out to see what had happened and promptly closed their doors. Came a police squad to gaze in startled incredulity at the face of Dion O'Banion's principal killer, stiffening now in a red puddle that was widening across the sidewalk.

A wagon bore Alterie to the hospital. Then came janitors with mops to restore the neighborhood to some semblance of quiet and respectability. Capt. Gregory Moran and a squad from the Town Hall station followed the janitors and made a canvass of the street. They had no trouble locating the flat where the ambushers had lived, but there was no trace of the marksmen save the abandoned shotgun and automatic rifle and some bullets and shells.

The face that Capt. John Stege had slapped after the killing of Dion O'Banion when Alterie had pledged himself loudly to carry on the vendetta was badly damaged when the doctors got around to look at it. There was a slug in the hand that had shot John Dougherty, the Philadelphia gunman, as he and Alterie sat side by side in Dion O'Banion's auto. The broad brown chest that had swelled so proudly under boiled shirts in the nightclub racket was well perforated. And life was flowing rapidly from a dozen holes.

The police found Mary Wittusen, sister of Mrs. Alterie, in the apartment. She told them that a phone call had come as the pair left the apartment. She had looked out to call him and had seen the body lying under the window. She had not recognized him. His face was like that.

Mrs. Wittusen, when the police called, was holding her seven-month-old baby, George.

The motivation of the killing was a little hazier than it might have been five years ago, but Captain Stege thought it would not be difficult to find. Alterie, during the reign of the rackets, had organized the Theatrical Janitors' Union and had made himself president of the organization for life. Captain Stege thought it just probable that somebody in the union had decided upon the killing as a sort of recall.

As a matter of fact, nobody seemed to be much interested in why Alterie was killed. The reaction in most public places was that the morning's tragedy was merely an inevitable event, miraculously postponed.

Time marched on and other stories cropped up—Louie shot a couple of gents in a quarrel in a Denver hotel; Louie was going to enter the movies as the lead in "When Gunman Meets Gunman"; Louie was glad to hear that Mayor Thompson had fired Captain Stege, and so on.

Alterie was brought back to Chicago when the government was investigating Ralph Capone's income tax. Because of a lapse of memory on Louie's part, the government indicted him for perjury, but Louie later talked, and the charge was dropped.

The state tried him on a charge of kidnapping Edward Dobin, a North Side gambler, but, despite an identification by another kidnapper, the jury let Louie go. Another jury decided that Louie was a vagrant when the public enemy vagrancy prosecutions drive was under way, but the Supreme Court decided otherwise.

Lately, Louie had been living quietly, running his Theatrical Janitors' Union and a few gambling houses. Just why he was killed police haven't yet decided, but no stations will be draped in mourning.

As the inquest got under way in the county morgue, a police message was sent out describing the man who had rented the ambush flat. His name was given as "J. Sullivan," and he was described as twenty-eight to thirty years old, 5 feet 7 inches, weight about 140 pounds. The message called him "a good dresser, looks like an American, and may be driving a maroon sedan or coupe."

At the inquest, Mrs. Alterie, who said she learned for the first time today that her husband was the notorious "Two-Gun Louie," wept with some freedom but could offer police no information in the who-did-it sector.

Police picked up Thomas Burke, an official of Alterie's union. After some questioning, they learned that Alterie received his mail at union headquarters.

The inquest was continued to August 15 by police request.

Mrs. Alterie said she and her husband were leaving the hotel bound for his office.

"He was at the curb, about twenty feet ahead of me," she said. "Suddenly the shots rang out, and he dropped. I ran to him. He said: 'I can't help it, Bambino, but I'm going.' He was unable to talk after that."

Murder Most Foul

She said she and her husband had returned from Valparaiso, Florida on July 7, after a month's stay there. Jerry Horan, head of the janitors' union, was with them, she said.

Frances Kern, maid in the rooming house at 927 Eastwood Terrace, where the killers lay in wait, said that "Sullivan" had rented the room a week ago and that he spent his nights there. This morning, she said, he left the house at eight o'clock. After the shooting, two men brushed past her in the hall and disappeared. Neither was the man who had rented the room.

* * *

This is the story of "Two-Gun Louie" Alterie, one-time pugilist, one-time policeman, one-time robber, one-time lieutenant of Johnny Torrio and Dion O'Banion, erstwhile rancher and union business agent, and today the subject of a coroner's inquest as to who shot him and why not sooner.

Alterie's real name was Leland Varain. He was forty-nine, and Chicago had known him off and on, and never favorably, for thirteen or fourteen years.

Legend has it that he came here from Los Angeles, and that in his early days he was a ham-and-egg pugilist known as Kid Haynes. Legend has it further that after his fighting days ended, he joined a police force in a West Coast city and rose, so some say, to be a lieutenant.

Alterie, so the story goes, put out his hand, palm up, once too often and was caught, and so he left the life of an ersatz law enforcer and hied himself to Chicago.

The first time police interested themselves in Alterie was in June, 1922, when they seized him and Terry Druggan, who was then emerging into power as boss of "the valley," on a charge of having robbed Mrs. Clara Weinberger, 5826 Wayne, and Mrs. Joseph Mendelson of the Sherburne Beach Hotel of $50,000 in jewelry. The women thought they recognized the two, but when the case finally got to trial, the two were freed.

One of the city's first gangland "rides" was attributed to Dion O'Banion and Alterie. A tough mug had arrived in Chicago from Philadelphia late in 1923. His name was Johnny Dougherty, alias Johnny Duffy, and he had fled here to escape a murder charge.

118

Dougherty lived with a woman named Maybelle Exley in a flat at 1216 Carmen.

One day in February Dougherty took on too much liquor and stole an auto belonging to a friend of the O'Banion gang. After driving here and there, bragging how tough he was and how he had turned down an offer to hire out to kill O'Banion, Dougherty went on to the Carmen Avenue love nest and in playful mood shot and killed Maybelle.

O'Banion, Alterie, and another man, hot on his trail, arrived at the flat shortly afterward. They escorted Dougherty to an auto, took him out to the Far Southwest Side, shot and killed him, and tossed his body into a snowbank.

Police got around to arresting Alterie and O'Banion, but they were unable to prove they had done the killing, and so the two were released.

A few months later Capt. William H. Schoemaker, then chief of detectives, and Capt. John Stege, then his first assistant, staged a raid on the Sieben brewery and seized Johnny Torrio, O'Banion, and Alterie and turned them over to Prohibition men.

While Alterie was out on bail in August of the same year, he and Johnny Phillips and another or so of the gang were whooping it up in the Northern Lights cafe. Phillips cast a come-hither eye on Dorothy Kressner, one of the entertainers, but Dorothy said, "No." Phillips put on a caveman act and cuffed Dorothy about the handkerchief-sized dance floor, much to Alterie's amusement.

Police were summoned and, thinking it an ordinary nightclub brawl, entered with their guns in their holsters. The gangsters thereupon "h'isted" the policemen and marched them out of the cafe, hands in air. Policeman Frank Sobol, who was sitting in the squad car awaiting his comrades' return, thought the procedure a bit undignified and cut loose with his pistol. In the battle he shot and killed Phillips, and Alterie high-tailed it down the street and escaped.

By the time Alterie came to trial on assault charges, witnesses had an attack of amnesia and again he went free.

Alterie, a handsome, black-haired, strapping fellow, was doing rather well financially in those days. He was the muscle man, laughingly called the president, of the Theatrical Janitors' Union, which Con Shea, ancient labor racketeer, and Jerry O'Connor,

Loop gambler, had formed to uplift the lowly wielder of mops and brooms and, incidentally, their own fortunes.

Alterie also was high in the counsels of the Torrio beer syndicate. He had a part ownership in several breweries, an alcohol distillery, several gambling places, and other racket spots.

O'Banion got a bit too ambitious, according to Torrio's notions, and Scarface Al Capone, then a rising young gent, decided that something would have to be done about it, which was this: Mike Merlo, first boss of the Unione Siciliana and one of the few to die a natural death, lay in a coffin up in a building in Diversey Parkway, and all "the boys" were buying floral pieces.

Two men strolled into O'Banion's floral shop, across from Holy Name Cathedral, that day back in November, 1924, and while one shook O'Banion firmly by the hand, the other pumped lead into him. And then they went away without their floral piece. O'Banion, it seemed, needed it more.

Alterie, never close-mouthed, received newspapermen and told them, with many a gesture and none too softly, that nothing would please him more than to meet O'Banion's killers at, say, State and Madison and there shoot it out.

"If I go I'll go with a smile," he said, "because I'll know that two or three of them will go with me. If I knew who killed Dion, I would shoot it out with the gang of killers before the sun rose in the morning, and some of us, maybe all of us, would be lying on slabs in the undertaker's place."

The wily Mr. Torrio and the fat-faced Mr. Capone didn't accept the challenge, and so Dion O'Banion was buried in handsome style with Mr. Alterie lending a hand with the coffin.

Chicago didn't see so much of Alterie after another six months or so. Captain Stege ran upon him one night in the Midnight Frolics cafe, took three guns away from him, and smacked him about. Shortly thereafter Alterie departed for a ranch near Gypsum, Colorado and soon became known to the neighbors and tourists as Diamond Jack, the big cow man. The ranch, in addition to catering to tourists, also became a hideout spot for Chicago gangsters fleeing other gangsters or, occasionally, the authorities.

Police never located the mysterious "Sullivan" who rented the room across the street.

Chapter IV

THE FLEECE

Ponzi was unbalanced on one subject—thought he was worth millions

"Who's the greatest Italian who ever lived?" someone once asked Charles Ponzi. "Columbus, because he discovered America," Ponzi replied. "No, you are," Ponzi was informed, "because you discovered money." Ponzi promised investors he would return fifty per cent on their money every forty-five days. He contended he was buying international postal coupons in nine unspecified European countries and redeeming them in the United States for six times what he paid for them. Although the scheme might have worked, Ponzi apparently never sent a cent to Europe or received a cent from Europe. Instead, he paid the promised interest with the proceeds from the hordes of new investors who thought he would make them rich. But the Ponzi bubble burst, and thousands of small investors lost their shirts, after William H. McMasters, a public relations man hired by Ponzi, caught on to what was happening and wrote the following story for the *Boston Post* of August 2, 1920.

After this edition of the *Boston Post* is on the street, there will be no further mystery about Charles Ponzi. He is unbalanced on one subject—his financial operations. He thinks he is worth millions. He is hopelessly insolvent. Nobody will deny it after reading this.

Murder Most Foul

If any money is paid out today at Ponzi's office, 27 School Street, Boston, that money will be paid out at the expense of those who are foolish enough to hold Ponzi's notes, thinking that he will meet all maturing obligations as fast as they come due.

He is more than $2 million in debt, even if he tried to meet his notes without paying any interest. If the interest is included on his outstanding notes, then he is at least $4.5 million in debt.

Here are the indisputable facts as disclosed by Ponzi's consecutively numbered notes. I print the dates and serial numbers so that any noteholder can check them:

June 8. No. 6,901
June 17. No. 8,965
June 18. No. 9,056
July 14. No. 21,000
July 24. No. 37,000

It will be seen that from June 8 to June 18 Ponzi was issuing only 200 notes every day. Between June 18 and July 14 he was issuing about 500 notes per day. Between July 14 and July 24 he had jumped to 1,600 notes per day.

Dist. Atty. Joseph C. Pelletier stopped him, at my suggestion, on Monday, July 26. The district attorney wanted to make sure that Ponzi wasn't lying to him about his fabulous profits in international postal coupons.

During Ponzi's last forty-five days of operation preceding the day he stopped receiving money, he issued about 29,000 notes. Since he stopped receiving money, he has paid out money to 4,000 holders of notes at the very highest estimate. All the payments have been made in Boston, and the line has been growing smaller every day.

The reason is simple. All the badly frightened noteholders who were willing to waive their fifty per cent profit were taken care of so quickly that confidence was restored. There are now about 25,000 noteholders who think that Ponzi will pay every note with interest. The fact that he can now pay $60,000 or so per day to noteholders whose notes are now maturing means nothing as to his solvency. He was issuing 200 notes a day forty-five days ago. The line will get bigger every day. It will take a full month before he is unable to meet his notes if only maturing notes are presented.

No wonder Ponzi is confident. He sees an apparently unlimited pile of cash in the banks and only a paltry $60,000 or so going out every day, the public dippy about him, suits for $5 million being brought in his name, and Wall Street "experts" who never did anything like it themselves offering "sure-thing" explanations of his "operations"—is it any wonder the thing has gone to his head?

Don't lose sight of this one fact: Ponzi issued more notes and for larger amounts during the last twelve days of his receiving money than he did in all the previous seven months. It would drive off his balance a man of stronger mentality than Ponzi.

By his own admission, Ponzi hasn't sent a dollar abroad or received a dollar from abroad during the last sixty days. His explanation is that his surplus abroad is so big that he doesn't need to send any money over. As long as his surplus abroad would enable him to meet his obligations over here, he is perfectly safe. He told U.S. Dist. Atty. Daniel J. Gallagher that story, and it sounds very plausible.

The reason I know that it is a lie is that he took it from a suggestion I made to him while walking from District Attorney Pelletier's office to U.S. District Attorney Gallagher's office last Monday. He amplified it considerably when he reached Atty. Gen. J. Weston Allen's office later in the afternoon.

This much is absolutely sure. Ponzi has not put into a Boston bank a dollar that he received from operations outside this country. He has not deposited a dollar with the Tremont Trust Company, the Fidelity Trust Company, the Cosmopolitan Trust Company, or the Hanover Trust Company—except what he received from the public in exchange for notes issued at 27 School Street or sent to his agents from 27 School Street. He has deposits in a few other banks, but these were his main depositaries up to thirty days ago. At that time he decided to buy an interest in a Boston trust company and did so, taking over a large number of shares. He was made a director and became the largest depositor in the bank.

The information that Ponzi has not operated in foreign drafts or anything else that would show any income except from the sale of notes to the public comes to me from Simon Swig of the Tremont

Trust Company. Swig agrees with me that Ponzi is mentally unbalanced on finance. I quote Swig:

"The large sums of money pouring in on Ponzi from the public turned his head. I sent for him and told him that I couldn't stand for the continual requests for information from people who wanted to make fifty per cent on their money and that he would have to take his account out of the Tremont Trust.

"He said that he saw my viewpoint, and he took his accounts over to another trust company. There was about $300,000 here under attachment that had to stay, subject to the order of the courts. During the entire time that this account was here, the only money involved at any time was the money the public gave him for notes. He never issued or received a foreign draft, a New York draft, or anything that looked like a profit.

"Any man who can pay ten per cent to agents for bringing in money on which he agrees to pay fifty per cent in forty-five days and then not to put the money to work to earn something must have a bankroll bigger than Rockefeller's. The same criticism that I make of his account here holds good for his account at other banks. If he had been operating on a big scale with his funds then that, too, would be news to me, as he has been carrying around a certified check for $1.5 million on a Boston trust company that required thirty days' notice to release."

Swig's reference to the certified check is correct, as I saw the check, shown to District Attorney Pelletier, U.S. District Attorney Gallagher, and Attorney General Allen, in consecutive order, on Monday when I accompanied Ponzi on his tour of investigation. Being the only one with him at these three separate conferences, I was able to note many deductions. A brief resume of his talks with the three officials will show the state of his mind.

He was introduced to Pelletier by me at 11:00 A.M. The first thing the district attorney did was to give him a severe call-down for allowing foolish rumors about the district attorney's being personally interested in the enterprise. Ponzi lost no time in making a cringing apology for anything of that nature, and the examination continued.

After assuring Pelletier that he was conducting a legitimate enterprise and making big profits in foreign operations, Ponzi was asked to name the bank through which he carried on his deals. Ponzi finally gave the name of an Italian bank in New York. He couldn't recall the number on Broadway where the bank was, but he was quite sure it was on Broadway. He then was asked when he had received any profits from this bank to meet his notes, and he startled the district attorney by telling him that he didn't need to get back any profits because he had plenty of funds on hand to pay everybody.

"Will an audit of your books show that you can pay all your notes and fifty per cent interest?" asked Pelletier.

"Absolutely!" replied Ponzi. "And I would have a surplus of $2 million." I am not quite sure of this figure. He shifted it so during the past week that I doubt if Roger Babson [a noted economist] could keep track of him. Ponzi then suggested to Pelletier that he would continue operations along the regular lines until Saturday and then allow an audit of the books. The district attorney gave me a look and then turned to Ponzi.

"See here, Ponzi, I think your scheme is crooked. If you think for a minute that I am going to allow you to take in money for the rest of the week, you are crazy. Why, if I did that you would, at the speed you are now going, take in $10 million and pledge yourself to pay back $15 million. Your operations stop today, and my auditor goes to work as soon as possible."

"Very well," said Ponzi. "I shall start paying back money tomorrow and will not accept any more until the auditor makes his report."

The district attorney then called his stenographer and dictated the statement that was given to the press regarding Ponzi's agreement to cease operations.

We next went to U.S. District Attorney Gallagher's office. A stenographer, three post office inspectors, and Gallagher's assistant were present. Gallagher has released all the interview that he cared to give to the public. Repeating it here would be old stuff. Ponzi ran true to form, however, and developed several new operations in international coupons, hitherto unmentioned.

We next went to Attorney General Allen's office in the State House. There we found Attorney General Allen, his two assistants, and three stenographers. Ponzi was elated to see the array of talent. He entered into the examination with gusto. It started at 2:45 and finished at 6:00 P.M., with Ponzi in the fourth dimension of finance and romance.

Most of his replies were along the lines of his talks with Pelletier and Gallagher, but he was absolutely insistent that he could not give the name of his New York bankers. Having heard him give the name to Pelletier only a few hours before, I couldn't see the reason for holding out on the attorney general, but, as I had been engaged as a publicity man and not as a lawyer, I didn't go into the matter with him.

After leaving the attorney general's office, Ponzi asked me what I thought of the way he had conducted himself, and I told him I thought he needed a good lawyer and needed him bad.

"Do you think so?" he asked.

"I do, and I will phone him tonight."

"Who is it?" he asked.

"I'll tell you in the morning," I answered, and he appeared to be satisfied. We then went to the office, and I collected funds to pay for an advertisement covering the arrangements made with Pelletier. I wrote the advertisement and inserted it into the *Post* and another paper.

The run on Ponzi's office in School Street started the next morning. It continued at feverish heat all day. The office announced that more than $1 million was paid out, and the crowd the next day was more easily handled. Further to allay the public mind, I had a sign posted on the wall of the old Bell-in-Hand at Williams Court, where the line formed, telling the public to "Beware of Speculators." This served to double the efforts of the speculators and immediately put a premium on notes maturing in a few days. The line on Thursday was smaller still and on Friday and Saturday had practically been reduced to those who held notes issued forty-five days before.

It may be asked why the 25,000 holders of notes don't rush in and demand back their money. The answer is this: Every noteholder went into the Ponzi scheme because he was eager to make fifty per cent in forty-five days. Strange as it may seem, the investors are more interested in making the fifty per cent than they are worried about the original investment.

If all Ponzi's 25,000 noteholders were to try to get into line today, the line would be more than five miles long.

Every noteholder must realize that he is one of more than 25,000. If he waits for his note to mature and everybody else does the same, there will be no excitement at Ponzi's office until he runs out of money and the payment of money is stopped by the authorities. I think payment should be stopped at once. Otherwise, I wouldn't be writing this story for the *Post*.

It might be good to make my position clear in this whole affair. I have been named in the press as Ponzi's publicity man. It is true that I engaged to do some publicity for him, about ten days ago. Soon after that the first news story appeared in the *Post*, one week ago Saturday. This story was not written by me, nor did I know of it until I read it in the *Post*. It was the first time that the general public had ever heard of him except in a hazy way. Since the appearance of that story, Ponzi has been on the front page of every newspaper in the United States. I was given at first to understand by prominent men that Ponzi was all he claimed to be. On Saturday I reached the conclusion—after developments of a week—that he was hopelessly insolvent.

As a publicity man, my first duty is to the public. I want it distinctly understood that my responsibility for Ponzi closed when I took him into Pelletier's office and arranged to have him stop receiving money from the public.

I understand that numerous schemes to defraud, using the Ponzi story as the basis for operations, are springing up all over the country. Every day of delay in reaching an official determination of Ponzi's hopeless condition is being used by the crooks all over the United States to "prove" that there is a way of making fifty per cent every forty-five days, after taking out ten per cent for agents' fees before the principal is set to work.

These fake schemes must be stopped. The quickest way to stop them is to stop Ponzi. That is why I am telling the people what I know.

Don't worry about Ponzi. If he is worth all the money he claims, he will be glad to save $2.5 million in interest on outstanding notes.

For a general summing up, let me say that I accepted a

commitment to handle publicity for a man who evidently was all right financially. I learned, little by little, that most of his associates were taking his word in everything because he backed it up with fees and generous bonuses. He gave one lawyer $5,000 for some unimportant work. He gave a policeman $500 for getting him a permit to carry a revolver. I understand he was paying money to some strong-arm men for keeping stories out of the newspapers.

The restored confidence of his noteholders was due to my own efforts. I issued the statements; I directed the stories; I shifted the drawing of all checks on one trust company to a reasonable number on another; I planted the sign that induced sure-thing money sharks to buy hundreds of his notes.

Ponzi has stopped operations for a week. He hasn't sent a cable abroad. He hasn't sent a dollar to New York or received a dollar from New York, in spite of his claim that he is operating in millions, and he hasn't dug up a new dollar to meet the drain that must come to settle the $7.5 million in notes outstanding, all of which must be paid within thirty-eight days.

It would seem like a joke if there were not 25,000 noteholders involved in it, thousands of whom had put their last dollars into the scheme and think that because Ponzi hasn't been arrested he must be all right.

Ponzi was indicted on federal charges of mail fraud and state charges of larceny and was convicted and sentenced to two jail terms. After serving ten years in prison, Ponzi, then fifty-two, was deported to Italy. In 1942, Mussolini offered him a job in Brazil with the Italian national airline. Ponzi moved to Rio de Janeiro, where he died, a hospital charity patient, in 1949.

"The thing that amazes us about Charley is that he never ended up in a trunk"

The exploits of Charles E. Leggett became known when word leaked to Chicago newspapers that Baltimore Federal Savings & Loan Association was about to file a civil suit to recover a huge potential loss for which it blamed the Justice Department. Following up the story, Jonathan R. Laing wrote this account for the *Wall Street Journal* of October 14, 1975.

Even normally cynical law enforcement officials seem almost awe-struck when they talk about the exploits of Charles E. Leggett.

They use such terms as "master con man" to describe the dapper, fifty-two-year-old Chicagoan, who has a criminal record dating from the 1930s. Their awe arises in part from Charley Leggett's courage and resourcefulness as an informer for the Justice Department's Organized Crime Strike Force in Chicago since 1971.

Justice Department sources say Leggett, an ex-convict, has used his extensive underworld connections and knowledge of the stolen-securities market to help recover some $11 million in stolen stocks, bonds, and Treasury securities. His undercover work, and even his testimony in court in some cases, has helped convict eight hoodlums, the Justice Department says, including some

Charles E. Leggett. (Courtesy U.S. Department of Justice)

with ties to organized crime.

"The thing that amazes us about Charley," a strike-force lawyer says, "is that he never ended up in a trunk. We offered him protection a number of times, but he always turned us down." (Of course, Leggett didn't turn down government rewards of $4,000 to $5,000 for each $1 million of stolen securities recovered.)

Although they don't like to talk about it, law enforcement officials are especially amazed by Leggett's latest caper, in which he parlayed a worthless piece of paper into a palatial California estate plus more than half a million dollars of pocket money. This time, they say, Charley Leggett's victims weren't the larcenous marks on whom he preyed in the past but several large financial institutions—and the Chicago strike force itself.

The trail in the case leads from Chicago to southern California to Baltimore to Zurich to Montreal, with various stops between, and it involves a $1.5 million bank loan Leggett obtained with startling ease, some vanishing Swiss francs, and some new questions about lawmen's use of undercover figures in gathering evidence. Strewn along the trail are about a dozen lawsuits, a Justice Department investigation, an IRS study, and a grand jury inquiry.

As federal investigators now reconstruct the Leggett tale, the scheme began in the spring of 1973 when he asked the Chicago strike force to provide him with "flash money" that he could show off in posing as a wealthy buyer of stolen securities. Leggett had used such flash money successfully in the past to help recover stolen securities, so the investigators complied.

The Chicago strike force, then headed by Sheldon Davidson, got Chicago's Continental Illinois National Bank, the nation's eighth-largest bank, to issue Leggett a non-negotiable $1,750,000 certificate of deposit. Although the CD was a dummy, with no deposit backing it up, the strike force provided the bank with a letter signed by Davidson stating that the strike force would assume responsibility for the CD "in the event that it is negotiated," as long as Continental Illinois wouldn't honor the certificate.

But Leggett didn't use the CD to recover stolen securities, authorities say. Instead, he used it months later as part of a deal to buy a lush La Jolla (California) estate with a thirty-five-room house with twelve bathrooms, tennis and handball courts, and a mammoth swimming pool.

Seller of the estate was Earl Gagosian, one-time head of Royal Inns of America and a former construction worker. Gagosian says that after long negotiations, Leggett agreed to buy the property for $1.8 million, with a $704,000 down payment. Under a complicated sales agreement, Gagosian says, Leggett gave him an unsecured note for $1.1 million in Swiss francs payable within two weeks of the closing.

Leggett made the down payment using funds he got from a $1.5 million loan negotiated through a mortgage banking company from Baltimore Federal Savings & Loan Association in Maryland. Backing the loan was Leggett's phony CD and the La Jolla estate.

But Leggett never paid Gagosian the $1.1 million in Swiss francs, and he defaulted on the Baltimore S & L note when it came due in August, 1974. Although the Maryland institution foreclosed on the estate this spring, it hasn't been able to evict Leggett's wife and daughter or sell the house, and it is also stuck at least for now with the bogus CD, which Continental Illinois refuses to redeem.

The Baltimore S & L has sued Continental for $1.7 million in federal court in Chicago, charging fraud and negligence. Continental, in turn, has sued the government and Leggett, asking that they be ordered to assume any of the bank's liability in the matter. Among the dozen other suits swirling around the case is a Justice Department action against Leggett, filed in federal court in San Diego, seeking to recover the $590,000 it says Leggett pocketed, representing the difference between the proceeds of the Baltimore Federal S & L loan and Leggett's down payment to Gagosian and other expenses in the real estate transaction.

Besides these civil actions, the case has stirred a storm over Leggett's tactics and his relationship with law enforcement officials. Robert Feldkamp, a Justice Department spokesman, says the agency is investigating to determine what happened and whether "any criminal liability was involved, not only on Leggett's part but on the part of anyone else connected with the matter."

Separately, a California grand jury is investigating the case, and Sen. Charles Mathias of Maryland says he may seek a Senate Judiciary Committee investigation of Leggett and the Justice Department's use of informants.

Leggett, meantime, has dropped out of sight, although he hasn't yet been charged with any crime in this case. Justice Department sources confirm he is traveling about the country in a $70,000 motor home, surfacing briefly in such places as Houston, Las Vegas, and Phoenix. A request for an interview, relayed to him through a third party, was declined. A Las Vegas lawyer, who refuses to confirm reports that he represents Leggett, says, "If I did represent him, I would recommend that he not talk to the press."

However, talks with dozens of persons connected with the case and perusal of court reports tell something about Leggett's career and the fringe world of stolen securities and government informants.

Leggett was reared in Chicago. His father, an accountant, and his mother, an interior decorator, were divorced when he was a toddler, but they later remarried. Although the Leggetts were Presbyterians, they sent Charles to Catholic schools, where he would get "more discipline," a relative says.

Always short and slim, Leggett even today is a trim 150 pounds. A stylish dresser with a penchant for $70 shoes and sporty clothes, he is almost universally described by associates as "charming."

But long before his undercover association with the Chicago strike force, law enforcement officers say, he was in frequent trouble with the law, and he went to prison on several occasions.

His so-called rap sheet shows he was sentenced to a one-year term in federal prison in 1959 on charges of interstate transportation of stolen cars, and he received an eighteen-month term in 1962 for interstate transportation of stolen property and wire fraud.

In 1971, he was sentenced to an eighteen-month term for income-tax evasion, but the record shows he served less than two months in the Cook County jail before he was set free. Justice

Department sources now say that his release from jail was part of the arrangement for Leggett to become an informer on a regular basis, although he had previously become a government witness in cases against others to win reduced charges or sentences for himself.

In his undercover role, Leggett posed as a "paper hanger," the term applied to financially sophisticated operatives used by organized crime to fence stolen securities, which often end up at reputable banks or financial institutions. Strike-force members say Leggett would contact sources of stolen securities around the country, make a deal to buy the securities, and set up a meeting in some Chicago hotel. At the meeting, the FBI would swoop in, grabbing the securities and the couriers.

"Charley turned out to be one of the best informants anywhere in stolen securities," a strike-force attorney says. "You have to be really good to sell yourself as many times as Charley did and stay alive," he adds.

Among those he helped convict, Justice Department sources say, were two couriers of $6 million of securities, part of the loot in a $50 million heist at Kennedy International Airport. Leggett in 1973 fingered the couriers, Frank Scarbaci and Murl Ingram. The government also got a guilty plea in the same case from Robert Perrette, an alleged lieutenant in the Joe Colombo Mafia family.

Leggett became something of a hit with Justice Department operatives for reasons beyond his brilliant undercover work. He showed up at a strike-force convention in San Diego several years ago in his opulent motor home, for example, and gave several strike-force officials a ride to the beach. He and a woman who was a former Las Vegas lounge singer also entertained FBI agents and Justice Department lawyers at a home he maintains in Las Vegas.

At one party, the lawyers recall, Leggett proudly displayed personally autographed pictures from Presidents Truman and Kennedy. "Who knows whether the pictures were authentic or not," says one of the lawyers, "because with Charley you can never be sure of anything."

So confident was Leggett of his position with the Justice Department people, sources in the department recall, that he once proposed that the government make a multimillion-dollar investment in a Las Vegas casino and put him in charge of it, so he could collect information of interest to the department.

The department turned down that idea, but the strike force didn't turn down Leggett's request for the $1,750,000 certificate of deposit in May, 1973. In fact, Justice Department sources say Davidson of the Chicago strike force violated the department's standard practice by providing Leggett with the original instrument rather than just a photocopy, at Leggett's request. (Leggett previously had used an original $8.6 million CD as flash money in a successful attempt to recover stolen securities.) Davidson, who has since left the Justice Department for private law practice, declines to comment on the Leggett case.

In any event, the CD given to Leggett surfaced sixteen months later, in late 1974, when Baltimore Federal S & L tried to redeem it at Continental. By this time, Leggett had struck up an acquaintance with Gagosian. According to Gagosian, Leggett represented himself as a successful gold speculator with some $32 million in Swiss banks.

Gagosian says Leggett told him he wanted to buy the Gagosian estate and also had a syndicate of fourteen investors interested in making a sizable investment in Royal Inns. Gagosian was interested in all this, especially because Royal Inns, once a high flyer on the American Stock Exchange, was having trouble with its bank lenders because of heavy losses. (During the time of the Leggett-Gagosian negotiations, Gagosian was ousted as chairman and president of Royal Inns, and the company ultimately started bankruptcy proceedings.)

"The first time he telephoned me, Leggett told me he was calling by radio telephone from his 102-foot yacht in the Pacific," Gagosian says. "Months later, I found out that he had actually called from his motor home."

In May, 1973, after Leggett got the bogus CD from the strike force, he agreed to buy the La Jolla property from Gagosian. Leggett's $704,000 cash down payment, part of the $1.5 million Leggett received from the Baltimore S & L, was paid in August, and Gagosian says the funds went to pay off mortgages and other liens on the property.

Because Leggett contended he was having tax problems and

therefore kept his money overseas, Gagosian says he agreed to take payment on the rest of the money in Switzerland.

"I regarded Leggett as the future savior of Royal Inns," Gagosian says, "so I didn't even insist that the Swiss franc note be secured by the property."

But he was soon sorry. The note proved uncollectible, and the syndicate never materialized. Gagosian says Leggett strung him along for more than a year with excuses—his health was deteriorating, and only he could withdraw the $1.1 million in Switzerland to pay the balance of the $1.8 million for the La Jolla property. Finally, Gagosian says, Leggett agreed to meet him in Zurich in September, 1974.

"He never showed up," Gagosian says, "but I was notified that he had suffered a heart attack and had been pulled off the plane in Montreal. I flew back to Montreal and checked all the hospital intensive-care units. There was no Leggett. Then I knew for sure that I had been conned."

(Gagosian may face still more problems. Federal sources say the Internal Revenue Service is investigating Gagosian's role in the transaction, including why he agreed to take the money in Switzerland.)

Meantime, Leggett had gotten his $1.5 million loan from the Baltimore S & L, using the phony CD and the La Jolla property as collateral. Despite the red tape that normally accompanies such a transaction, Leggett apparently had no trouble.

He first went to San Diego lawyer Richard Gerry, showed him the CD, and asked him to help line up a $1.5 million mortgage loan. Gerry recalls, "Leggett said that he wanted his name kept secret. He implied that he was having tax problems and didn't want to draw the IRS' attention to himself by openly buying a large estate."

Acting through Gerry, Leggett applied for a loan at several San Diego financial institutions. In August, the loan was granted by Curtis Coleman Company, a San Diego mortgage banking concern, which in turn sold the loan to Baltimore Federal. Under the arrangement, the loan was secured by secret trusts holding the CD and the deed to the Gagosian estate. The trusts afforded Leggett anonymity, protecting him from standard background and credit checks. Neither Coleman nor Baltimore Federal was to learn of Leggett's identity until after he defaulted on the loan a year later.

How Coleman and Baltimore Federal came to accept the fake CD as collateral is a subject of much dispute. In its lawsuit against Continental Bank, filed in federal court in Chicago, Baltimore Federal claims that shortly before the loan was made, Continental was telephoned by Title Insurance & Trust Company, which was the trustee of Leggett's secret trusts and handled the closing on the Gagosian property, and was asked about the CD. The suit claims that the bank confirmed the validity of the CD. Continental Illinois officials deny that the bank received any such call.

In any event, Baltimore Federal apparently failed to ask for written acknowledgment from Continental of the change in ownership of the CD. Such a verification step is considered a standard banking practice with non-negotiable CD's such as Leggett was issued. Had the acknowledgment been sought, Baltimore Federal presumably would have been tipped off that the CD was bogus and the strike force alerted to Leggett's unauthorized use of the CD, Continental Illinois officials claim.

"It's our position that we did more than necessary to verify the validity of that CD but were flimflammed because of negligence on the part of Continental and the U.S. Justice Department," contends Robert E. Hecht, president of Baltimore Federal.

Adding to Baltimore Federal's woes is its inability to sell the Leggett property or even evict Leggett's wife, Vivian, and their twenty-two-year-old daughter, Lisa. The two women have kept Baltimore Federal process-servers at bay by means of an electronic security gate and a German shepherd attack dog. The Leggett family also filed a clutch of lawsuits against the Baltimore S & L disputing everything from the validity of the foreclosure to the constitutionality of California's eviction law.

Leggett himself continues to roam about in his motor home. He has made several trips to Chicago and still visits his strike-force contacts. Says one Justice Department lawyer, "We plan to use him as a witness in one more trial and then get rid of him" as far as strike-force work is concerned. "The publicity has burned him as an undercover agent, and, besides," he says as an afterthought, "he took us for a hell of a ride."

In October, 1976, Charles E. Leggett was sentenced to one to ten years in San Quentin after his conviction on California charges of grand theft of Baltimore Federal Savings & Loan Association funds.

Ettelson and Gleason: how upper-crust swindlers cashed in on LaSalle Street

This story is reprinted by permission from the
Chicago Tribune of June 19, 1977. It was written by
R. C. Longworth.

If any two men belonged in the executive suites of Chicago they
were Leonard B. Ettelson and John S. Gleason, Jr.

Ettelson: The white-haired, patriarchal head of one of the city's
most prestigious law firms. Owner of an exclusive resort in
California. Board member of the Boy Scouts of America. Trustee
of Henrotin Hospital. Director of the Bob Hope Desert Classic
golf tournament. Chairman of the board of Barat College.
Chauffeur-driven car, Lake Shore Drive condominium. Very
conservative. Very wealthy. "We held him in awe," a former
partner says.

Leonard Ettelson, 71, died of uncertain circumstances last
December 9 as his financial house of cards was collapsing. He
already had left his firm in disgrace. He was about to be
disbarred. He was accused of defrauding banks, looting the estate
of a close friend, bilking other friends, even forging his wife's
signature.

He was at least $10 million in debt. Maybe $22 million. And
most of the loans were tinged with fraud.

Gleason: A major general in the U.S. Army Reserve.
Businessman and banker. Politically connected. Director of the

Murder Most Foul

Veterans Administration under President Kennedy. Former president of the Mercantile Bank of Chicago. Rancher and wine grower. Member of many presidential commissions. Former commander of the American Legion. A trustee at Loyola and owner of honorary degrees from Notre Dame to Tokyo. A sixteen-room house near the lake in Winnetka. A private railroad car. "He could talk anybody into anything," an associate recalls.

Jack Gleason, 62, was indicted last week on three counts of bank fraud. He earlier quit the Mercantile Bank in disgrace and filed for bankruptcy.

He says he is at least $16 million in debt. His creditors and the government say some of these loans were fraudulent.

Ettelson and Gleason. Between them, they ran up anywhere from $26 million to $38 million in debts in one of the biggest financial scandals in Chicago history.

They were friends; indeed, Gleason is a trustee of Ettelson's estate. And there is mounting evidence that they were partners in fraud, using their insiders' connections to arrange easy loans for each other, overriding bank and government rules with quiet phone calls to friends or underlings.

"You wouldn't believe the chaos left behind by those two guys," says Wallace Carroll, chairman of Katy Industries of Elgin, who is trying to collect on a $788,000 loan to Gleason. "They arranged loans for each other. They rubbed each other's backs."

In the process, apparently, they dragged in others. The federal grand jury that indicted Gleason is still sitting, and legal sources say more indictments are coming—not of Gleason, but of other persons involved with him and with Ettelson.

"You can't indict a dead man," one source acknowledged. But he confirmed that Ettelson's doings are very much linked to the jury's probe.

Gleason and Ettelson were elders of Chicago's upper crust. The cracks they caused in that crust are far from repaired. They appear to have broken almost every code and standard, violated almost every trust, hurt their friends and partners, and left behind widespread bitterness and seething anger.

At least nineteen banks and some of Chicago's leading citizens

142

are fighting for the crumbs from Ettelson's empty estate. Thirty-seven banks—including some of the ones in the Ettelson case—are involved in Gleason's debts.

Some old friends believe the men simply got in over their heads on bad business ventures and, desperate for money, began to bend the law. Others, including some who knew them best, refuse them even this benefit of the doubt.

"This guy really hit people close to him pretty hard," says another lawyer of the financial and personal damage Ettelson left behind him. "It's so venal, it's mind-boggling."

In his bankruptcy file, Gleason blamed his losses on fluctuating market prices that hurt his grape and cattle businesses, plus the energy crisis and "inadequate long-term financing." But there's no indication at all where Ettelson's money went.

"What the hell happened to it?" one banker said. "That's what's driving everybody around town nuts."

There is a theory, widely held on La Salle Street, that Ettelson salted millions away in a numbered Swiss account during three trips he made to Switzerland in 1975-76.

"I can't believe that," says his former law partner, James R. Frankel. "I can't believe he would be putting money away and hurting his friends this way at the same time." Frankel and others think the Swiss trips were meant to raise more loans, but one lawyer connected with the case scoffs, "Why go to Switzerland when this whole city lay open to him?"

With the bitterness, the affair has left a legacy of distrust.

"There are a hundred, maybe 200 men in this town with the connections and entree these two guys had," one shaken lawyer said. "And we're betting that each and every one of them is honest. Well, we bet on Ettelson and Gleason and lost.

"If you can't trust men like that, who can you trust?"

How did it happen? How does fraud of this scale take place in a business that is thought to be tightly regulated? Why didn't the banks get suspicious before it was too late?

The background of the Ettelson-Gleason affair is still murky. But rapidly growing files in county and federal courts, plus dozens of *Tribune* interviews with principals in the case, give some picture of what the two men may have done and how.

143

As far as is known, Gleason and Ettelson met in the late 1950s, when Gleason was a vice president of the First National Bank of Chicago and helped Ettelson with some loans. Ettelson already was a senior partner in his law firm, Ettelson, O'Hagan, Ehrlich & Frankel, and—as the brother of a former city corporation counsel and as one-time lawyer to the late Chicago Archbishop Bernard J. Sheil—a power in the local Establishment.

In 1961, Gleason—once campaign manager for Democratic Sen. Paul Douglas and a former commander of the American Legion—went to Washington as Veterans Administration chief. He stayed for four years, then returned to the First National Bank. In 1970, he became chairman and chief executive officer of the Mercantile National Bank at 222 South Riverside Plaza, a medium-size bank with current assets of about $87 million.

Some sources say Ettelson used his connections to help Gleason get the job.

By 1975, Gleason was making $81,000 in salary and bonuses, plus another $100,000 annually in "consulting fees," mostly from companies in which he held stock.

Among other things, Gleason was a director of Katy Industries, headed by his friend Carroll. Carroll is a dominant shareholder in the holding companies that control both the Mercantile Bank and the Drovers National Bank of Chicago. Gleason also was a director of the First State Bank of Northern California and a major shareholder and a director of Chicago Helicopter Industries.

All these companies were to play parts in the story.

At the same time, Ettelson, an expert in investments and tax law, was expanding his contacts in the banking world. He was chairman of First Drovers Corporation, which owned Drovers Bank. His law firm was counsel for Drovers, First Bank of Oak Park, and Water Tower Trust & Savings Bank. He owned part of the holding company that owned the Lawndale Trust & Savings Bank. Another part owner of Drovers and Lawndale was the Michigan Avenue Bank.

These names, too, were to appear again.

With such connections and links, the two men knew nearly every prominent banker in town. These top men saw each other regularly—over lunch, at board meetings, socially—and they trusted each other.

"They'd been borrowing from us for years, and they always repaid," one banker said. "At the end he [Ettelson] had several loans with us, and some of them were given on no more security than his high reputation. If you have a customer with that kind of reputation, and he has been good about repaying, well...."

Was it as simple as that—million-dollar loans on a handshake?

Basically, it was, according to several sources.

"Ettelson would talk to Gleason about arranging some financing at the Mercantile," says a lawyer who knew them both. "Then somebody from his firm would go over to the Mercantile and sign a note in the name of one of his companies."

Ettelson had a number of "shell companies"—one-man outfits set up to control some of his property or to act as vehicles for more loans. They go by a variety of names—Elkee, Emme, Manop, Cranallister, RLC, Macme—and there are scores of lawyers in Chicago today who are earning their pay trying to sort them all out.

Several of these companies handled various aspects of Ettelson's pride and joy, the La Quinta resort he owned at Palm Springs, California. It is one of America's most beautiful resorts and a magnet for movie stars and sportsmen. It, too, figures prominently in the story.

Gleason had his own companies, with such names as Gleaco and Josy. They managed his expanding interests—a 150,000-acre ranch at Austin, Nevada; a 2,178-acre vineyard in California; the Toiyabe resort in Wisconsin, and some 2,300 acres in Michigan and elsewhere in Wisconsin that he planned to turn into recreational property.

Life, to all appearances, was grand. A limousine ferried Ettelson daily between Lake Shore Drive and La Salle Street, where a barber came to his office to trim his white hair each week. To most people, he was "Mr. Ettelson," not "Leonard." Charities sought his aid. Clubs boasted his memberships.

Ettelson was also leading a double personal, as well as financial, life. He took a mistress in California and had a daughter by her in

1970. None of this was known to Chicago friends, who remember him as "strictly early-to-bed" on business trips and still find accounts of the affair "bizarre." Ettelson and his wife of forty years, Luela, had no children of their own; their only daughter, Leanne, now thirty-two and living in Virginia, was adopted.

Old acquaintances describe Ettelson as "the perfect black-silk-stocking La Salle Street lawyer...a friendly, lovable sort of man...the kind who inspires confidence." But one lawyer who lost money on a loan to Ettelson now calls him "the consummate con artist." And a friend who was bilked by Ettelson sits sadly in his panelled legal offices and says:

"I just can't understand it. What sort of man was this? Why would he do this to his oldest friends?"

Gleason, more flamboyant, carted friends to Notre Dame football games in his private rail car and told tales of modern-day cattle rustlers on his Nevada ranch. He is, by all accounts, a great talker. "He could look you in the eye and tell you you were in China," one former associate said. "And you'd believe it."

This was in the early seventies. Was it sour even then? Had the high living turned to fraud?

Insiders either don't know or won't say. But most men who were closest to Gleason and Ettelson think things began to go wrong during the recession, from 1973 on.

As Gleason said in his bankruptcy petition, earnings from his agricultural property plummeted just as loans became harder and more expensive to get.

Ettelson gave no hint that anything was wrong. But he had been borrowing heavily over the years, for La Quinta and other projects.

"If you're in hock for millions of dollars, and the prime rate [the best loan rate] goes to twelve per cent and you're paying even more than that, it's quite a burden," a former partner says.

In Gleason's case, the alleged illegalities date from November, 1974.

From then until February, 1975, according to the grand jury, he converted about $528,745 of Mercantile's money to his own use. He was chairman of the bank at the time and, according to the indictment, told the bank's loan committee that he had a two per cent interest in a Wisconsin firm named Earthwatchers, Inc., which had applied for a loan in that amount. In fact, the indictment said, he owned sixty per cent of it and ran it.

During the same time, on January 29, 1975, he allegedly had a $60,000 check issued as a loan to a man named I. Irving Davidson. According to the jury, Gleason took the money.

Six months later, on June 12, 1975, Gleason allegedly broke the law by putting himself up for re-election as a director of Chicago Helicopter Industries, which owned Mercantile, without disclosing his misuse of Mercantile funds.

Another charge against him has been filed by the Jefferson State Bank of Chicago, which says Gleason got a $50,000 loan from it on March 13, 1975 by pledging one of the condominiums he owned at Ettelson's resort, La Quinta. The bank says that condo already was pledged to a loan at the First State Bank of California.

Things were closing in on Gleason. On February 1, 1976, he resigned all his positions at the Mercantile Bank, ostensibly for "health reasons." He had $268,500 coming in deferred compensation from previous years, plus a hefty pension, but all this was "rescinded and abrogated" by agreement between him and the bank, according to records at the Securities and Exchange Commission (SEC).

Less than three weeks later, Gleason filed for bankruptcy.

Included in the file is a financial statement dated October 29, 1974, showing Gleason's net worth as $3,670,000. But by early 1976, he reported a staggering list of debts.

He owed $3,315,000 to a Los Angeles firm for the vineyard; $1,436,742 to a Nevada bank for funds to run his ranch, and $1,120,825 to the John Hancock Insurance Company for a mortgage on the ranch. Other loans—$375,000 from the Eagle River (Wisconsin) State Bank and $308,474 from the Citizens State Bank & Trust in Wausau, Wisconsin—went to finance his woodland properties.

But what caught the eye of bankers and prosecutors were his loans locally. He owed the Drovers Bank—Ettelson's bank—$685,084 on two loans, only partly secured.

He owed his former employer, the First National Bank,

$40,000. And he owed money to banks in which Ettelson had connections—$65,150 to the Michigan Avenue National Bank, for instance, and $42,269 to the Water Tower Trust & Savings.

Gleason's wife, Mary Jane, shared in his bankruptcy. Among her listed debts are $350,000 to the Oak Park bank, where Ettelson was counsel. The $788,000 loan from Wallace Carroll of Katy is in her name.

Dozens of other creditors, most of them smaller, have filed claims against Gleason in Bankruptcy Court. They range from a $207,795 debt to the Union Bank in Los Angeles to a $176 bill from Winnetka for garbage and water service to their house. [The house has been sold. So have the railway car and the La Quinta condos, and his other properties are on the block.]

One other Chicago bank—the mighty Continental Illinois National Bank & Trust Company—may be holding the biggest bag of all.

Between 1969 and 1971, Helicopter Air Service, which Gleason controlled, borrowed $5.6 million from Continental to buy eighty per cent of the stock in Mercantile Bank, which Gleason headed. According to SEC documents, the loan has been in default since November, with $5,567,330 left to pay.

Gleason is one of the guarantors of that loan. The other is Carroll, who says of that aspect of the affair only that it "has not been good for me." Continental says it is negotiating with all parties to get its money.

Gleason is to be arraigned in federal court here this week. His lawyers have told him to make no statement until then, and efforts by the *Tribune* to reach him were unsuccessful.

As the federal government began to look into Gleason's affairs, Ettelson was also about to come to grief.

His friends think now that Ettelson had been reduced, by early 1976, to a frantic search for new loans to pay off old ones. Interest rates were still high. Credit was plentiful, but not limitless.

La Quinta was losing money. Another La Salle Street lawyer, William Friedman, had owned part of the resort but sold out to Ettelson in 1973 in protest against the latter's extravagant management—two servants for every guest, for example. Ettelson promised to pay Friedman $1 million—beginning this year.

Almost without exception, all the claims filed against Ettelson in court stem from short-term loans, sixty or ninety days, that he obtained from a number of banks from February to May of 1976. The dry legal file gives off the unmistakable whiff of panic, of a man seeking money wherever he could find it.

This need probably led to two frauds so shocking that they still baffle and infuriate his friends.

Charles F. Jarrard, owner of the Allied Structural Steel Company in Chicago Heights, had been one of Ettelson's closest friends until he died in 1972. Jarrard's will named Ettelson as trustee, with the specific job of making sure that Jarrard's widow "never wants for any material thing."

The will went on to give a warm posthumous salute to Ettelson for "his friendship, advice, and loyalty" over the years. Jarrard said he would have left Ettelson part of his estate, except that "he is otherwise well provided for." It is a phrase of deep irony, considering what happened next.

Lawyers for the Jarrard family have sued, contending Ettelson looted his friend's estate of more than $1 million. Legal sources in Chicago say the true figure is nearly $1.9 million.

Among other things, according to the charges, Ettelson pledged 40,104 shares of Allied stock from the Jarrard estate for a loan from the Mercantile Bank—Gleason's bank—and then kept the money for himself.

Ettelson's former law partners say they got wind of this and confronted him with the evidence. In July of last year, he quickly and quietly resigned from the law firm he had headed for forty years.

At the same time, the partners told the Attorney Registration and Disciplinary Commission of the Illinois Supreme Court what was going on. The commission confronted Ettelson and, after considerable wrangling, he signed a motion voluntarily disbarring himself. The specific charge was theft of 22,384 shares of Allied, worth $400,000, from Jarrard's estate.

[Jarrard's widow is still provided for, according to her son, Charles, Jr., who said the Ettelson affair "didn't take the food out of her mouth; but all this has worked a hardship on our family, and not necessarily in a financial way."]

The disbarment motion was sent to Springfield. The Supreme Court, according to sources, was to rule on it December 9, 1976.

Meanwhile, allegations of another betrayal of trust were mounting. William J. Campbell, the former chief federal judge in Chicago, and his wife, Marie, filed suit charging that Ettelson stole $250,000 worth of securities owned by Mrs. Campbell.

Campbell was one of Ettelson's oldest friends. The judge had appointed the lawyer to positions of trust, among them the job as receiver in the sensational City Savings Association case ten years ago.

So when Ettelson came to them on April 26, 1976 asking for a $250,000 loan to tide him over until he could swing a large loan to consolidate his La Quinta debts, Campbell and his wife never hesitated. They gave him the securities in exchange for shares of the La Quinta Water Company, which Ettelson said he owned, and his promise to repay the money in six months.

The repayment date, October 26, came and went. Campbell, who was getting suspicious, pressed for payment. Finally, he says, Ettelson admitted that he had illegally sold the securities to pay other debts.

Campbell, flabbergasted, threatened to tell the FBI. Ettelson promised to make good on the debt. The two men agreed to meet December 9—the same day as the Supreme Court session.

Other chickens were coming home to roost in early December. Dozens of Ettelson's short-term loans were in default. Banks were pressing. Despite his attempts to dodge them, process-servers had delivered subpoenas. He had court appearances and meetings with lawyers scheduled for the 9th.

That morning, December 9, Ettelson was found dead in his bathroom by his maid. He was pronounced dead at Northwestern Memorial Hospital some four hours later. Many men who knew him say the timing was so "convenient" that they suspect he committed suicide, but there is no evidence to back this up and the death certificate lists "heart disease" as cause of death.

Even after his death, news of Ettelson's debts seeped out only slowly. But files in various courts and the bitter memories of friends tell an astounding story.

There is the $250,000 owed to the Campbells. There's the $1 million owed to lawyer Friedman. There's a copy of loans from members of his law firm, including Frankel. And there is scant chance any of these will ever be paid.

Ettelson owed a $2.3 million mortgage on La Quinta, and the banks involved have foreclosed. Most of that was owed to the United Bank of California.

Mercantile Bank—Gleason's bank—says Ettelson owed it $740,000 on a personal loan, plus a staggering $19.4 million on loans guaranteed by him, mostly to his various companies.

Drovers Bank—Ettelson's own bank—holds court judgments totaling $2,322,931 on defaulted loans to Elkee, Cranallister, and Manop, all companies owned and controlled by Ettelson.

["With all the regulatory rules we have, how could a guy borrow from banks where he was a director?" one lawyer asked.]

Other banks connected with Ettelson say he defaulted on loans—a personal loan of $128,016 from Lawndale and loans both personal and to Elkee, totaling $724,816, from the First Bank of Oak Park. Legal sources say Ettelson also owed money to the Michigan Avenue and Water Tower banks when he died.

The First National Bank says Ettelson owed it $379,000, and it plans to sue to collect. The Continental Bank is said to have a large loan outstanding to Ettelson, but it will not say how much.

Other banks, including the Ashland State Bank of Chicago and the Forest Park National Bank, already have filed claims.

Legal and banking officials say Ettelson pledged some stock—the La Quinta Water Company stock, for instance—more than once, in violation of the law. Several creditors are holding identical copies of the same shares, leading to suspicion that Ettelson kept duplicate portfolios.

Some of the loans, including the corporate loans from Drovers Bank, were guaranteed both by Ettelson and his wife. But Mrs. Ettelson has filed court statements denying that she signed the guarantees, implying that her husband forged her signature.

Attorneys for Drovers Bank say the bank apparently bent the rules by allowing Ettelson to take the guarantees home for his wife to sign. As for Mrs. Ettelson, they say, "she professes not to remember anything."

151

There is only limited sympathy for Mrs. Ettelson on La Salle Street. She has sold the condominium on Lake Shore Drive and has moved into the Ritz-Carlton Hotel, and she has kept up her membership at the Saddle & Cycle Club ($100 per month dues, plus assessments). It's a life-style that would seem to be beyond the income from the sale price of the condominium, and the insurance she is known to have collected.

For one bank, it is too late. The First State Bank of Northern California in San Leandro was closed by state authorities on May 21, 1976 after being caught in a series of bad loans. The SEC says the Mercantile Bank, under Gleason, arranged large loans to the San Leandro bank, which in turn lent $580,000 to Ettelson and his companies.

The mystery of where the money went remains.

One theory is that La Quinta ate it up. But persons familiar with the resort's operations said it lost $1 million a year at the most, "and there is no way he could have sunk $10 million to $20 million into it."

There is no sign that much money went to Ettelson's second family in California. One friend who has been in touch with the mother of his child says she is living in modest circumstances and needs money.

A former employee who lost money to Ettelson thinks the lawyer built a "paper castle" of loans, pyramiding them, hocking all his stock to finance new loans, until it simply collapsed on him.

Amid all the chaos, one victim is taking the long view.

Jerry Pritzker, one of Chicago's shrewdest real estate men, says he lent Ettelson $50,000 "but even then I had a visceral feeling that I'd never see that money again.

"Leonard had a problem," Pritzker says. "La Quinta was like a sewer for money. But it was a way of life with him. He felt like a duke out there.

"I don't feel put on. I liked Leonard very much. Everybody liked Leonard."

Gleason pleaded guilty to misapplying more than $500,000 while he was board chairman of the Mercantile National Bank and accepted a three-year-and-one-day prison sentence. "I never thought that I would appear before the court and admit that I've committed a crime," he told U.S. District Court Judge Alfred Y. Kirkland. "I have done so and I am sincerely sorry."

153

A 1788 woodcut of William Brodie.
(Courtesy Newberry Library, Chicago)

Chapter V

THE HEIST

The execution of the gentleman who inspired "Dr. Jekyll and Mr. Hyde"

William Brodie was born September 28, 1741 in Edinburgh of prominent parents. As an adult, he was a neighbor and friend of poet Robert Burns and a member of the Cape Club, composed of Edinburgh's male elite. But he gambled away his fortune on cockfights, and that, according to an account in the *London Chronicle* of July 12, 1788, "led him into a set of connections that depraved his morals and finally engaged him in a confederacy of desperadoes who tempted his last fatal act." He broke into the General Excise Office for Scotland on March 5, 1788 and stole L16. He was linked to other robberies totalling L800. His last hours and his hanging on September 30, 1788 are described in this story from the *Chronicle* of October 7 of that year.

At a quarter past two o'clock, William Brodie and George Smith were brought out upon the platform at the west end of the Luckenbooths, attended by two Edinburgh magistrates, and proper officers.

Brodie had a full suit of black, his hair dressed and powdered; Smith was dressed in white, with black trimming. They were assisted in their devotions by the Reverend Mr. Hardie, one of the ministers of this city; the Reverend Mr. Cleeve, of the Episcopal persuasion, and Mr. Hall, of the Burghers.

Having spent some time in prayer with seeming fervency, they put on white caps; and Smith, whose behavior was highly penitent and resigned, slowly ascended a kind of table raised a few feet above the platform and placed immediately under the beam where the halters were fixed; he was followed by Brodie, who mounted with briskness and agility and examined the dreadful apparatus with attention, particularly the halter designed for him, which he pulled with his hand.

It was then found that the halters had been too much shortened, and they were obliged to be taken down to alter. During this dreadful interval, Smith remained on the table, but Brodie stepped lightly down to the platform, took off his nightcap, and waited patiently till the ropes were adjusted. He then sprung up again onto the table, but the rope was still improperly placed, and he once more descended to the platform, showing some little impatience, and observed that the executioner ought to be punished for his stupidity.

Having again ascended the table, and the rope being at last properly adjusted, he deliberately untied his cravat, buttoned his waistcoat and coat, and helped the executioner fix the rope; then pulling the nightcap over his face he folded his arms and placed himself in an attitude expressive of firmness and resolution. Smith, who during this time had been in fervent devotion, then let fall a handkerchief as a signal, and a few minutes before three, the table dropped from under them.

This execution was conducted with more than usual solemnity. The magistrates and ministers were dressed in their robes and the great bell tolled during the ceremony, which had an awful and solemn effect.

The crowd of spectators was immense; and, it is believed, much greater than ever assembled on a similar occasion, great numbers having come from all parts of the country.

Thus ended the life of William Brodie, whose conduct, when you consider his situation in life, is equally singular and contradictory. By the low and vicious connections he formed, he had everything to lose—he could gain little even if successful; for, from the moment he embarked in the enterprise of his desperate associates, his property, his life, were at their mercy.

Indeed, his crimes appeared to be rather the result of infatuation than depravity; he seemed to be more attracted by the dexterity of thieving than the profit arising from it.

To excel in the performance of some paltry legerdemain or sleight-of-hand tricks, to be able to converse in the language of thieves, or to chant with spirit a song from "Beggar's Opera" was to him the highest ambition.

Those who knew him best agree that his disposition was friendly and generous, and that he had infinitely more of the dupe than the knave in his composition; and was indeed admirably fitted for designing and wicked men to work upon.

But the grand source from which all his crimes and misfortunes sprung was gaming; a vice, indeed, too prevalent in all ranks; leading, in the most opulent, to bankruptcy and suicide; and, in the middle and lower classes, to crimes hurtful to society, and fatal to themselves.

The fate of this unfortunate man, distressing as it must unavoidably prove to many respectable individuals, formed, however, an example highly important and beneficial to society. It points out the difficulty of eluding, by the most artful means, the steady and persevering hand of justice; it shows that when guilt is once brought home, the rank of the individual rather aggravates than softens the crime; and that the laws are distributed with an equal and impartial hand to all.

For the month preceding his execution he appeared to possess an undaunted resolution, and at times even a daring boldness, frequently turning to ridicule his situation and the manner of his exit, by calling it "a leap in the dark," and that even within a few days of his suffering.

He declared that, notwithstanding the censures and opinion of the world, he was innocent of every crime excepting that for which he was condemned; and endeavored to extenuate his guilt by saying that the crime for which he suffered was not a depredation committed on an individual, but on the public, who could not be injured by the small trifle the excise office was robbed of.

A considerable time before his death, he employed himself chiefly in writing, and complained much of the interruption he met with from the ministers attending him, and his fellow convicts' singing of psalms.

He remarked that his temporal concerns required his attention, and that the best of men had not thought it improper to employ

157

even their last moment in the concerns of this world; that he was standing on his last legs, and it behooved him to employ his time most sedulously; that he was determined to die like a man and recommended the same to his fellow sufferers.

He lamented to a friend the impropriety of his first pursuits in life; that his inclination at an early period led him to wish to go to sea; and though he did not possess much bodily strength, yet his courage and resolution were undaunted; that, instead of being in that disgraceful situation, his country might have looked upon him with admiration, and he might have been an honor to himself and family.

He appeared to have no hopes of a pardon, and expressed himself satisfied at the exertions his friends had made on his behalf. On the Friday before his execution, he was visited by his daughter, a fine girl of about ten years, and here nature and the feelings of a father were superior to every other consideration; and the falling tear, which he endeavored to suppress, gave strong proof of his sensibility; he embraced her with emotion, and blessed her with the warmest affection.

On the Sunday preceding his execution, he appeared to possess the same courage, the same undaunted resolution, that had attended him through the whole of his imprisonment; and, on the other prisoners, being informed of a respite being granted them for six weeks, Brodie appeared as well satisfied, and declared that it gave him as much pleasure as if mercy had been extended to himself; and on its being observed by the other criminal, George Smith, that six weeks was but a short period, Brodie, with some emotion, cried out, "George, what would you and I give for six weeks longer? Six weeks would be an age to us."

He made frequent inquiries about the alterations that were being made at the place of execution, which his friends declined answering out of tenderness. He observed that the noise made by the workmen was like that of shipbuilders; but, for the short voyage he was going to make, he thought so much preparation was unnecessary.

On being visited by a friend on Sunday evening, Brodie, with great calmness and composure, gave the needful directions respecting his funeral, and acknowledged with gratitude the attention that had been paid him during his confinement.

On the Monday preceding his death, at the request of Smith, the two prisoners for whom a respite had been obtained were removed from the room in which they had all been confined. They parted from their companions in misery with great feelings of sensibility; and, during the process of taking off their chains, Brodie remained an unaffected spectator.

He was frequently denied being allowed to receive the visits of his friends by an order from the magistrates, a report having been propagated of his meditating his own destruction; but he appeared to have full conviction of the dreadful consequences attending the crime of suicide, declaring that if poison were placed on the one hand and a dagger at the other he would refuse them both, and not launch into eternity with the horrid crime of self-murder to account for; that he submitted to the sentence of the laws of his country and would wait his fate with calmness and composure.

The nearer the fatal moment approached, the greater his resolution and fortitude appeared, without any adventitious aid, his manner of living being rather abstemious. He astonished everyone who conversed with him; and his courage and magnanimity would have rendered his name immortal, had he fallen in a good cause.

The day before his death, on being visited by a friend, and the conversation turning upon the female sex, he began singing, with the greatest cheerfulness, from "Beggar's Opera," " 'Tis woman that seduces all mankind."

Late on Tuesday evening, while he was inveighing with some acrimony on the cruelty of not admitting his friends to him, a noise was heard in the prison, when suddenly starting, he turned to his fellow prisoner Smith, "George, do you hear that noise? That's the fatal beam going on which you and I are to suffer tomorrow."

On the night preceding his death, he retired to rest about eleven o'clock, slept till four in the morning, and continued in bed till near eight o'clock, without any symptoms of alarm at his approaching fate. At nine o'clock on Wednesday morning, he had his hair full dressed and powdered; and, upon a minister requesting to pray with him, Brodie desired he might use dispatch and make it as short as he possibly could.

During the remainder of his time, he was employed in the most painful of all trials, parting with his friends, which he did with the utmost fortitude and composure. About a quarter past two, he was conducted to the place of execution by a few friends, who to the last paid him every attention; and here, in this trying and awful moment, his courage and composure did not forsake him; he viewed the apparatus with the greatest calmness and indifference, and conversed cheerfully with steadiness to those about him.

When the executioner proceeded to bind his arms, he requested that it might not be done too tight, as he wished to have the use of his hands, at the same time assuring his friends that he should not struggle. He twice ascended that platform, which was raised much higher than at former executions.

Before he ascended the platform the last time, he was addressed by his fellow sufferer, Smith. They then shook hands and parted. Brodie took off his neck cloth, opened his shirt collar, and mounted with great alertness; he then adjusted the rope about his neck, put the cap on, and, taking a friend who stood close by him by the hand, bade him farewell, and requested that he acquaint the world that he was still the same and that he died like a man.

The platform dropped, and he was launched into eternity without a struggle.

Thus fell William Brodie, a just sacrifice to the laws of his country; and, while we lament his fate, we cannot but admire that impartiality, that integrity with which justice is administered; for, however great, respected, or exalted the culprit, it affords no shield to protect from punishment or save from disgrace.

His untimely fate claims the tribute of a peer; for, if those who possess fortitude, courage, benevolence, and humanity claim our admiration, such was William Brodie.

Nearly a century after Brodie's hanging, Robert Louis Stevenson studied the case and became fascinated by the gentleman burglar's "double being," which inspired him to write "The Strange Case of Dr. Jekyll and Mr. Hyde."

Boston Brink's robbery: a $1.5 million haul, the biggest ever in U.S.

The 1950 Boston Brink's heist was a gangland masterpiece—patiently plotted, brilliantly executed. This story of the caper—at the time, the biggest robbery in history—is from the *Boston Herald* of January 18, 1950.

Nine bandits seized an estimated $1.5 million, at least $1 million of it in cash, last night from the second-floor office of Brink's, Inc. armored-car firm in the company's North End garage.

The final check-up of the theft will show the total taken "will go $1.5 million all right," Police Comr. Thomas F. Sullivan said.

The gunmen left another million dollars behind.

It was the biggest cash robbery in the nation's history.

Seven of the bandits, disguised by Halloween masks, cowed and disarmed five employees and scooped the money from an open vault. They carried it away in two large Federal Reserve Bank moneybags and cursed because they were unable to take more.

The seven entered the second-floor office at Prince and Commercial streets at 7:10 P.M. Twenty minutes later they were driven away by confederates who had waited outside in two cars.

They left the five Brink's workers bound and gagged on the floor, and they left police bewildered by the million dollar-plus theft.

The loot the bandits carried away in their two cars was money that had been collected from various firms yesterday by the armored cars and was to be delivered to the Federal Reserve Bank of Boston this morning.

Police Supt. Edward W. Fallon said that, of the sum left behind, $880,000 was the payroll of the General Electric Company and $120,000 was from Filene's department store.

Immediately after the robbery, the police sent out a description of two former Brink's employees, one from Somerville and the other from Back Bay, for questioning. As the night passed, police throughout the eastern states were asked to look for two ex-workers of the concern, presumably the same two men.

Search for the former workers came after the investigators discovered the holdup men unlocked six doors before reaching the grilled-in vault where the money was being sorted and tabbed for distribution today.

Officials of the firm said they presumed some former workers had keys to the doors.

Police Commissioner Sullivan ordered all captains and detectives to headquarters last night for a briefing on the robbery. Watches were posted at bus terminals, the airport, and hotels.

Early today one of the former employees who had been sought appeared voluntarily at police headquarters. He was questioned at length, but the police said they were satisfied he had nothing to do with the robbery. The other former employee who has been mentioned in police radio orders was picked up in the South End about an hour later. He also was taken to headquarters for questioning.

Investigators were exploring the possibility that the gunmen may have used a gray 1948 Cadillac with white sidewalls on the front and snow treads on back stolen yesterday in the Back Bay.

This car, equipped with license plates stolen from another car, was seen on Memorial Drive in Cambridge last night. All police cruising cars were directed to be on watch for it.

The bandits apparently were frightened away by the persistent pressing of a buzzer by a Brink's garage man who did not know the robbery was in progress.

In the vault room, surrounded by an eight-foot wire enclosure, when the bandits entered were Thomas Lloyd of 11 Merritt Avenue, Braintree, and James C. Allen of 26 Crandall Street, Roslindale, both cashiers, and guards Sherman D. Smith of 40 Hancock Street, Somerville; Herman E. Pfaff of 163 Chestnut Street, Cambridge, and Charles S. Grell of 205 Spring Avenue, Arlington.

All five were armed, but so quickly and efficiently did the robbery take place that they were unable to draw.

Allen gave the following account:

"One of them said, 'Don't move, boys, or we'll let you have it.' The others talked, too, but in voices so low you couldn't make out what they were saying.

"The vault door was open. There was money in the vault, a lot of it, and a lot of money on the floor in the cage.

"The bandits made us open the cage door, and then they made us lie down. They took our pistols. They tied us up and put adhesive tape over our mouths. One of them ripped my glasses away from me."

As reconstructed by police, the bandits entered a side door leading upstairs from Prince Street. Since all wore rubbers, with the exception of one wearing crepe-soled shoes, they made no sound as they passed through the upstairs corridor and a counting room on their way to the vault room.

On the way they must have had the services of a confederate who had slipped in to the garage to open the doors before them or made use of pass keys. They passed through no fewer than six doors before reaching the vault room.

There they flashed their guns — black, long-barrelled, Army-type .38-caliber revolvers — and ordered the five employees to "Get 'em up," while they stood beyond the wire enclosure.

Then the leader ordered: "Open the door."

Lloyd told Grell, standing nearest the door, to comply.

The bandits, working with precision, snatched the employees' guns, took short lengths of wire wrapping cord, carefully knotted at each end, from their pockets, and tied the five employees. They taped the employees' mouths with adhesive and then looted the vault of as much as they could carry.

They took with them bags and envelopes delivered to the money-collecting firm to be held for deposit this morning. Police were hopeful last night that disposition of those bags and envelopes might give them a clue to the bandits.

Lloyd was the first to free himself. He tore away Allen's bonds and ordered him to sound the burglar alarm while he telephoned police headquarters.

The only description of the bandits that police could get was that they all wore Navy pea coats and concealed their features with orange and black masks "like kids use."

Witnesses were found who saw two men, sitting at the wheels of two cars parked on Commercial and acting nervously at about the time of the holdup, and it was assumed that the getaway was made in these cars. There was no description immediately forthcoming from police, however, of the cars or drivers.

Police even lacked a description of the voices of the robbers. Only the one who gave the original command for the Brink's men to put up their hands spoke loudly and even he, according to Lloyd, had no accent or peculiarity of speech that might be helpful in identifying him in a lineup.

The others spoke softly or not at all, and coming through the cardboard masks the intonations of their voices were dulled and indistinct.

Timing of the robbery was extraordinarily precise. Drivers for the firm had all reported in, parked their trucks in the gloomy cavern of the first floor, and turned in their day's receipts.

Upstairs in the vault room, which contained the huge concrete block of a safe, whose heavy doors probably would withstand a good-sized charge of dynamite, the employees were busy counting money into envelopes and stacking them into piles for deposit at the Federal Reserve Bank.

The physical layout of the offices provides a maximum amount of protection, but the bandits managed to outwit those who had planned it so.

Just to get to the vault room they had to open a heavy, lead-lined door.

Then they mounted a short flight of concrete steps, opened a second heavy door and were in a short hallway, from which a wooden door with a doorknob lock led into a corridor and the counting room.

They passed through a fourth door into the long counting room running parallel to Commercial Street at the back of the building, and then through two doors in the wire cage that separated the vault room from the other sections of the building.

Knowledge that the building was deserted, their wearing of

rubbers, and the childish simplicity of the masks and uniformity of costumes showed a clever mind behind the robbery.

The Brink's heist had one flaw—the lack of honor among thieves. But for that, it would have been perfect. The brain behind the plot was Anthony Pino, a stickup man who always had trouble deciding whether a job called for a shotgun or a machine gun; Joseph F. McGinnis, a hijacker and rum-runner whose trademark was smashing his enemies' fingers with a crowbar; and Joseph (Specs) O'Keefe, a gambler who once said he would do absolutely anything but work. They spent two years pulling together eight unlikely accomplices to make the haul. All agreed "that if anyone did anything to endanger the life or liberty of another he was to be exterminated." Three years after the robbery, O'Keefe got caught with a pistol in Pennsylvania and went to jail for two years. When he got out, he returned to Boston to claim a share of the still undivided money. But his colleagues tried to cut him out, and there was an abortive attempt on his life. Shortly after that he was jailed on another weapons charge. In prison, he confessed to the Brink's job and identified the others, who were indicted just four days before the statute of limitations would have expired. Two of them died before the trial and the eight others, including McGinnis and Pino, were sentenced to life in prison.

Société Générale heist: picnicking with wine in the strong room

The 1976 robbery of the Société Générale in Nice, France was truly *le fric-frac du siècle* (the heist of the century). The take was more than twice the previous record of $4.3 million taken two years earlier from Purolator Security in Chicago. The French crime was in a class of its own in daring and imagination, as this story from *Nice-Matin* of July 21, 1976 shows. It was written by René Cenni, Maurice Huleu, P. F. Leonetti, and Daniel Curzi, and translated for this anthology by Armand Petrecca.

The afternoon stretches out toward evening but does nothing to diminish the torrid and oppressive heat of this scorching summer.

Along the Avenue Jean-Médecin, in the heart of Nice's business center, flows the uncertain stream of the idly curious. On the sidewalk, in front of the head office of the Société Générale—a would-be palace enclosed by heavy grillwork and faced with stucco—the employees of the strong room have just emerged from their air-conditioned basement, trying, like fish out of water, to regain their breath in the sticky air.

It is three or four minutes past 5:00 P.M. Little by little, as the final transactions are concluded, the large bank is emptied of its personnel.

Between 5:15 and 5:30, all the cash boxes having been secured, the vault is locked for the weekend, behind several hundredweights of steel armor, controlled by a mechanism designed to survive the most violent onslaughts.

At 7:00 P.M. within the high walls, so elegantly adorned with diaphanous greenery, statues, glasswork, and glistening metal, where the scent of tobacco still hovers, the caretaker makes his routine rounds to see if the lights are out, if the doors are locked, if everything is in order. He is unperturbed. Technology has taken over his tasks of vigilance. He glances only casually, in passing, at the huge panel that guards the treasure room. He can even, if it suits his mood, put on his slippers and wait for Monday...

When he returns to his quarters—not a part of the bank, and located in the adjoining building—he is far from suspecting that a few meters from him, crouched in the fetid darkness of the sewer that drains the Rue Gustave-Déloyé, behind the bank, resolute men are preparing to bring off the heist of the century. A monumental stroke, it will even wipe away memory of the raid on the Glasgow-London mail train, the nimble burglary of the Rothschild Bank in Paris, and the break-in of the main post office in Strasbourg.

It is easy to visualize these men today, in the light of what their "labors" have revealed about them. They are five or six, no doubt. A commando unit. They have prepared their venture with exceptional attention to detail. They are ready for action, not the least bit on edge, as, their eyes fastened upon their watches, they await zero hour. The night is suited to their plan.

Making good use of their time, they have readied the way for the final assault. From the sewer main, beneath the midline of the Rue Déloyé, they have excavated a tunnel eight meters long, calculated to meet the rear wall of the vault at the point where it is weakest.

This being their tunnel to fortune—their base camp, their avenue of access, and their route of withdrawal—they have spared nothing in the way of precautions to shore it up with metal stanchions, to apply cement to the weakest portions of the roof, to protect it from human wastes by spreading a fiber mat along the base, to ventilate it by means of air vents, and even to illuminate it by laying, for nearly a kilometer, an electric cable that has been inconspicuously hooked up to the power supply of the underground parking lot at the Place Masséna.

They find it easy enough to penetrate the wall. Its thirty centimeters, however strongly reinforced, cannot resist for long the thrusts of their impact drills, which are likewise connected to the power supply of the Masséna parking lot. But behind it, another obstacle awaits them: a formidable safe, placed back-to-back against the wall. Without hesitating, without a single superfluous movement, the commando unit marshals its hand drills and, by a skillful interaction of wedges and a pneumatic jack, causes the object to tilt forward. A centimeter at a time. Just enough to enable a man to pass through, but not so much as to trigger the ear-splitting collapse of those hundredweights of hardware. Now that this delicate phase has been completed, it remains only to enter the first of the three distinct rooms that make up the vault.

No time has been lost in turning the *sanctum sanctorum* into a beehive of activity, disciplined down to the most minute details. Using a special saw, one man cuts into the bars of the two gratings that separate the three compartments, after having first cut through a door of hardened glass, without leaving splintered fragments to endanger their subsequent movings about. Another applies a synthetic resin to seal off whatever openings that might allow light or smoke to filter through. And finally, the bulk of the gang must draw on their utmost energies to haul inside, from the tunnel, the imposing equipment that has been assembled to provide for all contingencies. In fact, they have brought twice, no three times, the necessary equipment, and only an improbable combination of circumstances could cause their efforts to fail for technical reasons. In the space of perhaps an hour, the six oxyacetylene torches, the twenty-seven large gas cylinders, the innumerable jumper drills, crowbars, screwdrivers, and chisels, all conveyed (very likely the night before) through the sewers, are in place, ready to function.

While the drill operators prepare their work site, the cook sets up his kitchen and prepares the menus for the duration of the campaign. The quartermaster corps would do well to pay heed. For the most part, there are no sandwiches, cold dishes, or emergency rations, but rather ready-cooked meals heated on camping stoves, sausages, cheeses, desserts, and even soups. And to go with everything: wine, cases of mineral water, milk for breakfast time, and cigarettes to suit the tastes of each. Shades of Byzantium!

With no nervousness whatsoever, the men begin the burglary. It has three well-defined objectives: first of all, the "pillbox" into which drop—from the special intake accessible on the Rue de l'Hotel-des-Postes [General Post Office]—the after-hours receipts of the big businesses that are regular users of this system of deposit. Next, the safe where the cash reserves of the bank are kept. And finally, the armored cabinets containing the safe-deposit boxes rented by private parties. Of these, 317 out of 4,000 will be emptied of their contents.

The specialists work quickly, but without excessive haste. They know that they have about fifty hours ahead of them and that, if anything, they have too much to choose from: they can even afford to be connoisseurs. Above all, they know that they have nothing much to fear and that there is no risk of their being given away by an unluckily triggered alarm signal. Insofar as can be judged today, from the sworn statements of the investigators, the vault—which was designed half a century ago—has no such alarms. So great is the confidence that its armor inspires!

And now for the inventory, the meticulous sorting, as armor plating and locks give way. Assured of a fabulous first prize in the form of cash, gold coins, ingots, and bars—all negotiable without the slightest risk—the thieves do not hesitate to pass up the greater part of the jewels, the stock certificates, and even those bearer instruments that are most easily convertible into cash. Having picked and chosen, they scatter their discards about the floor.

Full of toil and monotony, the hours go by. The loot takes on unhoped-for dimensions, and fatigue is forgotten. For relaxation, the commandoes refresh and amuse themselves with the discovery of the sometimes astonishing and sometimes even scandalous contents of certain safe-deposit boxes, whose owners believe that they have placed their least admissible secrets out of reach.

With the salacious photos that they have gotten their hands on, the euphoric gangsters set up a rather explosive display—as a prank for the benefit of those who will enter the vault after them. And they restrain themselves, for reasons of their own "convenience," from taking the loveliest pieces of family silverware.

They have saved for last—for their supreme pleasure—the task of plundering the night-deposit chute: a colossal piggy bank, glutted with the weekend receipts of business establishments whose pouches read "Les Nouvelles Galeries," "Casino Supermarkets," "Prisunic," "Manufrance," "Les Rapides Côte d'Azur." Stuffed and giddy, tottering under their wealth, they call a halt to their digging. They will forget a bundle of a hundred 500-franc bills (a pittance).

That's it. It's finished. The dawn is about to break over the most sumptuous Monday of their lives. Before departing, they administer a few spot-welds to the mechanism of the vault door. With a little luck it will look like a breakdown, and the alert will be delayed for as long as it takes to get it open.

The bags sway as they move through the tunnel. A final, searching glance backward at the scene of the plunder. Nothing that might become a clue do they dare forget. Their worn and soiled gloves are the last to be discarded, just to make sure there will be hardly any hope of finding even a single interesting fingerprint. Before departing, the last man draws—in full view—the peace symbol and, in quite anonymous block letters, this inscription: "Without weapons, without hatred, and without violence." The ultimate in nose-thumbing....

The night of the cloaca engulfs the multimillionaire sewer-diggers.

Up above, Nice is awakening. Another week's activities are resuming their course. In a very short while the bank will reopen. The same old routine. But the day's usual progress is halted as the chief teller presides over the opening of the strong room. The door stands fast against all manipulations. Efforts are redoubled, but to no avail. Still, it seems that nobody is getting excited: on a recent occasion, this huge apparatus already showed signs of failure to function properly. For the sake of peace and quiet, a call goes out for the services of technical experts, who arrive at a grave diagnosis: it will be necessary to perform "open-heart surgery." And so it is that, at 3:00 P.M. sharp on Monday, after prolonged efforts by the safebreakers, the managers of the Société Générale are horror-struck at the magnitude of the disaster revealed before them.

It only remained to begin the investigation. From scratch. The investigators are directed at the scene by Police Inspector Besson, acting chief of the Criminal Investigation Detachment of Nice, with the co-operation of officials from the Central Office for the Suppression of Banditry in Paris, under the supervision of Inspector-General Mathieu, head of the Criminal Investigation Department of Marseilles.

In an investigation, it would appear that one is reduced to conjectures, on all levels. Conjectures, first of all, as to the underground route taken by the thieves, both to transport their heavy equipment to the work site and then to vanish into thin air with their loot. Subject to evidence that has yet to be turned up, it seems logical to suppose that, following the network of the sewers both coming and going, they operated from the bed of the Paillon River, beneath the covering of concrete and asphalt that assured them of complete secrecy. It is possible, by way of the open banks proceeding upstream, to reach the half-drained bed of the river, and to descend from there in a vehicle as far as a sewer outlet located at the level of the Rue Chauvain, roughly a few hundred meters from the bank. Resourceful and far-seeing, the thieves had dreamed up a convenient method for transporting first their equipment and then their loot with less effort: the sewer men found a fully inflated inner tube for a truck, which (along with others) could be used as a boat.

And now for further conjectures as to the total value of the "transaction." While awaiting an exhaustive inventory, which doubtless will require days, one must be content to calculate the probabilities, which are supported by certain data. In circles close to the Société Générale, there was talk of ten million francs for just the night-deposit chute used by businessmen and large stores, and of five million francs (all of it in cash, naturally) as the liquid reserves of the bank. Starting from that, well-informed sources were placing the final take at between forty million and sixty million francs.

Conjectures, in short. But on one thing everyone agrees: the superior organization of the foray, which implies the alliance of a team of specialists with a high level of preparation in disciplines as diverse as those of earthworks, civil engineering (the experts have

171

admired unreservedly the step-wise layout of the tunnel, its infrastructures, its fittings, its ventilation system like that of the strong room, consisting of a flexible air duct some twenty meters long, with a pump), topography, economics (for selection of the loot), and, of course, the opening of the safe-deposit boxes.

Into this complex undertaking, did some small failing creep in? Does the commando unit have its weak point, minor participants who might spill the beans? For the moment, the police are proceeding cautiously in all directions, even beyond our borders. The burglars—enjoying, thanks to the jammed door, a head start of a good ten hours—must have succeeded in going into hiding quite tranquilly after stashing their loot. For an exploit of this great scope, the gang must have been international.

French police later identified Albert Spaggiari, a photographer and former paratrooper, as the "brain" behind the crime. The plot apparently was hatched to provide money for a shadowy international rightist organization. Spaggiari was arrested and confessed. But, early in 1977, the forty-five-year-old master thief leaped from a window in a magistrate's office and vanished on a motorcycle. He is still at large. Police said they recovered an "important part" of the loot in a raid on a villa outside Nice, but never revealed how much.

Fear on 47th Street: murder and madness haunt diamond district

In 1974, Leo Dershowitz and Howard Block were murdered in Puerto Rico. In 1977, Abraham Shafizadeh was murdered in Puerto Rico and Haskell Kronenberg was murdered in Florida. The victims were carrying diamonds—probably $1.5 million worth all together. Authorities made no connection between the crimes until a fifth victim, Pinchos Jaroslawicz, was found murdered in New York on September 20, 1977. He may have been carrying as much as $1 million in diamonds. Since the four earlier victims worked in or frequently visited New York's diamond block—47th Street from Fifth Avenue to Avenue of the Americas—police surmised that the murders were related, that someone had broken the honor code of the street where million-dollar deals are sealed with a handshake and *mazel un brucha* (good luck and blessing). The Jaroslawicz murder and the diamond district are described in the stories reprinted here. The first is by Leonard Buder from the *New York Times* of September 29, 1977, and the second by David Behrens from Long Island's *Newsday* of October 4, 1977.

The body of a twenty-five-year-old diamond broker who vanished last week with up to $1 million in gems was found yesterday, his head smashed by blows with a wooden plank. The body was bound and stuffed inside a small box in the Manhattan office of a diamond cutter.

There was no trace of the gems he had been carrying in a wallet.

The police were led to the body of the broker, Pinchos Jaroslawicz, by a thirty-one-year-old diamond cutter, Shlomo

173

Tal, himself the object of a police search since his wife reported him missing on Monday. Tal, whom the police found sleeping in his wife's car in Queens yesterday morning, was held as a material witness.

The diamond cutter told the police that the murder had been committed by two masked men who struck Jaroslawicz on the head and by whom he himself was abducted and robbed several days later. An autopsy showed that Jaroslawicz died of head injuries and asphyxiation after a plastic bag was put over his head.

Tal told detectives that he had kept silent about his associate's murder and had concealed the body in a box under a workbench out of fear that the murderers might harm his own family.

"His story is that he had no part in the robbery and murder, that he was also a victim," said John L. Keenan, New York City's chief of detectives. "We are certainly not accepting his story or any story at face value."

One of the points detectives said they found puzzling is why, according to Tal's account, the murderers let him go unharmed after driving him around in his own car for three days.

Tal led the police to the body of the missing broker after being found asleep on the floor of his parked station wagon by two radio-car officers on regular patrol in Queens.

The cutter had been reported missing by his wife, who said she last saw him on Sunday morning when he left for the office with a pouchful of gems.

Jaroslawicz, who was the object of a wide search after he disappeared on September 20, was highly respected in Manhattan's busy diamond district and in the Orthodox Jewish community in the Parkville-Midwood section of Brooklyn, where he lived with his wife and two-year-old daughter.

A slightly built man—he stood 5 feet 6 inches tall and weighed 117 pounds—he looked years younger than he was.

His body, when discovered, was wrapped in layers of plastic, with the head covered with a thin plastic bag. The body, knees to chest, had been crammed into a wooden box about two feet high, two feet wide, and three feet long. The hands and feet were tied in a fetal position, Keenan said.

Dr. Yong-Myun Rho, a deputy medical examiner, said that Jaroslawicz had died of head injuries and asphyxiation, and that the broker was still alive but unconscious when the plastic bag was placed over his head.

On Monday, detectives had visited Tal's office on the fifteenth floor of 15 West 47th Street, west of Fifth Avenue—and spent hours there—after his wife, Aviva, had reported him missing. But no one looked inside the wooden box that once held an air conditioner and now contained the body. It had been shoved, along with other boxes, under a workbench.

Keenan said that the detectives had gone to the office looking for Tal and were not conducting the kind of search that might have discovered the body.

He said there had been no reason to make a thorough search, although the office was dusted for fingerprints in connection with a report—which now appears unfounded—that Tal's office might have been burglarized.

Jaroslawicz had been scheduled to see Tal on the evening he disappeared. It was to have been his last business call before going home.

Witnesses have told the police that they saw the broker in the elevator of the building at 15 West 47th Street at 5:30 P.M., and one diamond merchant said he saw Jaroslawicz knock at the outer door to Tal's office. Tal, however, originally said that he was not in at that time and thus did not see the broker.

According to police sources, Tal had given various closing times to different investigators— ranging from 5:00 to 7:30 P.M.—to show that he was not in the office when Jaroslawicz called.

But yesterday Tal gave the police a different version. He told them that shortly before Jaroslawicz arrived, two masked men entered his office. There are two doors to the office, and both are usually locked from the inside. The inner door contains a small window, which was discovered smashed on Monday, that permits occupants to see who is outside.

Lt. Earl J. Campazzi, who is in charge of the missing-persons squad, said that Tal told them yesterday that when Jaroslawicz got there, one robber pulled a gun and the other hit him on the head with a two-by-four. The robbers, he said, then fled with the diamonds that the broker had been carrying.

According to the police, Tal said he wrapped the body in plastic, stuffed it into the box "and continued doing business" for the rest of the week. He told investigators that he had said nothing because he was "scared" for his life and the safety of his wife and children.

Last Sunday, members of Jaroslawicz' Orthodox Jewish community mounted an unsuccessful search for him through the diamond district, a search that took them to the door of Tal's office.

On that day, Tal told police yesterday, he was abducted by the same two masked men shortly after he left his Plainview, Long Island home.

First, he was quoted as saying, the two men jumped into his 1972 Buick station wagon as he stopped at the intersection of Woodbury and South Oyster Bay roads. Later, the police said, he added that the killers had first called him to arrange the meeting and that, in terror, he complied.

He said the two drove him around Nassau County, Brooklyn, and Queens for most of three days, spending one night at a motel. On Tuesday night, he said, the men gave him something to drink—he thought it contained "a drug potion."

The next thing Tal said he knew, two policemen were knocking on the window of the station wagon. It was 2:15 A.M. yesterday and the vehicle was parked at 68th Road and Grand Central Parkway in Forest Hills.

After Tal produced his driver's license, the officers, Joseph Wukich and Carmine Lofaso, immediately realized that they had found one of the two missing persons in the diamond mystery.

Tal told the police that his abductors had taken $180 from him, but had overlooked $30,000 in gems that he had hidden under the driver's seat.

The discovery of Jaroslawicz' body and the account given by Tal shocked their Brooklyn and Plainview neighborhoods.

In front of the white-pillared, six-story building at 760 West 10th Street in Brooklyn, where Jaroslawicz lived, sorrowful neighbors spoke of the slain young man.

"What can I say?" commented Israel Borg, a friend. "He was

just a wonderful man, an exceptional person. He was devout, always in the synagogue, always observing the Sabbath and all the holidays."

Jaroslawicz' absence from his family and from the synagogue on Yom Kippur last weekend had stirred fears among his friends and family that he might have been murdered.

* * *

It is only one block long, an island of sorts surrounded by the New World.

Just a few streets to the north, the shoppers stroll past St. Patrick's Cathedral and Saks Fifth Avenue and Rockefeller Center. But for those who drift down to 47th Street and turn westward to the Hudson, modern Manhattan vanishes.

There, between Fifth Avenue and the Avenue of the Americas, the hustling, bustling past comes alive again on 47th Street. There, as the hours of the business day unwind, two strands of time meet and intertwine: the history of diamonds and the history of Jews.

The events that linked Jews with the world of diamonds go back more than 600 years. After centuries of peace under Moslem rule, Jews in Spain and Portugal again became the target of Christian massacres in the 1300s. In 1492, they were banished by a royal Spanish edict. Expulsion from Portugal came a few years later.

Vast numbers of Jews fled to North Africa, Turkey and Italy, but many turned to the north, to the more tolerant societies of Belgium and Holland. It was there that the roots were first planted—in the guild shops of Antwerp and Amsterdam, both places emerging as great trading ports and the first great diamond centers of the new Europe.

Antwerp blossomed in the early 1500s when most of the world's diamonds still came from India. By 1608, there were 104 cutters in the Belgian seaport, and in less than a century the number rose to more than 200, many of them Jews. Diamond cutters and goldsmiths handed down their craft father to son, but later, Jews from East and West were welcomed to Antwerp from such cities as Frankfurt, Hamburg, Warsaw, London, and Paris to perfect the art of diamond cutting.

Today, one merchant on 47th Street puts it this way: "Now *we* are Antwerp."

It is West 47th Street that now plays a part in nearly ninety per cent of all American diamond sales, perhaps $2 billion worth. It is West 47th Street where the Jews in the world of diamonds have again found sanctuary.

Along the street, merchants estimate that seventy-five per cent of the street's population is Jewish: the brokers and salesmen, the cutters and polishers, the setters and jewelers, as well as the insurance agents and lawyers. All along the street, the names are Jewish. Fabrikant, Schneider Jewelers, Murray Blauweiss, Aaron-Faber, Rakowsky Antiques, Saul Drexler.

Why did Jews find security in diamonds? Many merchants echoed Bill Fabrikant's answers: "First there was silver and gold." Fabrikant operates one of the largest centers on the street, the International Jewelry Exchange at the strategic corner of Fifth Avenue and 47th Street, where more than eighty jewelers offer their wares.

"Gold and silver were something you could escape with," Fabrikant said. "But diamonds, they were the easiest to carry, to run with. Not bulky, easy to hide. How many escaped by giving someone a diamond?" He shook his head, a touch of amazement and sadness in the one movement.

"So what does a Jew do? He sells everything for as much as he can get, even at a sacrifice. And he says: 'Give me diamonds.' Then, if he gets out, he either sells them and goes into another business or he sells them and stays. A lot of people stayed in the business," Fabrikant said.

"But always it's the smartest who escape. Always. That's why Jews are so smart. Only the smart escaped the inquisitions, the pogroms." The Russian word, which means "riot" or "devastation," is an echo of the nineteenth century, when czarist authorities refused to halt public uprisings in which thousands of Russian and Polish Jews were killed. Fabrikant's ancestors survived.

But not all the survivors who have created this New Antwerp are alike. West 47th Street is a diverse scene, reflecting the divisions within Jewish culture itself.

There are ultra-orthodox Hasidim in knee-length, loose-fitting black coats and black ritual hats. Some trim their beards and some do not. Some wear earlocks and some do not. Some are Zionists and some violently oppose a Jewish state in Israel.

But the Hasidim, as highly visible as they are, make up only about twenty per cent of the Jewish community on the street. There are also Orthodox Jews and Conservative Jews and Reform Jews. There are assimilated Jews who speak with no accent and Orthodox Jews who may or may not wear skullcaps. There are Jews who buy hot dogs from the street vendors, and there are Jews who lunch only in the kosher restaurants.

Regardless of spiritual shading, 47th Street is a world of single-minded intensity for almost everyone.

There are deals on the street, in the shops, in the hundreds of tiny, often dingy offices that fill the old buildings on the block, in the cubicle-filled exchanges, offering the wares of dozens of jewelers, all eager to make a deal.

At lunchtime, the streets are jammed. On one afternoon, a bearded Hasidic Jew brushed through the noontime crowd, his newspaper folded to the story of the diamond center murder story. All day, merchants had been saying: "Crazy, just crazy, the kind of world we live in."

As the bearded man passed, he glared disapprovingly at an intruder, a press photographer snapping a picture of two men in front of Mendelsohn Brothers' shop. One of the men peered up, looking at the very blue sky refracted through the facets of a small diamond, pinched between his thumb and forefinger.

The diamond glinted, and a small crowd watched the scene.

"This is not as good even as that," the man with the diamond said, pointing down to a satchel another man braced between his knees. The man with the satchel shrugged. Such was business.

Meanwhile, a young woman rushed by, greeting another dealer in front of a neighboring exchange. She whispered: "I need to talk to you." And she was gone.

But if there is madness and mystery, there is also much

hand-shaking. And often it is followed by business as usual, with earnest conversation in doorways and along the curb, with men standing with their square-cut jewelry boxes between knees or leather pouches tucked firmly under arms. And who knows what is inside the traditional thin wallets beneath the baggy coats and the half-hidden vests?

Today, perhaps not much, a merchant shrugged, now that the street had murder and violence on its mind. But, as they say here, Business is business. The street talk is often in Yiddish, spoken with gusto and gestures. There is also a promise of, yes, very, possibly, a really big deal.

According to Gilbert Mitchell, managing editor of Jewelers' Circular-Keystone, the industry's largest publication, there are about 200 bona fide diamond brokers on the West 47th scene, not counting the dozens who come in every week.

It is big business. Diamonds for engagement and wedding rings, for example, accounted for more than $1 billion in sales last year, Mitchell said, and that was only about forty-five per cent of the annual diamond sales at about 30,000 retail outlets across the country, according to his magazine's recent surveys.

But life on West 47th Street is not lived in the billions. It is filled with hard work for one or two per cent profit and an appreciation for haggling and needling and nudging.

For example, two salesmen were negotiating at an exchange counter.

"How much'll you give me for the small ring?" the first one asked.

"I'll give you, maybe, $400," said the second, after a long pause.

"Good," replied the first salesman. "Now I know it's worth more!"

Irony is a precious mettle along 47th Street.

Down the street, for example, Bill Fabrikant was talking about security. He lives on Long Island, but he won't say where. "I have no listed phone, no name on the mailbox, I don't carry diamonds home with me." At night they go back into the vault. In the exchange, he said, he feels secure. In fact, he does not even carry insurance on his own stall near the front door. The exchanges are very open and visible. There are uniformed and undercover guards. They do not get robbed, Fabrikant said. That's how safe it is, he said. No insurance, no fears.

"So why do I dream all the time I'm being held up?" he asked with a flourish. Then he paused and added: "Ehhh. So what! So I dream. At least I don't get held up."

On the street itself only a few city police officers are visible. One of them, Patrolman Lewis J. Weshner, stood in front of the Mr. Diamond shop.

"We Buy Diamonds...Highest Prices Paid," the sign above the display window promised. A card in the display case read: "Marquise." That's a style of cut, Weshner explained to a reporter. A police officer for nineteen years, the officer has spent the last five years on the diamond beat. He glanced at the window, a glitter of affluence in all shapes: ovals, pears, little hearts. A tray below the ovals was filled with emerald cuts.

"Not worth anything," Weshner said, pointing to the emerald-styled diamonds. "See right through them...flaws show right up," he said. "With a ten-power lens, you can see no flaws. With a twelve-power, you see it," he said, squeezing the reporter's elbow for emphasis, like a rebbe making some Talmudic point or a salesman closing in on a deal.

As Gilbert Mitchell predicted, along West 47th Street, everyone becomes a diamond maven.

"We Buy Diamonds," the signs chorus along the street. "Top Prices Paid at This Window."

"Sadie, the Polisher," one of them announced, competing with the "Best Jewelry Polisher" sign across the street.

As the day ended, buses chartered by the Hasidim pulled up along the street, to carry the black-frocked men back to Hasidic enclaves. On Fridays, the buses come earlier, so that the Hasidim may reach home before the Sabbath begins at sundown.

Some Hasidic Jews, a merchant said, trickled in before World War II, when the diamond center was downtown in the Wall Street area. But the Hasidim were not really visible in great numbers until the early 1950s, he said. Now there is conflict between some pro-Zionist Hasidim and Israelis, on the one hand, and anti-Zionist Hasidim. It is ironic because the Hasidim, founded in Poland in the 1700s, were themselves persecuted by Orthodox Jews who criticized them for rejecting the traditional scholarship.

Elsewhere on the street, there are other survivors. One concentration-camp survivor works in the Jewelers and Dealers Exchange not far from the Yahalom. "He has his number, tattooed on his arm," said Saul Drexler, who has a shop in the exchange.

Drexler entered the business in 1938 when he was nineteen, an apprentice cutter working for three dollars a week. Then, after he had served in the Army during the war, the union wouldn't let him return as a cutter. Another echo of the Antwerp guild system. "They just told me my father wasn't a cutter." So Drexler became a salesman, and now is also a respected appraiser.

"I'll tell you why Jews got into the diamond business. You might be a butcher or successful in some business. But you were always prepared to run. With a diamond, you could put everything in your pocket and run. And you knew you could sell it anywhere. Not like a ruby or an emerald, which you could not be sure of. So they ran from Poland to Belgium, and from there to England and the United States. Some were never in the diamond business before they had to run, but, being Jewish, you always had the fear that you would have to run. You were always prepared for it. In Europe at least. Not here. Here we're more secure."

"For now," someone said.

"For now," Drexler echoed.

Outside almost no one wanted to talk about murder. But there was a drunk staggering along 47th Street just as a photographer was taking pictures of a jeweler outside his shop.

"He did it," the drunk said, waggling his finger at the jeweler. It was just a whiskey joke. But no one had to explain what the drunk was talking about.

Police refused to accept Tal's account, which varied considerably in his many tellings. On March 30, 1978, Tal and another diamond cutter, Pinhas (Pini) Balabin, 29, both Israeli citizens, were arrested on charges of murdering Jaroslawicz and taking $500,000 worth of gems from him. The two men, who had criminal records in Israel and had been in the United States as resident aliens for six years, were sentenced to 25 years to life in prison for the murder. Police said that a grand jury would look into the possibility of a link between the Jaroslawicz case and other diamond murders.

Chapter VI

THE GETAWAY

Dale Otto Remling's daring helicopter escape from Jackson Prison

A spectacular helicopter escape similar to one in the movie "Breakout" occurred at Southern Michigan Prison on June 6, 1975. These two stories from the *Detroit Free Press* describe the escape and the escapee. The first, reported by Tom Hennessy, William J. Mitchell, Ron Ishoy, and Jim Neubacher, appeared June 7. The second, by David Johnston and Bill Michelmore, appeared June 8.

A forty-six-year-old bad-check artist made a daring escape Friday from the Southern Michigan Penitentiary at Jackson, flying to freedom in a hijacked helicopter after it landed behind the prison walls to pick him up.

Two persons were arrested within hours, including the man police say was the knife-wielding hijacker who commandeered the private helicopter used in the escape.

But the inmate, Dale Otto Remling of Sidney, Michigan, remained at large late Friday in the second successful escape in less than three months from the nation's largest walled prison.

The dramatic escape, similar to the plot of the recent movie "Breakout" and to real-life breaks in Mexico and Ireland, caught guards at Jackson completely by surprise.

The first indication guards had of the escape came when they saw the helicopter flying away from the prison shortly after 11:05

A.M., said Capt. Lee McCoy, of the prison staff.

Not a shot was fired in the episode.

Police believe that at least three persons helped Remling escape and at least three getaway cars were used to decoy pursuers.

Arrested Friday were Don Hill, 23, of Howell, and Jolyne Lou Conn, 32, of Webberville.

The plot began Friday when a man believed to be Hill arrived at Mettetal Airport near Plymouth, posing as a businessman who needed a hurried helicopter ride to Lansing.

About ten minutes into the flight, pilot Richard Jackson told police later, the passenger pulled a black-handled knife from his briefcase, pressed the five-inch blade to the pilot's throat, and ordered him to change course to Jackson.

The pilot said the hijacker pulled out the radio wires in the plane. Following orders, Jackson said he flew low toward the prison walls to escape detection and dropped the helicopter in a grassy clearing marked by a red handkerchief inside the prison at precisely 11:05 A.M.

Remling, on a lunch break from his job in a prison factory building nearby, made a quick dash into the helicopter, and the craft immediately lifted away.

That part of the prison is guarded by electronic surveillance only, with the nearest manned guard post nearly 300 yards away, McCoy said.

With the knife still to his throat, Jackson said, he flew the men to a site five miles northeast of Jackson, along M-106 near the junction of North Meridian Road. There the men sprayed chemical irritants in Jackson's face and abandoned the helicopter.

A man who lives near the site said he saw one man run to a yellow Volkswagen waiting on M-106. The other man, apparently Remling, ran to a red car parked along North Meridian.

Jackson said he recovered after sixty to ninety seconds from the temporary blindness caused by the spray. He fixed the radio, made a call to a nearby airport to report the hijacking, then got the helicopter airborne again in time to spot a third car, a red Plymouth, driving slowly from the area.

Jackson notified authorities, and state troopers stopped the car, which was driven by Mrs. Conn. Police, who questioned Mrs.

Conn Friday afternoon, believe she was deliberately acting as a decoy while Remling escaped in another red car.

She was charged with aiding and abetting the escape. Another Webberville woman, Gertrude Woodbury, was being sought Friday, suspected of driving the Remling getaway car.

However, the FBI said it had information that Miss Woodbury was in the prison complex at the time of the escape, waiting to visit Remling.

When the escape alarm went off, Miss Woodbury vanished in the confusion.

Hill was charged with kidnapping after being arrested near Howell by Livingston County sheriff's deputies on a probation-violation warrant.

State police Lt. B. H. Garrison said Hill was implicated in the escape plot by Mrs. Conn. The FBI said Hill took five hours of practice helicopter flying in May at a Greenville (Michigan) flight school.

Witnesses said Friday that a fifth person may have been involved in the getaway—the person who was seen driving the yellow Volkswagen that met Hill, the alleged hijacker, as he abandoned the helicopter.

Livingston Sheriff Charles Hands said a helicopter stolen in Howell several weeks ago, and recovered at a crash site near Jackson, may be linked to Friday's escape plot.

That helicopter crashed near the site where Remling met his getaway car, police said. Police believe Hill may have been practicing for Friday's escape.

Garrison said Miss Woodbury, a cook until last fall at the Delta Delta Delta sorority house at Michigan State University in East Lansing, leased the car Mrs. Conn was driving Friday in the getaway decoy plot. Miss Woodbury was described by neighbors in Webberville as the mother of eight children and a divorcee.

A spokesman for the FBI in Detroit, which entered the case because of the hijacking, said Friday he expects charges of air piracy to be filed against Remling and his accomplices.

Remling, born in Hooker, Oklahoma, has been in and out of prisons and jails since 1947, when he was first arrested for grand larceny in California.

His general practice had been to steal valuable items or buy them with bad checks, then attempt to sell them for cash.

Remling escaped from Soledad Prison in California in 1955, but was caught three days later.

In 1971, while serving a prison sentence in a medium-security facility in Sonora, California, he escaped again. He was a fugitive from Sonora when arrested in Sidney, Michigan in 1973 on a variety of fraudulent-check charges.

He was sentenced by an Ionia County Circuit Court judge to a maximum term of six years and eight months to ten years for the attempted check purchase of a $2,440 car.

While at Jackson, Remling was serving a concurrent term for grand larceny and auto theft in Nebraska. He is still wanted in California.

Police used dogs and their own helicopters, and made a house-to-house search in areas near Jackson, but were unable to apprehend Remling Friday.

The helicopter that freed Remling landed in an area called the "Back Forty" by officials at Jackson Prison. It is actually the ten least-used of the 57.5 acres of land inside the walls of the prison. The prison houses 4,959 inmates.

Captain McCoy said the "Back Forty" is generally unmanned because of recent personnel cutbacks at the prison. The site where the helicopter landed is partially hidden from view of the nearest guard by a large tree, McCoy said.

The walls in the area are guarded by electronic sensing devices, television cameras, and an electric alarm beam.

"All these were operating. It would take something like a helicopter to beat the system, and that's what they did," said McCoy.

"This was very well planned," he conceded.

If guards had manned the towers on that end of the prison, McCoy said, the escape might have been prevented.

"A man running to the helicopter would have been shot," he said. "The pilot probably would have been shot, too."

But state corrections director Perry Johnson said in Lansing Friday he does not anticipate bolstering manpower in the area of the prison where the escape occurred.

"It costs the state $80,000 a year for five men—one on each shift and two on relief—to man one tower around the clock seven days a week," he said.

Johnson said, however, he may consider anti-aircraft cables or other devices that would make it difficult or impossible to land a helicopter safely in the prison yard.

"We will re-evaluate," Johnson said. "We don't want to tempt anyone else to try this scheme."

After a March escape from Jackson, Kenneth Oliver, 35, of Detroit, was captured in Los Angeles last month. Oliver, serving a life sentence for killing a state trooper near Niles, Michigan in 1973, apparently escaped by hiding in a truck leaving the prison.

* * *

It was three years ago this week that a handsome cowboy with an engaging smile that inspired confidence in his honesty rolled into Sidney, Michigan.

A year later he had married the beautiful daughter of the town's richest citizen, won the affection of the 100 residents, and written $53,000 in bad checks.

Saturday there was not a person in town with a bad word to say about Jimmy Mangan, better known to the rest of the world as Dale Otto Remling, con man extraordinaire who pulled off a daring helicopter escape Friday from inside Southern Michigan Prison.

Remling, posing as Mangan, earlier had met James Hansen, owner of a saddle shop, at a horse auction in nearby Crystal, Michigan, and so impressed Hansen with his riding skill that Hansen brought him to Sidney.

Remling said he was a wealthy Colorado cattleman, and he had the personal documents to prove it. Remling was using the name and identification papers of James J. Mangan of Glenwood Springs, Colorado, who had lost his wallet in Wichita, Kansas in 1951 when he was a hotel bellhop.

"This guy has really used me," said the real Mangan, contacted by phone at his home Saturday.

It was only two years ago that the real Mangan finally found out about the con man who had been misusing his good name for more than two decades.

"I found out he was using my credit rating and even had a dishonorable discharge from the Navy using my name," Mangan said.

He said he became suspicious when he received a letter from a stranger who said he was an old Navy buddy. Mangan had never been in the service.

About the same time, Mangan said he learned from a local credit bureau that someone was using his credit rating to buy cattle in Colorado. It was later learned that Remling and his bride from Sidney were at the time living in Rifle, Colorado, about eighteen miles from the Mangan home.

Mangan, 44, a land appraiser with the U.S. Forest Service, said he had never met Remling. The two men are similar in appearance. With only two years separating their ages, both are 5 feet 10, about 180 pounds, and have brown hair and green eyes.

"All this has upset me," said Mangan. "For years I had a good name and now I don't know what crimes are associated with it."

To Mangan, Remling is "a leech and a parasite," but to the people of Sidney, from whom he borrowed thousands of dollars that were never repaid, he's still a "nice fellow."

"You won't find anybody who'll say a bad word about him," said Don L. Petersen, whose daughter Kay married Remling in January, 1973.

"He was a very nice fellow and everyone liked him; even the littlest child loved him," Petersen said.

Petersen said that despite what Remling did to him, his daughter, and half a dozen other people in Sidney, a town with one bank, one real estate office, one insurance office, one general store, and one gasoline pump—all owned by Petersen—he still has high regard for the man.

"You couldn't get mad at him," said Seafred Jensen, a retired factory worker, whose driveway Remling used to plow for free.

"He was a real swell guy. He always smiled, and you just seemed to place your confidence in him."

Remling told everyone he had a cattle ranch in Colorado. His skilled horsemanship and renown as a master blacksmith who could easily shoe the most troublesome horse lent credence to his tale.

According to Dorothy Rogers, a friend who lost $3,000 to Remling, he had a photo album with pictures of what he said were his son who was killed in a car crash and "his wife who had to go in an iron lung for six months before she died and it cost him all his money."

Gerald Petersen, no relation to Don, said Remling once told of spending a winter snowed in with a herd of cattle in a remote Colorado valley.

"Once he got to talking, he could get people to believe him and to do just about anything he wanted them to do," Petersen said.

After a wedding at the Sidney Christian Church in January, 1973 to Kay Petersen, an attractive schoolteacher and horsewoman, Remling took his bride to Colorado to show off his spread, according to half a dozen town residents.

Remling even had documents to show he had money coming to him from the sale of cattle and reportedly showed his bride a broken gate at the ranch he claimed to own and angrily told about how a fence gate he had carefully built was damaged.

At one point Remling had his bride getting together a group of men to go to Indiana to pick up cattle he claimed he owned, residents here said. The trip never came off.

Another time, after borrowing money from several people because he said proceeds from the sale of his cattle were tied up in escrow, he reportedly flew to Las Vegas to win a big stake to pay off the loan but instead lost all the borrowed money.

Jo Hansen, whose husband owns the saddle store, said Remling "was a real nice man. He was smart, polite, and could do anything—ride a horse, build a stall, tool beautiful leather purses, run a bulldozer, and once he even flew in here in an airplane and gave Kay and some other people a ride."

Remling had a few too many drinks at the Sidney Tavern once shortly after arriving in town and "shot off his mouth," Gerald Petersen said.

Remling complained of ulcers and after that incident drank only sparingly, residents said.

"He always did everything the best," recalled Kenny Mitchell, Sidney Township constable, who said that, while others bought inexpensive liquor, Remling drank only the best.

Not long after the wedding, Remling's stories about the cattle and the money that was supposed to come and the loans he made but couldn't repay began catching up with him.

He and another man, Dennis Gerbracht, 30, of nearby Greenville, Michigan, went to Hooper, Nebraska, where they took a family hostage, stole 383 hogs, and took the animals to Iowa. Because they forgot to take certain health records for the hogs, they were unable to sell them and abandoned the scheme. Gerbracht since has been convicted of that crime and was imprisoned in Nebraska.

Upon returning to Sidney, Remling seemed troubled and continued to complain about ulcers, Mrs. Rogers said. To others he was unchanged, continuing to work in the basement of the neat white farmhouse he rented from his father-in-law, a few hundred feet from Sidney's only intersection.

Remling wrote a number of checks without funds in the bank, but his father-in-law, chairman of the local bank's board of directors, covered them.

One day about $35,000 in bad checks came in that his father-in-law would not cover, and police began moving in on Remling, who had begun buying merchandise with bad checks and selling it elsewhere.

Police finally arrested Remling, 46, revealing his true identity to the shocked citizens of Sidney, on a bad-check charge that sent him to Jackson Prison from August, 1973 until his dramatic escape. His marriage was annulled after that arrest.

In 1971 Remling escaped from Soledad State Prison in California, where he was serving time for grand larceny in connection with the theft of an airplane.

He was on the run from California authorities when he met Hansen at the horse auction.

He is also wanted in Kansas in connection with the sale of stolen cattle in March, 1969.

Asked why Remling's carefully constructed world as smiling cowboy Jimmy Mangan began falling apart after things had gone so well, people in Sidney just shake their heads.

"He sure could have made a lot of himself," said Ruth Jensen,

Seafred's wife, "because he was the kind of person who could sell anything."

"He was sitting on top of the world," Seafred Jensen observed, "with a nice wife—the pretty schoolteacher—a well-to-do father-in-law with just two daughters, everyone in town liking him, and then it all went wrong."

"He could've stayed here ten years," Ruth Jensen said, "and done very well, and nobody would have ever known."

Soon after the escape, notices appeared mysteriously on bulletin boards throughout Southern Michigan Prison: "Helicopter rides 75 cents." And on official job-posting forms: "Six anti-aircraft gunners (two for each shift) to shoot down aircraft, helicopters, and other flying objects." Remling was arrested in a bar in Leslie, Michigan—fifteen miles from Jackson—thirty hours and eight minutes after his daring flight. State police said Remling put down the groceries he was carrying and smiled when they grabbed him. "I'd smile more," he said, "but I have a missing tooth." He told reporters he had "heard some birds sing, water trickle, and a fox bark" in his night of freedom. That made it all worthwhile, he said. Hill's arrest turned out to be a case of mistaken identity. Morris Eugene Colosky, 20, was arrested and charged with the helicopter hijacking.

"Garage-door opener" unlocks prison gates; five inmates get away

There have been several escapes from the Marion (Illinois) federal penitentiary, which was built in 1963 to replace Alcatraz. But none was more intriguing than this one, reported by Linda Eardley in the *St. Louis Post-Dispatch* of Sunday, October 12, 1975.

A convicted bank robber described as "highly intelligent and about as bad as they come" apparently masterminded the escape of five prisoners Friday night from the federal penitentiary near Marion, Illinois.

The convict, Edward P. Roche, is believed to have made a hand-size transmitter, similar to an electronic garage-door opener. The device triggered a series of electronically controlled metal doors, allowing the convicts to walk out through the prison's main door.

Roche, 39, an electrician in the prison electrical maintenance shop, was serving thirty-nine years for two bank robberies and carrying a dangerous weapon. "Because he's much smarter than the average bird, our assumption is that he made the thing," a senior prison official said.

About 100 law enforcement officers from the U.S. Bureau of Prisons, the FBI, the Illinois State Police, and local police departments are searching for the five escapees, all of whom are considered extremely dangerous. "Any would kill at the least provocation," a prison officer said.

The FBI is examining the transmitter that the prisoners used to open three electronically controlled doors called "security grills." The device was left behind by the convicts.

Prison officials determined that the transmitter activated a small receiver in the master control panel that opens and closes the grills. The receiver did not belong in the control panel. It probably was installed a month ago when the panel was in the prison's electrical maintenance shop, where Roche worked.

The security grills are designed so that only one is supposed to open at a time, but the transmitter-receiver combination overrode the safeguards in the control panel and opened the three doors at once.

The five men were attending a prison historical society class in the visitors' room when one of them feigned a cut on the finger and asked the teacher, Loren Dees, to get a bandage from the storeroom.

The five overpowered Dees in the storeroom and took his keys to the visitors' room. Once they let themselves out of the visitors' room, only the three electronically controlled sets of bars stood between them and freedom.

The prisoners connected the transmitter to the wires of an intercom near the first set of bars. This apparently caused the three securing grills to open.

Prison personnel watching television monitors saw activity in the hallway and sounded an alarm, but by the time the searchlights were turned on by the prison's two control towers the men had fled over a hill and into the woods.

"It's black after you go over the hill, very black," said Bill Tolson, the prison safety officer.

The prison, built in 1963 to replace Alcatraz, is the newest and most modern facility in the federal penitentiary system. It sits in the middle of rolling hills eight miles south of Marion and adjacent to the Crab Orchard National Wildlife Refuge.

Less than two miles from the prison is Interstate 57, which runs north to Chicago and southwest to Sikeston, Missouri. Only a few scattered farms and half a dozen homes occupied by prison personnel are near the prison.

Nearby residents were comforted by their proximity to the prison. "The guards are all around. I feel I'm as safe here as anywhere else," said Velma Lockhard, who rents a small house about a mile from the prison. "If I lived away where the guards weren't so close I'd be afraid."

Don Smith, owner of the Motel Marion and Restaurant, said: "Those prisoners are going to get as far away as they can. I'd rather be next door to the prison than twenty miles away."

The night after the escape, police spotted the fugitives in a stolen car and gave chase near Salem, Illinois, seventy miles from the prison. The car hit an embankment, and the escapees sprinted into the woods. Arthur T. Mankins, 37, serving life for killing an FBI agent in a previous escape attempt, was hit by a patrolman's bullet and captured. Maurice J. Philion, 40, doing fifty years for bank robbery, was captured nearby two days later after he knocked at two farmhouses, asking for water. An hour later, Edward P. Roche, carrying an unloaded shotgun, was caught a mile away. "He said the only reason we caught him was he was hungry and thirsty," one official told reporters. "He said they were afraid to drink the water in the creeks. They thought it was polluted. They're city boys." Henry Michael Gargano, 43, a convicted cop killer and most feared of the fugitives, was docile and almost childlike when captured near Bloomfield, Indiana the next day. The fifth escapee, Dennis Dale Hunter, 26, serving twenty-five years for kidnapping, made it all the way to Winnipeg, Manitoba, where he was arrested on October 30 after trying to rob a bookstore.

Soldier of fortune raids Mexcian jail, frees fourteen U.S. citizens

This story, by Hugh Aynesworth and Robert Montemayor, is from the *Dallas Times Herald* of May 9, 1976.

The Mexican border-town jail breakout that freed fourteen American prisoners last March was directed and financed by a Dallas psychologist and executed by a former Marine sergeant turned soldier of fortune, the *Times Herald* has learned.

The psychologist, Sterling Blake Davis, financed the raid to free his son, who had been in Mexican jails for twenty-three months. The doctor earlier had attempted more conventional methods to gain his son's release.

The breakout at the Piedras Negras jail, believed to be the largest in Mexican history involving American prisoners, was executed by a three-man team led by Don Fielden, 31, a Dallas truck driver who says he was with the First Marine Division in Vietnam.

Fielden, now unemployed, said he did the job "because I was hungry. I don't give a damn about who was in jail or why they were there. I needed the money."

He said he ended up losing money on the daring raid.

The plot was initiated in February when Dr. Davis was put in touch with Fielden by an intermediary.

Dr. Davis' son, Sterling (Cooter) Davis, Jr., was in jail on drug charges and claimed to have been beaten and harassed by the Mexican guards. Dr. Davis wanted him out.

Young Davis had been in jail since 1974 and faced another seven or eight years in prison.

Dr. Davis said he had a patient who had "connections" and

197

offered to help the psychologist get somebody to free his son. "I had exhausted all other options of the Mexican extortion system," said Dr. Davis. Many parents of Americans held prisoner in Mexican jails have told of paying bribes.

Dr. Davis said he had hired several other mercenaries— spending about $70,000 to $75,000 to no avail. Some went to the jail, reconnoitered the situation, and returned to say they couldn't do it. Others didn't even report back.

Then came Fielden. "He didn't believe I could do it," Fielden said. "But I told him I would go down at my own expense and see how I could work it out. I hocked everything I had.

"Finally I got enough bucks together and down I went. I went down three times. I studied it from every angle. Finally I knew what had to be done."

With that he came back to Dallas and collected $5,000 from Dr. Davis to do the job.

"I knew I had to have some help, at least a back-up man and a lookout," said Fielden. He said he contacted "about twenty-five different people" before he found his back-up man. "Not too many people wanted to get involved in something like that," he said.

Then, said Fielden, he hired a fifteen-year-old Dallas boy as the third man and prepared to carry out the escape plan.

He said he and the other two, whom he refused to identify, spent several days going over maps and drawings made by Fielden on his two previous trips—when he said he visited young Davis in the jail, posing as a relative. Dr. Davis also made trips there to help ascertain the dimensions of the scene and intelligence needed for an effective jail break.

"I was already in the hole," Fielden told the *Times Herald.* "I had to pay the second man the $5,000 we had gotten from Dr. Davis. Then I paid the West Dallas punk $500 out of my own money. But I had made a commitment, and when I make a commitment, that's it. I'll follow through."

He said Dr. Davis made it plain he didn't want any bloodshed unless there was no other way. Fielden agreed.

"I didn't go down there to kill anybody," he said. "That wouldn't have helped me any. It wouldn't have made me a penny more—and it might have caused me plenty of trouble afterward."

198

Fielden and his partners left for Eagle Pass to check into a motel and set the final preparations for the plan.

After making several trips across into Piedras Negras, Fielden and his two partners slipped across in the pre-dawn hours of March 12.

Though the whole operation took less than ten minutes from crossing to return, it did not go flawlessly.

In fact, Fielden said they were almost foiled before they made their last run.

A customs agent stopped their car hours beforehand as they returned with Fielden's sawed-off shotgun in the trunk.

"He said, 'Lemme look in the trunk,' " Fielden recalled, "and I thought, 'Oh, hell, this is it. We've had it.' " Fielden said the agent shined his flashlight directly on the shotgun, but apparently didn't realize what it was. "I had my guitar strap hanging on it. I guess he didn't notice. I couldn't believe it."

But after checking distances, times, checkpoints, and jail personnel, they decided to act.

Said Fielden: "I drew him (the fifteen-year-old boy) a diagram of what we were going up against. Hell, we ain't talking but maybe about a quarter of a mile from the front door of the jail to the border.

"He went over there with a walkie-talkie, and I had a CB radio in my car."

At 3:05 A.M. on March 12, they took hood masks, bolt cutters, a Browning 12-gauge pump riot gun, and a fifteen-inch sawed-off shotgun that Fielden had cut off and honed himself, and moved toward the Mexican jail.

Fielden described the scene:

"We cranked up, went across the border, and pulled up in front of the jail. He (the lookout) was instructed to get into the back seat of the car, get hold of the microphone from my CB radio, give my back-up shotgun man the walkie-talkie, and we go on.

"The last thing I asked him before we got out of the car was, how many were in there now. He said there are two, maybe three.

"I walked in on five city police, three *federales* and two secret police. At which time my butt drew up.

"I'd been studying this damn dictionary for seven weeks,

getting it down. And I went in there fixing to tell these Mexicans to put their hands up. I threw out, 'Palmo asente,' and they put their palms straight together and started praying. I said, 'Lord, there's ten of these mothers. You let me out of this jail, and I'll teach this kid how to count.'

"My partner had three of 'em on his side of the jail. They gave up immediately. And I had seven, and two of them pulled their pistols and got behind the desk and had them cocked at me, while I was fightin' this city policeman, trying to get his pistola.

"I finally slapped him up side the head one time and turned my shotgun on those other cats, and they gave up.

"And I went back there (toward the cells) with my bolt cutters, and I cut the first lock on the door to get back into the cells. Came like a charm. There are two locks on each cell, one on the door, a sliding bolt, the second a chain they had locked around the bars.

"Well, I had been up here in Dallas cutting everything I could get my hands on with those bolt cutters. The only thing I didn't get around to was that heavy-duty metal.

"I put my bolt cutters on it and started to cut it, and it wouldn't go. I put one arm to the bolt cutters next to the bars...and my man stuck his arms out and started pulling and another cat put his arms out there and the bolt cutters just snapped.

"When they snapped, my man just looked and all I could say was, 'Oh crap.' And then he said, 'Oh crap.' A second man that I was going to get if I had the time yelled out, 'Bring me the bolt cutters.' And this cat said, 'Well, they just broke.' And all they could say was, 'Oh crap.'

"It was a funny farm down there, man. We weren't too happy about the whole thing.

"Finally somebody said, 'Get the keys,' and I hollered, 'How do you say keys?' And I got three different answers.

"So I just grabbed me a Mexican, and I stuck this shotgun up in his throat, and I said, 'I want your keys.' He said he didn't understand. So I put it behind his head and somebody must've said the right words 'cause he showed me where the keys were."

Fielden described the jail as having six cells, with human excrement on the damp floors, and twice as many people inside as there were pallets to lie on.

He released the men first. They were on the front side of the jail. "In the meantime I sent one of the prisoners back to get the girls out. I had them all standing there. I instructed the man I was going after to tell everybody, 'Don't do anything unless you're told to do it.'

" 'Don't try to run because there'll be somebody in front of the jail who'll cut you in two'...and he would have. One man tried to break. He was a man they had just busted two days before, and they had his wife in that interrogation room. He tried to go and he got about three feet and this cat leveled off on him and I drew on him and he turned around and came back.

"The girls were out by then and I told them once more, 'Don't nobody try to pass me. I'm goin' outta here first.' So we came outside.

"Now this kid in the car...all he was supposed to do was get through to us if anybody starts to come in. He did a half-decent job there.

"So we got to the front door and I turned around....I don't care what the papers say, there were not sixteen comin' outta this jail. It kinda looked like Moses walking across that sea. There's about twenty-six or twenty-eight people. The whole office was full...belly-to-belly people.

"It was real simple, go out the door, take a right at the corner of the building, go down to the next corner, and take a right and run straight. When you hit water you know you're at the river; when you're out of the water, you're home.

"And I told 'em to go about 300 yards upstream and they could walk across and never get their knees wet.

"Anyway, I get my man out. And I got my two boys in the car, and I told the rest of 'em, 'Don't anybody move until I get my two people' and the rest of 'em split.

"One of the prisoners asked me, 'Would you take our girls with you?' and I said, 'No, I didn't come for 'em.'

"So there we were, the five of us in the car... and we didn't break no laws. We got to the toll bridge, and there was a red station wagon sitting at the toll area. We sat behind it for what seemed like three years.

"As we drove across I had it down, either the second or third light pole was where I planned to throw out the weapons. Because that was the deepest and swiftest part of the river.

"Well, everything was so confused, and he (Cooter) was hangin' out the window....I said, 'Throw,' and as I said it I saw that concrete marker that says 'Welcome back turkey,' and he threw it. As soon as he threw it (an M-1 they had taken from a guard), I knew it was going to hit the American ground.

"Sure enough, dirty, stinking soil. One of the masks landed on the bridge, 'cause I saw it in the rear view mirror."

They drove quickly to the Holly Inn Motel in Eagle Pass, and Fielden placed a collect phone call to Dr. Davis in Dallas. "William Green calling," Fielden said, the name he said Dr. Davis knew him by.

"He didn't believe I could do it," Fielden said. "He didn't believe it until I put his son on that phone."

Fielden said he was not fearful of any legal problems emanating from the raid. "If you don't commit a felony, there's no breaking of the law," he said.

Fielden's lawyer, Ernest W. Kuehne, Jr., said several publishing houses and movie companies already have contacted him trying to buy Fielden's colorful tale and his life story. Kuehne said no contracts had been signed yet.

Fielden said he feared no Mexican retaliation, but "had heard" that one famous investigator might come gunning for him.

"His name's Salvador Del Toro Rosales. They say he's a junior J. Edgar. It is my understanding," Fielden said, "that he said he would find out and get the people responsible. I don't know what he looks like, but I've got a general description of him. I don't figure there'll be any doubt in my mind when I walk into him. I'll know him."

(Rosales is a well-known federal police investigator in Mexico, often sent to the scene of major crimes to pull together the case.)

"I'm not afraid of him," Fielden said. "In fact, I'd kinda like for him to come up here so I can get rid of him."

Cooter Davis, 29, confirmed much of Fielden's story—the part he lived. Three days after the escape, young Davis turned himself in to federal authorities for violating parole.

Cooter originally was arrested in 1972 on the Arizona border in possession of 350 kilos of marijuana. He received a three-year federal sentence. He served fourteen months and was released on good behavior.

But during his parole in May, 1974, Cooter's Mexican prison ordeal began after he was arrested near Saltillo, Mexico, about 150 miles from the Texas border, for allegedly transporting eighty kilos of marijuana.

He told the *Times Herald* in several telephone conversations from El Reno (Oklahoma) Federal Reformatory of his "hell on Earth" in Mexican jails.

His escape ended what he described as a grueling, twenty-three-month ordeal in which he and some other Americans were subjected to cruel, arbitrary punishment at the hands of corrupt Mexican jail officials.

Cooter confirmed reports of jail officials applying physical abuse to prisoners in attempts to coerce them into signing "confession" statements written in Spanish, without the benefit of any translation.

"I was beaten right after my arrest," he said. "For three weeks I was interrogated, strapped down in a bed naked, with a rifle pointed at my head. I finally signed the papers."

Other prisoners who escaped also related tales of the traditional, sadistic use of cattle prods on genitals, rubber hoses, and oddly wired gadgets, all utilized to apply torture.

Inside the Saltillo prison walls, Cooter said his hassles first began with a $2,000 double-cross escape deal with the prison's assistant warden that blew up in his face.

"That dude told me and three others that for $2,000 apiece we could dig our way out and escape," said Cooter. "We paid and, sometime after we had begun digging, the dude screwed us by turning the guards on us."

Not counting the probable six-year marijuana sentence he already had coming, Cooter and his friends were slapped with an additional four years for attempted escape.

"I raised a big stink about it (the bribe), and the assistant warden then came to me one day and said, 'If you value your life, you'll shut up.' Then the word came to me through a guard that me and another American were marked men, that we were to be killed at the earliest convenience," Cooter said.

A "rough" Mexican gang of eight prisoners, led by a widely feared killer named Alfredo (Mafia) Alvarez, took up the chore, Cooter said.

Armed with knives and razors, the gang cornered Cooter and the other "marked" American, named "Spooky," in the prison's inner courtyard. Unarmed and fending off the slashing blows with only their arms, the two were backed against a wall, absorbing several slash wounds, Cooter said.

If not for a Mexican prison guard atop a wall who fired his rifle in between the men, the two would have been slashed to death, Cooter said.

Feeling his chances of survival were limited at Saltillo, young Davis and his father arranged a $5,000 payoff to get the "proper" people to have him transferred to Piedras Negras.

The elder Davis said he had been told by other mercenary groups that the jail's proximity to the Texas border at Piedras Negras was more advantageous for escape plans. His son waited there for about eight months before the breakout.

Both Dr. Davis and Fielden denied West Coast reports that a California activist group was responsible for the breakout.

"Look, I don't care who takes the credit for the break," Dr. Davis said. "If they or whoever wants to take credit, then that's fine. But I'm the one who knows better."

Dr. Davis told the *Times Herald* he began enlisting a variety of free-lance mercenaries under a "no violence unless absolutely necessary" condition as early as a year before the breakout.

The psychologist said one group "lost their guts" and backed off from the job. A second group was ordered by the doctor to pull out after jail security was dramatically increased and "it was very clear...the plan wouldn't work."

He said he also dealt with a Detroit outfit, supposedly equipped with heavy armament, which first contacted him during early summer last year. But he balked at "fully" using them because they were a "very dangerous group of sorts. I was somewhat afraid to use them because...they wanted to go down there and start blasting."

He contends he spent more than $70,000 commissioning these groups before the final $5,000 deal with Fielden's group proved successful. One of the groups wound up taking the psychologist for a $5,000 vehicle and $2,000 cash provided for weapons, a laser, and various other pieces of equipment.

"Why did I do it this way? What else was I supposed to do?" Dr. Davis asked. "They (the Mexicans) had beaten and damn near killed my son in those jails."

Dr. Sterling Davis was convicted October 1, 1976 at Del Rio, Texas on federal charges of conspiracy and was sentenced to five years in prison. Don Fielden, who pleaded guilty to conspiracy and illegally transporting a weapon, was sentenced to four years. Others involved drew shorter sentences.

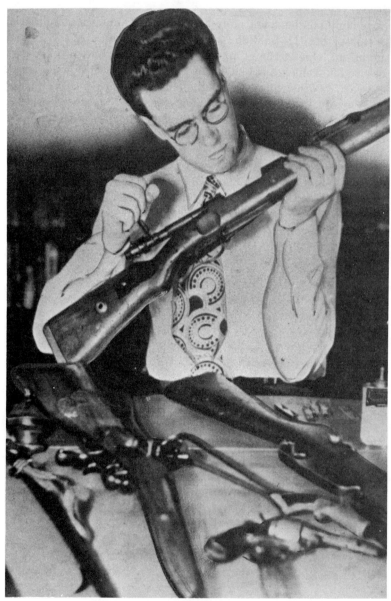

Howard B. Unruh with war souvenirs.

Chapter VII

MASS MURDER

Veteran goes berserk in Camden and kills twelve with a souvenir Luger

Most New York dailies dispatched teams of reporters to Camden, New Jersey the morning of September 6, 1949, after wire services bulletined that a murder rampage had occurred there. The *New York Times*, however, sent only one reporter—Meyer Berger, who won a Pulitzer Prize for the following story from the *Times* of September 7.

Howard B. Unruh, twenty-eight years old, a mild, soft-spoken veteran of many armored-artillery battles in Italy, France, Austria, Belgium, and Germany, killed twelve persons with a war-souvenir Luger pistol in his home block in East Camden, New Jersey this morning. He wounded four others.

Unruh, a slender, hollow-cheeked six-footer paradoxically devoted to scripture reading and to constant practice with firearms, had no history of mental illness, but specialists indicated tonight that there was no doubt that he was a psychiatric case, and that he had secretly nursed a persecution complex for two years or more.

The veteran was shot in the left thigh by a local tavernkeeper but he kept that secret, too, while policemen and Mitchell Cohen, Camden County prosecutor, questioned him at police headquarters for more than two hours immediately after tear-gas bombs had forced him out of his bedroom to surrender.

The blood stain he left on the seat he occupied during the questioning betrayed his wound. When it was discovered, he was taken to Cooper Hospital in Camden, a prisoner charged with murder.

He was as calm under questioning as he was during the twenty minutes that he was shooting men, women, and children. Only occasionally excessive brightness of his dark eyes indicated that he was anything other than normal.

He told the prosecutor that he had been building up resentment against neighbors and neighborhood shopkeepers for a long time. "They have been making derogatory remarks about my character," he said. His resentment seemed most strongly concentrated against Mr. and Mrs. Maurice Cohen, who lived next door to him. They are among the dead.

Mr. Cohen was a druggist with a shop at 3202 River Road in East Camden. He and his wife had had frequent sharp exchanges over the Unruhs' use of a gate that separates their backyard from the Cohens'. Mrs. Cohen also had complained of young Unruh's keeping his bedroom radio tuned high into the late-night hours. None of the other victims had ever had trouble with him.

Unruh, a graduate of Woodrow Wilson High School in Camden, had started a GI course in pharmacy at Temple University in Philadelphia some time after he was honorably discharged from the service in 1945, but had stayed with it only three months.

In recent months he had been unemployed, and apparently was not even looking for work.

His mother, Rita Unruh, 50, is separated from her husband. She works as a packer in the Evanson Soap Company in Camden, and hers was virtually the only family income. James Unruh, 25, her younger son, is married and lives in Haddon Heights, New Jersey. He works for the Curtis Publishing Company.

On Monday night, Howard Unruh left the house alone. He spent the night at the Family Theater on Market Street in Philadelphia to sit through several showings of the double-feature motion picture there—"I Cheated the Law" and "The Lady Gambled." It was past three o'clock on the morning of September 6 when he got home.

Prosecutor Cohen said that Unruh told him later that before he fell asleep he had made up his mind to shoot the persons who had "talked about me," that he had even figured out that 9:30 A.M. would be the time to begin because most of the stores in his block would be open at that hour.

His mother, leaving her ironing when he got up, prepared his breakfast in their drab little three-room apartment in the shabby, gray, two-story stucco house at the corner of River Road and 32nd Street. After breakfast he loaded one clip of bullets into his Luger, slipped another clip into his pocket, and carried sixteen loose cartridges in addition. He also carried a tear-gas pen with six shells and a sharp six-inch knife.

He took one last look around his bedroom before he left the house. On the peeling walls he had crossed pistols, crossed German bayonets, pictures of armored artillery in action. Scattered about the chamber were matches, a Roy Rogers pistol, ash trays made of German shells, clips of 30-30 cartridges for rifle use, and a host of varied war souvenirs.

Mrs. Unruh had left the house some minutes before to call on Caroline Pinner, a friend in the next block. Mrs. Unruh had sensed, apparently, that her son's smoldering resentments were coming to a head. She had pleaded with Elias Pinner, her friend's husband, to cut a little gate in the Unruhs' backyard so that Howard need not use the Cohens' gate again. Pinner finished the gate early Monday evening after Howard had gone to Philadelphia.

At the Pinners' house at nine o'clock, Mrs. Unruh had murmured something about Howard's eyes, how strange they looked and how worried she was about him.

A few minutes later River Road echoed and re-echoed to pistol fire. Howard Unruh was on the rampage. His mother, who had left the Pinners' little white house only a few seconds before, turned back. She hurried through the door.

She cried, "Oh, Howard. Oh, Howard. They're to blame for this." She rushed past Mrs. Pinner, a kindly gray-haired woman of seventy. She said, "I've got to use the phone; may I use the phone?"

But before she had crossed the living room to reach for it, she fell on the faded carpet in a dead faint. The Pinners lifted her onto a couch in the next room. Mrs. Pinner applied aromatic spirits to revive her.

While his mother writhed on the sofa in her house dress and worn old sweater, coming back to consciousness, Howard Unruh was walking from shop to shop in the 3200 block with deadly calm, spurting Luger in hand. Children screamed as they tumbled over one another to get out of his way. Men and women dodged into open shops, the women shrill with panic, men hoarse with fear. No one could quite understand for a time what had been loose in the block.

Unruh first walked into John Pilarchik's shoe repair shop near the north end of his own side of the street. The cobbler, a twenty-seven-year-old man who lives in Pennsauken Township, looked up open-mouthed as Unruh came to within a yard of him. The cobbler started up from his bench but went down with a bullet in his stomach. A little boy who was in the shop ran behind the counter and crouched there in terror. Unruh walked out into the sunlit street.

"I shot them in the chest first," he told the prosecutor later, in meticulous detail, "and then I aimed for the head." His aim was devastating—and with reason. He had won marksmanship and sharpshooters' ratings in the service, and he practiced with his Luger all the time on a target set up in the cellar of his home.

Unruh told the prosecutor afterward that he had Cohen the druggist, the neighborhood barber, the neighborhood cobbler, and the neighborhood tailor on his mental list of persons who had "talked about me." He went methodically about wiping them out. Oddly enough, he did not start with the druggist, against whom he seemed to have the sharpest feelings, but left him almost for the last.

From the cobbler's he went into the little tailor shop at 3214 River Road. The tailor was out. Helga Zegrino, 28, the tailor's wife, was there alone. The couple, incidentally, had been married only one month. She screamed when Unruh walked in with the Luger in his hand. Some people across the street heard her. Then the gun blasted again, and Mrs. Zegrino pitched over, dead. Unruh walked into the sunlight again.

All this was only a matter of seconds, and still only a few

persons had begun to understand what was afoot. Down the street at 3210 River Road is Clark Hoover's little country barber shop. In the center was a white-painted carousel-type horse for children customers. Orris Smith, a blond boy only six years old, was in it, with a bib around his neck, submitting to a shearing. His mother, Catherine Smith, 42, sat on a chair against the wall and watched.

She looked up. Hoover turned from his work to see the six-footer, gaunt and tense, but silent, standing in the doorway with the Luger. Unruh's brown, tropical worsted suit was barred with morning shadows. The sun lay bright in his crew-cut brown hair. He wore no hat. Mrs. Smith could not understand what was about to happen. Unruh walked up to "Brux"—that is Mrs. Smith's nickname for her little boy—and put the Luger to the child's chest. The shot echoed and reverberated in the little twelve-by-twelve shop. The little boy's head pitched toward the wound, his hair half cut, stained with red. Unruh said never a word. He put the Luger close to the shaking barber's hand. Before the horrified mother, Unruh leaned over and fired another shot into Hoover.

The veteran made no attempt to kill Mrs. Smith. He did not seem to hear her screams. He turned his back and stalked out, unhurried. A few doors north, Dominick Latela, who runs a little restaurant, had come to his shop window to learn what the shooting was about. He saw Unruh cross the street toward Frank Engel's tavern, then he saw Mrs. Smith stagger out with her pitiful burden. Her son's head lolled over the crook of her right arm.

Mrs. Smith screamed, "My boy is dead. I know he's dead." She stared about her looking in vain for aid. No one but Howard Unruh was in sight, and he was concentrating on the tavern. Latela dashed out, but first he shouted to his wife, Dora, who was in the restaurant with their daughter Eleanor, 6. He hollered, "I'm going out. Lock the door behind me." He ran for his car, and drove it down toward Mrs. Smith as she stood on the pavement with her son.

Latela took the child from her arms and placed him in the car's front seat. He pushed the mother into the rear seat, slammed the doors, and headed for Cooper Hospital. Howard Unruh had not turned. Engel, the tavern keeper, had locked his own door. His customers, the bartender, and a porter made a concerted rush toward the rear of the saloon. The bullets tore through the tavern door's paneling. Engel rushed upstairs and got out his .38-caliber pistol, then rushed to the street window of his apartment.

Unruh was back in the center of the street. He fired a shot at an apartment window at 3208 River Road. Tommy Hamilton, two years old, fell back with a bullet in his head. Unruh went north again to Latela's place. He fired a shot at the door, and kicked in the lower glass panel. Mrs. Latela crouched behind the counter with her daughter. She heard the bullet, but neither she nor the child was touched. Unruh walked back toward 32nd Street, reloading the Luger.

Now the little street—a small block with only five buildings on one side, three one-story stores on the other—was shrill with women's and children's panicky outcries. A group of six or seven little boys and girls fled past Unruh.

They screamed, "Crazy man!" and unintelligible sentences. Unruh did not seem to hear or see them.

Alvin Day, a television repairman who lives in nearby Mantua, had heard the shooting, but driving into the street he was not aware of what had happened. Unruh walked up to the car window as Day rolled by and fired once through the window, with deadly aim. The repairman fell against the steering wheel. The car seemed to wobble. The front wheel hit the opposite curb and stalled. Day was dead.

Frank Engel had thrown open his second-floor apartment window. He saw Unruh pause for a moment in a narrow alley between the cobbler's shop and a little two-story house. He aimed and fired. Unruh stopped for just a second. The bullet had hit, but he did not seem to mind after the initial brief shock. He headed toward the corner drugstore, and Engel did not fire again.

"I wish I had," he said later. "I could have killed him then. I could have put half a dozen shots into him. I don't know why I didn't do it."

Cohen, the druggist, a heavy man of forty, had run into the street shouting, "What's going on here? What's going on here?", but at sight of Unruh he hurried back into his shop. James J.

Hutton, 45, an insurance agent from Westmont, New Jersey, started out of the drug shop to see what the shooting was about. Like so many others, he had figured at first that it was some car backfiring. He came face to face with Unruh.

Unruh said quietly, "Excuse me, sir," and started to push past him. Later, Unruh told the police: "That man didn't act fast enough. He didn't get out of my way." He fired into Hutton's head and body. The insurance man pitched onto the sidewalk and lay still.

Cohen had run to his upstairs apartment and had tried to warn Minnie Cohen, 63, his mother, and Rose, his wife, 38, to hide. His son, Charles, 14, was in the apartment, too. Mrs. Cohen shoved the boy into a clothes closet and leaped into another closet herself. The druggist, meanwhile, had leaped from the window onto a porch roof. Unruh, a gaunt figure at the window behind him, fired into the druggist's back. The druggist, still running, bounded off the roof and lay dead in 32nd Street.

Unruh fired into the closet where Mrs. Cohen was hidden. She fell dead behind the closed door, and he did not bother to open it. Minnie Cohen tried to get to the telephone in an adjoining bedroom to call the police. Unruh fired shots into her head and body, and she sprawled dead on the bed. Unruh walked down the stairs with his Luger reloaded and came out into the street again.

A coupe had stopped at River Road, obeying a red light. The passengers obviously had no idea of what was loose in East Camden, and no one had a chance to tell them. Unruh walked up to the car, and, though it was filled with total strangers, fired deliberately at them, one by one, through the windshield. He killed the two women passengers, Helen Matlack Wilson, 43, of Pennsauken, who was driving, and her mother, Emma Matlack, 66. Mrs. Wilson's son John, 12, was badly wounded. A bullet pierced his neck, just below the jawbone.

Earl Horner, a clerk in the American Stores Company, a grocery opposite the drugstore, had locked his front door after several passing men, women, and children had tumbled breathlessly into the shop panting, "Crazy man... killing people." Unruh came up to the door and fired two shots through the wood paneling. Horner, his customers, the refugees from the veteran's merciless gunfire, crouched, trembling, behind the counter. None there was hurt.

"He tried the door before he shot in here," Horner related afterward. "He just stood there, stony-faced and grim, and rattled the knob, before he started to fire. Then he turned away."

Charlie Petersen, 18, son of a Camden fireman, came driving down the street with two friends when Unruh turned from the grocery. The three boys got out to stare at Hutton's body, lying unattended on the sidewalk. They did not know who had shot the insurance man, or why, and, like the women in the car, had no warning that Howard Unruh was on the loose. The veteran brought his Luger to sight and fired several times. Young Petersen fell with bullets in his legs. His friends tore pell-mell down the street to safety.

Helen Harris of 1250 North 28th Street, with her daughter, Helen, a six-year-old blond child, and a Mrs. Horowitz with her daughter, Linda, 5, turned into 32nd Street. They had heard the shooting from a distance but thought it was auto backfire.

Unruh passed them in 32nd Street and walked up the sagging four steps of a little yellow dwelling back of his own house. Madeline Harrie, a woman in her late thirties, and two sons, Armand, 16, and Leroy, 15, were in the house. A third son, Wilson, 14, was barricaded in the grocery with other customers.

Unruh threw open the front door and, gun in hand, walked into the dark little parlor. He fired two shots at Mrs. Harrie. They went wild and entered the wall. A third shot caught her in the left arm. She screamed. Armand leaped at Unruh to tackle him. The veteran used the Luger butt to drop the boy, then fired two shots into his arms. Upstairs Leroy heard the shooting and the screams. He hid under a bed.

By this time, answering a flood of hysterical telephone calls from various parts of East Camden, police radio cars swarmed into River Road with sirens wide open. Emergency crews brought machine guns, shotguns, and tear-gas bombs. Sgt. Earl Wright, one of the first to leap to the sidewalk, saw Charles Cohen, the druggist's son. The boy was half out the second-floor apartment window, just above where his father lay dead. He was screaming, "He's going to kill me. He's killing everybody." The boy was hysterical.

Wright bounded up the stairs to the druggist's apartment. He saw the dead woman on the bed and tried to soothe the druggist's son. He brought him downstairs and turned him over to other policemen, then joined the men who had surrounded the two-story stucco house where Unruh lived. Unruh, meanwhile, had fired about thirty shots. He was out of ammunition. Leaving the Harrie house, he had also heard the police sirens. He had run through the back gate to his own rear bedroom.

Edward Joslin, a motorcycle policeman, scrambled to the porch roof under Unruh's window. He tossed a tear-gas grenade through a pane of glass. Other policemen, hoarsely calling on Unruh to surrender, took positions with their machine guns and shotguns. They trained them on Unruh's window.

Meanwhile, a curious interlude had taken place. Philip W. Buxton, an assistant city editor of the *Camden Evening Courier*, had looked up Unruh's name in the telephone book, and he called the number. It was just after 10:00 A.M., and Unruh had just returned to his room. To Buxton's astonishment, Unruh answered. He said "hello" in a calm, clear voice.

"This Howard?" Buxton asked.

"Yes, this is Howard. What's the last name of the party you want?"

"Unruh. I'm a friend," the newspaperman said. "I want to know what they're doing to you down there."

Unruh thought a moment. He said, "They haven't done anything to me—yet. I'm doing plenty to them." His voice was still steady without a trace of hysteria.

Buxton asked how many persons Unruh had killed.

The veteran answered: "I don't know. I haven't counted. Looks like a pretty good score."

"Why are you killing people?"

"I don't know," came the frank answer. "I can't answer that yet. I'll have to talk to you later. I'm too busy now."

The telephone banged down.

Unruh was busy. The tear gas was taking effect, and police bullets were thudding at the walls around him. During a lull in firing, the police saw the white curtains move, and the gaunt killer

215

came into plain view.

"O.K.," he shouted. "I give up. I'm coming down."

"Where's that gun?" a sergeant yelled.

"It's on my desk up here in the room," Unruh called down quietly. "I'm coming down."

Thirty guns were trained on the shabby little back door. A few seconds later the door opened, and Unruh stepped into the light, his hands up. Sergeant Wright came across the morning glory and astor beds in the yard and snapped handcuffs on Unruh's wrists.

"What's the matter with you?" a policeman demanded hotly. "You a psycho?"

Unruh stared into the policeman's eyes—a level, steady stare. He said, "I'm no psycho. I have a good mind."

Word of the capture brought the whole East Camden populace pouring into the streets. Men and women screamed at Unruh, and cursed him in shrill accents and in coarse anger. Someone cried, "Lynch him," but there was no movement. Sergeant Wright's men walked Unruh to a police car and started for headquarters.

Shouting and pushing men and women started after the car, but dropped back after a few paces. They stood in excited little groups discussing the shootings and the character of Howard Unruh. Little by little, the original anger, borne of fear, that had moved the crowd began to die.

Men conceded that he probably was not in his right mind. Those who knew Unruh kept repeating how close-mouthed he was, and how soft-spoken. How he took his mother to church, and how he marked scripture passages, especially the Prophecies.

"He was a quiet one, that guy," a man told the crowd in front of the tavern. "He was all the time figuring to do this thing. You gotta watch them quiet ones."

But all day River Road and the side streets talked of nothing else. The shock was great. Men and women kept saying: "We can't understand it. Just don't get it."

Unruh was adjudged incurably insane and never was tried. He was placed in the New Jersey State Mental Hospital.

Two-state murder spree ends with Starkweather capture in Wyoming

When Charles Starkweather and Caril Fugate were captured in Wyoming after a murder rampage that shocked the nation, the *Lincoln* (Nebraska) *Star* chartered an airplane to fly staff writers Virgil Falloon and Dell Harding to Douglas, Wyoming to report on the pair. This report appeared without a byline in the *Star* of January 30, 1958.

The Lincoln area's three-day reign of terror that saw nine persons wantonly slain in an almost unbelievable chain of events ended at 3:30 Wednesday afternoon when nineteen-year-old Charles Starkweather was captured by two Wyoming lawmen.

His empty .38-caliber revolver at his side, Starkweather told officers: "If I had had a gun, I'd have shot you."

He suffered head cuts during an exchange of shots with a deputy sheriff.

With Starkweather was Caril Fugate, the fourteen-year-old who fled with him from the Lincoln area where police say he killed nine persons. Included among the victims were Caril's parents.

A tenth murder victim was found not far from where Starkweather was captured. The dead man was Merle Collison, a thirty-seven-year-old shoe salesman from Great Falls, Montana.

There were rumors that Starkweather signed a statement admitting the slaying of Collison and wrote out an admission of the Nebraska killings. The rumors were not confirmed by any officials.

The two teenagers were run to earth in rugged country where Old West gunmen often holed up.

The girl was almost hysterical and ran to Casper (Wyoming) Deputy Sheriff Bill Romer crying out her fear that Starkweather would kill her. She was in a state of shock shortly afterward.

Romer said she screamed to him: "He's going to kill me. He's crazy. He just killed a man!"

Romer said the gunman, who likes to swagger in cowboy boots and black motorcycle jacket, had made a crude attempt to disguise his flaming red hair with shoe polish.

Wyoming, if it chooses, will have priority on prosecuting Starkweather in the slaying of Collison.

Despite Starkweather's capture, Lincoln Mayor Bennett Martin said, "We're still in a damn sick situation. We still don't know whether the number of victims will stop at nine."

The bloody trail began less than sixty hours ago in Lincoln when the slaying of Caril's parents and infant half-sister was discovered. As police pressed investigation, other killings were disclosed until the total reached nine. A frantic hunt was started for Starkweather, but he and the girl escaped.

As Nebraska National Guardsmen culled the byways of Lincoln, the stolen auto driven by Starkweather was speeding west across the state line and into Wyoming. Behind them police ran down false leads in a desperate effort to nab Starkweather before any further violence occurred.

Douglas (Wyoming) Sheriff Earl Heflin said Starkweather snarled after his capture: "They wouldn't have caught me if I hadn't stopped. If I'd had a gun, I'd have shot them."

Heflin said a first-degree murder charge would be filed Thursday morning against Starkweather in the killing of Collison.

No decision as to whether to try Starkweather in Wyoming or release him to Nebraska authorities has been reached, he said.

Starkweather faces multiple murder charges that could mean the death penalty in either state. Wyoming executes condemned slayers in the gas chamber, and, in Nebraska, death in the electric chair is the supreme penalty. In the latter state, the jury sets the death penalty.

In Wyoming, however, Gov. Milward Simpson opposes the death penalty and has said publicly he will continue to spare condemned murderers.

Converse County (Wyoming) Atty. William Dixon said that Collison apparently had been napping in his car when Starkweather drove up.

"Starkweather shot once through the window of the car and said, 'Come out,' " Dixon related. "Then he blasted him (Collison) five or six times." Dixon said Starkweather told him he wanted Collison's car because his own was "too hot."

An oil company worker, Joe Sprinkle of Casper, drove up to the scene while Starkweather was still there and stopped to investigate. The fugitive shoved a .22-caliber rifle in Sprinkle's face, and the two began to wrestle.

Casper Deputy Sheriff Romer was on a rent-receipt inspection job when he spotted two men fighting over a gun near two stopped cars. One was Sprinkle, fighting for his life. As Romer pulled up, Starkweather ran for his car. The Fugate girl fled from the getaway car and ran screaming to Romer.

Romer radioed for a roadblock, which was flung up hastily, but Starkweather roared through it at more than 100 miles an hour. Sheriff Heflin and an officer gave chase, firing at the fleeing car. It careened through Douglas, and five miles out of town pulled to a stop.

The sullen gunman offered no resistance. He had a revolver with him. It was empty.

Back at the scene of the struggle, Sprinkle stood near the parked car. Shoved down under the dashboard was the body of Collison.

The Casper oil employee, who had stopped because the two cars were parked and he thought somebody needed help, was short and to the point about why he jumped Starkweather.

"All I saw was the gun barrel, and every time I looked, it got bigger," he said. Sprinkle is a husky 185-pounder, and he won the deadly tug-of-war with the 5-foot-5-inch gunman. Then Sprinkle said he found the rifle already had been emptied.

In a Douglas jail cell, Starkweather slouched on his bunk glowering. A Casper newspaperman who was nearby said Starkweather asserted he had shot his Nebraska victims in self-defense.

"What would you do if they tried to come at you?" the newsman quoted Starkweather as saying.

As night closed in over this cattle town, a strict guard was set over Starkweather. The Fugate girl, who Starkweather said had been forced by him to go along, was under sedation.

"I hated the world with all the poison of a granddaddy rattlesnake ever since I was a youngster," Charles Starkweather wrote after he was extradited to Nebraska. The extradition, he said, was a blessing because Wyoming had a gas chamber and "I hate the smell of gas." He was convicted in Nebraska of one murder and was sentenced to die in the electric chair. Spurning an offer to see Caril once more before he died, Starkweather was executed in Lincoln on June 24, 1959. Caril was paroled on June 8, 1976 at age thirty-two, after eighteen years in prison. She moved to St. Johns, Michigan.

Out of the flophouses came Speck, with acne face, bent mind, and knife

The murder of eight young women by Richard
Franklin Speck in a townhouse on Chicago's South
Side probably was the most sensational crime of the
1960s. *New York Herald Tribune* columnist Jimmy
Breslin rushed to Chicago to cover the story. The
following column was published July 18, 1966.

He came out of the flophouses and bus terminals and prison
yards, and he went around with his shirtsleeves rolled up so the
tattoos on his arms would look sharp.

His world was whores and old men who were homosexuals and
meals from prison steam tables and hillbilly music in bars that
stink of cheap wine.

On Wednesday night, with an acne face and a bent mind, he is
accused of crawling out into the life that others lead and killing
eight young student nurses with a knife and with his hands. Back
in his flophouse world and on Saturday night, he tried to kill
himself.

Richard Franklin Speck was at 617 West Madison on Saturday
night. It is a seven-story building with a blinking red neon sign
over the entrance. "Starr Hotel, Fireproof Rooms," the sign says.
The sidewalk under the sign was crowded with derelicts.

Richard Speck was upstairs, on the fifth floor. He was in a
cubicle with a door on it. The number was 584. It cost him ninety
cents to rent. It has a concrete floor and olive drab walls. The
ceiling is a rusted wire mesh. The window is a tiny vent in a square
of greasy glass blocks.

Richard Speck was stretched out on an uncovered mattress that
smelled of other people. He watched the blood run out of the cuts
he had made in his wrists. The blood seeped through the mattress

and dripped onto the newspaper under the bed. The headline on the newspaper said, "Police Say Nurse Survivor Can Identify Slayer of 8."

The floor was filled with the noise of men coughing and being ill and dropping empty beer cans.

"Come and see me," Richard Speck called out. He was registered under the name of B. Brian, but nobody knew who he was.

"Leave me alone," George Gregrich called out from the next cubicle. Gregrich was sitting on the edge of his mattress. He had three cans of beer on the floor. A bottle of fifty-cent wine was in a brown paper bag next to him on the mattress. Gregrich did not want any company.

"Please come and see me," Richard Speck called out.

"I ain't comin' to see you," Gregrich said. "I work hard all day. I need rest."

"You got to come and see me. I done something bad."

"You're a hillbilly, you just want to get at me. I don't trust no hillbillies."

"I'm going to die here if you don't come and see me."

"Shut up."

"Please come in."

"You go to hell, you made me come in and talk to you last night. I ain't comin' in to see you tonight."

Gregrich reached for the paper bag with the wine bottle in it.

He didn't know how long he sat drinking his wine and telling Speck to keep quiet. He thought it was two hours. Then he heard Speck come out of his cubicle. Speck began to kick at Gregrich's door.

"Get away from here," Gregrich yelled. "Go back to your own bed, you hillbilly."

"I need water," Speck said.

"Go on or I'll kill you."

Gregrich heard other men out in the hall.

"Look at him."

"You're bleedin' all over."

"Look at the cuts."

"Hey! This guy's bleeding himself to death."

Gregrich opened the door. Two groping men were with Richard Speck. Speck stood in the dark, narrow hallway with his hands held up in front of his face. He was looking at the blood coming out of his wrists.

"Put him in his own bed," Gregrich said. "I'll go get somebody."

He stumbled down the hallway and pushed the elevator button. The elevator was down in the lobby. The operator, James Crubaugh, a bald man wearing a sweatshirt with the sleeves cut off, sat on a stool in the elevator. His hands shook when the register showed somebody on the fifth floor was buzzing him. He sat in the elevator and looked at the register and, finally, when it kept buzzing, Crubaugh reached out and shut the doors and started his elevator up.

When he got to the fifth floor, he heard the noise down the hall and came out. He walked down and saw Richard Speck bleeding to death on his bed while the three others watched. Crubaugh shuffled back to the elevator and went downstairs.

"A guy on the fifth floor is cut bad," he told Bill Vaughan, the tall desk clerk.

"I'll get the police," Vaughan said. He reached for the phone.

Crubaugh went back to the elevator and sat down. There is very little excitement about life and death in a flophouse.

It was midnight when two partrolmen arrived and went upstairs and took Speck out of his room on a stretcher.

"I want water," Speck kept saying.

"Wait'll we get you to the hospital," one of the patrolmen said.

The picture of Richard Speck, wanted for murder, was in the mind of every policeman in Chicago Saturday night. But this guy on the elevator, blood covering his face, was unrecognizable. It wasn't until later, when they were washing the blood from his arms in Cook County Hospital and they saw the tattoo, "Born to raise hell," that anybody realized that this flophouse guy, helpless and moaning for water, was the one they wanted.

On the fifth floor of the Starr Hotel, somebody took Speck's mattress and threw it into the hall. When people stepped on the mattress to get into the room, their weight forced blood to run out of it.

"He must have lost a quart and a half of blood," a detective was saying.

Inside, on a stool, was a tube of Gleem toothpaste, a pack of Gillette razor blades, a can of Old Spice after-shave lotion, and a smeared bottle of Max Factor Signature cologne for men.

"The razor is missing," a detective said.

"He could have used that. But there's a broken beer bottle in the garbage can. It has blood all over it. He might have cut his wrists with that."

The only other thing Speck had left in the room was a black wallet. There was no money in it. It had a folder of color pictures.

"Let me see them," somebody said.

"Forget them," a detective said. "It's family. Why should they go through any more than they have to because of him?"

George Gregrich was still sitting on the edge of his mattress in the cubicle next door. He had finished the wine, and he was drinking the three cans of beer. He was in a black shirt and pants. He used his heavy work boots to crush out the cigarettes he was chain-smoking.

"If I had been told that he done a thing like that, I wouldn't have had him living next door to me," he said. "I don't do things like he done."

"Shut up," a voice yelled.

"You shut up," Gregrich yelled.

He picked up a can of beer and held it to his mouth.

"I'm glad he's gone from here," Gregrich said. "I don't want no more trouble from that guy."

People who came in to talk to Gregrich breathed with their mouths open against the smell of his world and the world that Richard Speck had just been carried out of on a stretcher.

At 6:30 in the morning, Francis Flanagan, commander of homicide detectives in Chicago, stood under the trees on the empty sidewalk in front of Area 2 Homicide headquarters, which handled the murder case. Flanagan's red eyes kept blinking. He took quick drags on a cork-tipped cigarette.

"I took a look at him," he said. "I didn't say a thing to him. I just took a look at him."

"What did you think about when you looked at him?"

Flanagan closed his eyes. "I thought about why anybody bothered to call the police when he was bleeding in his room," he said. "Then, I don't know, I knew I couldn't think like that, so I just looked at him and I got tired. Very tired."

After a trial in Peoria, Illinois, Speck was convicted of murder and sentenced to die in the electric chair. But when the U.S. Supreme Court held existing death-penalty laws unconstitutional, he was re-sentenced to life in prison. Now he is eligible for parole.

Whitman hauls an arsenal up U. of Texas tower, starts shooting everyone

At twenty-five, Charles Whitman was a handsome, strapping young man, an ex-marine and University of Texas architectural engineering student who thirteen years earlier had been the youngest Eagle Scout in America. On the night of July 31, 1966, he sat in his Austin apartment and wrote notes saying he was going to kill his wife and his mother to spare them the embarrassment of what he was going to do the next day. Early the next morning, he killed them and pinned the notes to their bodies. Later that morning, he bought a .30-caliber carbine and several boxes of shells at a hardware store, telling the clerk he was "going to Florida to shoot wild hogs." He stopped at another store and bought a shotgun on credit. With these and other weapons, and with food rations, he climbed to the top of the university's tallest building and started killing everyone he could. This story, from the *Austin American-Statesman* of the afternoon of August 1, 1966, was written before the bodies of his mother and wife were discovered.

A sniper firing from the observation deck of the University of Texas Tower Monday killed at least nine persons and injured at least twenty-four more before being gunned down by police.

The entire campus area was bathed in blood as the sniper fired down on unprotected victims on every side of the tower from noon until 1:30 p.m.

Blood literally ran in the hallways of the tower and on the sidewalks throughout the sprawling campus, as the sniper used an arsenal of weapons to pick off victim after victim, some a block away.

The sniper was gunned to death by five police officers who went

226

onto the twenty-seventh-floor observation deck after the man quit firing.

Police said papers on the body of the man they gunned down carried the name Charles Whitman.

Police who shot the gunman said they found a .22-caliber rifle, a .38 pistol, a 7-mm. rifle, and a 30-06 rifle at different points on the observation deck.

They said the man, about twenty-five, clad in blue jeans under a set of cover-alls, had a shoulder-type field pack of ammunition, a trench knife, and a pair of binoculars with him.

He was gunned down at the northwest corner of the observation deck.

Bodies of the dead and injured, mostly those felled by the sniper's opening fire, were strewn about the university's famed main mall on the tower's south side.

The wounded could not be rescued for more than an hour as the sniper's high volume of fire covered the area. They finally were taken out by rescuers in an armored car.

Many of the injured staggered to ambulances ringing the campus as far away as two blocks from the tower, still in the sniper's range.

Every police officer and every ambulance in the city went to the scene. A Department of Public Safety airplane manned by city police officers was called to assist in spotting the man in the tower.

The known dead included a city police officer, Patrolman Billy P. Speed; Paul Sonntag, grandson of KTBC newsman Paul Bolton; Robert E. Boyer, an associate professor of geology and education; Roy Schmidt; Claudia Rutt, and Thomas Eckman. Among the wounded, his condition unknown, was Associated Press writer Robert Heard.

The emergency room at Brackenridge Hospital overflowed with the dead and wounded. Other victims were taken to Seton Hospital.

An urgent call went out for blood donors at the Travis County Blood Bank. The call was answered immediately, with lines of donors forming even before police stopped the gunman's fire.

At 12:30 P.M. *Statesman* reporter Jim Berry said he could see at least four wounded—two lying on the main mall and two more who had been pulled to cover but were still pinned down.

Most of the persons at Brackenridge had been removed from the university area after staggering to businesses, houses and police units near the campus.

The sniper opened fire shortly before noon. The firing continued unabated—as many as three shots every ten seconds.

Vera Palmer, a university elevator operator pinned inside the tower by the gunfire, said she was at the twenty-seventh floor of the tower at 11:55 A.M. when a man in a white shirt with tennis shoes in his hand told her:

"Lady, don't you dare get off this elevator. Go on down."

Mrs. Palmer did not mention seeing a gun.

For more than thirty minutes the man fired from every side of the tower, concentrating on the south side's main mall.

One girl, felled by a bullet, was dragged behind a concrete stairway by several men. One could be seen holding her across his lap. Shots from the tower prevented rescuers from reaching her.

About fifteen shots had been counted by observers hiding in buildings around the tower. Persons crouched against buildings to escape.

The campus was almost deserted when the firing began. Small groups of people ran out of buildings when the first shots were fired, then ducked back to safety as the bullets kept coming from the tower.

Officers, armed with rifles equipped with telescopic sights, sought to pick off the sniper from the high tower, located in the middle of the campus.

Associated Press newsman Heard was shot in the arm by the sniper as he followed two Texas Rangers to an open area near the tower.

"He got me," Ernest Strombeger of the *Dallas Times Herald* said Heard yelled. Heard was taken to a hospital.

Don Reeves, a graduate student in history at the University of Texas who lives at Brackenridge Apartments, said, "I came out of the north door of the west mall of the student-services building. I saw a man lying in the grass. I saw two more people on the pavement; one may have been a woman. I saw a girl run out to help the man lying in the grass. I heard a shot; the girl ran back behind a flagpole. She was pinned down. I ran in the east door of the historical library building."

University student Richard Embry said that between 12:15 and 12:20 P.M. shooting from the tower ceased, and he theorized that perhaps the man was reloading his gun.

"There is this concrete-and-iron sort of barricade that he hides behind," the student said, "and then he pops his head over to take another shot.

"You can see the gleam of the gun. He is firing down, and the police are firing up at him."

An employee on the tower's twenty-second floor said she could see a man and a girl lying on the south mall in front of the tower.

Another man was lying near the hedge around the flagpole. A small boy was reported down on the mall also.

As many as four persons were gunned down on the top of the computation center just east of the campus. University police were trying to bring in an armored car to rescue victims from the open areas.

Austin police said Texas highway patrolmen moved into the area immediately and began returning the sniper's fire.

Every rifle in the Austin police department was sent to the university, but officers could not get a good sight on the sniper.

As every available police unit moved into the area, officers took up positions around the tower.

Using high-powered, scope-equipped rifles, officers finally got a good bead on the man momentarily from the sixth floor of the business and economics office building just south and east of the tower.

"I can see him real good, walking back and forth," one officer told the police network.

Christ Whitcraft, an *Austin Statesman* reporter who was in the campus' Sutton Hall, southwest of the tower, said he counted "eight shots in less than three minutes."

The reporter said persons told him they had heard shots as early as 11:45 A.M.

"There are groups of students standing around in small knots of five and ten," Whitcraft said. "They are being very cautious.

They are hovering in doorways and at the sides of buildings."

Inside the tower, university personnel on the eighteenth, twenty-fourth, and twenty-sixth floors barricaded themselves inside their offices.

Amy Jo Long of the university's news and information service said she received a call at 11:55 A.M. from personnel at the Humanities Research Center saying, "Someone is shooting at people from the tower. There is blood all over the place. Don't come over here. We have locked ourselves in."

Francis Lucas of the Office of Naval Research locked himself in on the twenty-fifth floor of the tower.

He said he saw two young boys lying face down in front of Hogg Auditorium. Some people dragged them away. "They didn't move," he said. "They looked like sacks." The sound of firing could be heard over the telephone.

Whitman killed sixteen in all, counting his wife and mother. He was buried in his home town of Lake Worth, Florida, where his father, a wealthy plumbing contractor, still lived. Texas Gov. John B. Connally created a blue-ribbon committee to try to determine what made Whitman go berserk. An autopsy showed he had a small malignant tumor at the base of his brain, but the committee thought it unlikely that this interfered with his reasoning capacity. The full report on the committee's findings never was made public.

"Hello from the gutters of N.Y.C.," Son of Sam writes Jimmy Breslin

Donna Lauria, 18, was shot to death with a
.44-caliber revolver outside her family's Bronx
apartment on July 29, 1976. Christine Freund, 26,
was murdered in similar fashion in Queens on
January 30, 1977. But it was not until March 8,
1977, when Virginia Voskerichian, 19, was killed in
Queens, that New York police concluded the murders
probably were related and appealed to the public for
help. On April 17, Alexander Esau, 19, and
Valentina Suriani, 18, were shot to death in a car in
the Bronx. Attached to the steering wheel was a note
from the killer, who vowed to strike again. It was
signed "Son of Sam." In May, as the anniversary of
the first murder approached, the killer wrote a
taunting note to *New York Daily News* columnist
Jimmy Breslin, who had been writing about the
murders. Breslin showed the letter to the Lauria
family, and wrote this column for the *Daily News* of
June 5, 1977.

©1977 by Chicago Tribune - New York News
Syndicate.

We put the letter on the table and read it again. In his opening
paragraph he writes:

"Hello from the gutters of N.Y.C. which are filled with dog
manure, vomit, stale wine, urine, and blood. Hello from the
sewers of N.Y.C. which swallow up these delicacies when they are
washed away by the sweeper trucks. Hello from the cracks in the
sidewalks of N.Y.C. and from the ants that dwell in these cracks
and feed on the dried blood of the dead that has settled into the
cracks."

"He's a pretty good writer," somebody at the table said.

"Yes, he is," I said.

The letter was from the person who calls himself "Son of Sam." He prowls the night streets of New York neighborhoods and shoots at young girls and sometimes their boyfriends too, and he has killed five and wounded four. He sneaks up on victims with a .44-caliber pistol. Most of the young women had shoulder-length brown hair.

One of the victims was Donna Lauria, who was eighteen last year when the killer shot her as she sat in a car with her girlfriend outside the Laurias' apartment house on Buhre Avenue in the Bronx. Donna Lauria was the only victim mentioned by the killer in his letter, which was sent to me at my newspaper in New York, the *Daily News*. So yesterday I took the letter up to the fourth-floor apartment of Donna Lauria's parents, and I sat over coffee and read the letter again and talked to the Laurias about it.

The killer had sent one communication before this one. He left a note to police after murdering a girl and boy as they sat in a parked car at a place only five blocks from where Donna Lauria had been killed. Both notes were hand-printed.

Yesterday, in the sadness and tension of the Laurias' dining room, I read the letter again. After the first paragraph, it said:

"J.B., I'm just dropping you a line to let you know that I appreciate your interest in those recent and horrendous .44 killings. I also want to tell you that I read your column daily and find it quite informative.

"Tell me, Jim, what will you have for July Twenty-Ninth? You can forget about me if you like because I don't care for publicity. However, you must not forget Donna Lauria and you cannot let the people forget her, either. She was a very sweet girl but Sam's a thirsty lad and he won't let me stop killing until he gets his fill of blood.

"Mr. Breslin, sir, don't you think that because you haven't heard from (me) for a while that I went to sleep. No, rather, I am still here. Like a spirit roaming the night. Thirsty, hungry, seldom stopping to rest, anxious to please Sam. I love my work. Now, the void has been filled.

"Perhaps we shall meet face to face someday or perhaps I will be blown away by cops with smoking .38s. Whatever, if I shall be fortunate enough to meet you I will tell you all about Sam if you like, and I will introduce you to him. His name is 'Sam the Terrible.'

"Not knowing what the future holds I shall say farewell, and I will see you at the next job. Or, should I say you will see my handiwork at the next job? Remember Ms. Lauria. Thank you.

"In their blood
and
From the Gutter
'Sam's Creation' .44

"P.S.: J.B., please inform all the detectives working on the slayings to remain.

"P.S.: J.B., please inform all the detectives working on the case that I wish them the best of luck. 'Keep Em digging, drive on, think positive, get off your butts, knock on coffins, etc.'

"Upon my capture I promise to buy all the guys working on the case a new pair of shoes if I can get up the money.

"Son of Sam"

Directly under the signature was a symbol the killer drew. It appears to be an X-shaped mark with the biological symbols for male and female, and also a cross and the letter S.

When I finished reading the letter, Mike Lauria, the father, said to me, "What do you think?"

"Want to see for yourself?" the father was asked.

He pushed the letter away from him: "I don't want to see it."

"Let me," his wife, Rose, said.

"You don't want to see it," the husband said.

"Yes, I do. I have a lot of cards she used to get. Maybe the printing is the same."

The husband shrugged. "Go ahead then."

We took out the page that mentioned her daughter and gave Rose Lauria the rest. Her large, expressive brown eyes became cold as she looked at the printing. On the wall behind her was a picture of her daughter, a lovely brown-haired girl with the mother's features.

The mother put the pages down and looked up. "He's probably a very brilliant man, boy, whatever he is," she said. "His brain functions the opposite way."

She looked up at the picture of her daughter. "She was a dancer and a half. Every place you went, people used to praise her. Is it possible he saw her someplace and she didn't speak to him or something?"

Nobody knows. The .44 killer appears to be saying that he is controlled by Sam, who lives inside him and sends him onto the streets to find young people to shoot. He does this at close range: One young woman, walking home from college, held a textbook over her face, and he put the gun up to the book and killed her.

The detectives, whose shoes he would buy, walk the streets at night and hope for a match with the man with the .44. "He's mine," one of them, a friend of mine, was saying Friday night. "The man is Jack the Ripper, and I'm making a personal appointment with him."

The hope is that the killer realizes he is controlled by Sam, who not only forces him into acts of horror but will ultimately walk him to his death. The only way for the killer to leave this special torment is to give himself up to me, if he trusts me, or to the police, and receive both help and safety.

If he wants any further contact, all he has to do is call or write me at the *Daily News*. It's simple to get me. The only people I don't answer are bill collectors.

The time to do it, however, is now. We are too close to the July 29 that the killer mentions in his letter. It is the first anniversary of the death of Donna Lauria.

"She was sitting in the car with her friend Jody Valenti," Rose Lauria was saying. Jody Valenti was wounded and has recovered. "Mike and I came walking up. We'd been to a wake. I went up to the car and I said, 'Tell me, Jody, what happened tonight?' 'Donna'll tell you when she gets upstairs.' Now my husband says to Donna, 'What are you doing here at 1:00 A.M., you got to work tomorrow.' I said to him, 'What is she doing that's wrong?'

"So we went upstairs. My husband says, 'I'm going to walk the dog.' He goes with the dog to the elevator, and I hear Jody's horn blowing downstairs. I called out in the hall to my husband. He says to me, 'Well, go look out the window and see.' I look out and here's Jody screaming that Donna's been shot."

Rose Lauria, nervous now, got up from the table. "You know the last month when he killed the two more around here? My husband and I were at a wedding. We were supposed to meet some people after it. We left the wedding, and I said to my husband, 'I don't want to meet anybody. Something's the matter. I want to go home.' And we just got inside at the same time the two got killed.''

"She was pacing around here like a cat," Mike Lauria said.

He walked me downstairs to the street. He stood in an undershirt, with the sun glaring on his wide shoulders, and he pointed to the spot where his daughter had been shot.

"She was starting to get out of the car when she saw this guy on the curb. Right where we are. Donna said to Jody, 'Who's this guy now?' Then the guy did what he did. Jody, she can't get herself to come near my wife. Forget about it. I saw her a couple of weeks ago. She spoke to me from the car. Told me she got engaged. She couldn't even look at me. I told her, 'All right, Jody, go ahead, I'll see you.' I let her go home."

He turned and walked back into his building. I took my letter from his daughter's killer and went down the street and out of his wounded life.

On June 26, 1977, the killer wounded a young couple in a car in Queens. Police braced for the July 29 anniversary of the Lauria killing, but Son of Sam didn't strike until two days later, when he killed Stacy Moskowitz and wounded Robert Violante, both twenty, in a car in Brooklyn. It was the first time the killer had struck outside the Bronx and Queens, and terror gripped all New York City. "NO ONE IS SAFE FROM SON OF SAM," the *New York Post* blared on August 1. But the killer had made a mistake. While stalking the Brooklyn victims, he had left his car in front of a fire hydrant, and police ticketed it. They traced the license number—561 XLB—to David Berkowitz, 24, of Yonkers, postal worker and former auxiliary policeman. Suspicious about what a Jew from Yonkers would be doing in a quiet Italian neighborhood in Brooklyn at that time of night, detectives went to his apartment on August 10. They found the car in front and, peering through the window, saw the butt of a sub-machinegun and a letter addressed to police. Berkowitz was arrested when he came out to start the car. "I'm Son of Sam. O.K., you've got me," he said. The letter in the car indicated that he had planned a machine-gun raid that night on a Hamptons discotheque and that authorities "would be all summer counting the bodies." In the car, police also found a loaded, .44-caliber Bulldog revolver, the weapon that had killed six and wounded seven. Later, in taped interviews with a psychiatrist, Berkowitz said that "howling and crying demons demanding blood" had ordered him to kill. "I'm the Son of Sam, but it's not me," he said. "It's Sam who works through me. I'm David Berkowitz. That's all I want to be. They use my body." In April, 1978, Brooklyn Supreme Court Justice Joseph Corso ruled that Berkowitz was competent to stand trial for the murder of Stacy Moskowitz. Berkowitz pleaded guilty to all six murders and was sentenced to 315 years in prison.

Chapter VIII

KIDNAP

The Lindbergh ransom note warns: "Don't publish this letter"

Four years after Charles A. Lindbergh flew the Spirit of St. Louis across the Atlantic, a tragedy befell the Lindbergh family that aroused passion and sympathy rarely equalled for millions of hero-worshipping Americans. From the Lindbergh country estate near Hopewell, New Jersey, the aviator's twenty-month-old son and namesake was kidnapped on March 1, 1932. While a horde of newsmen waited outside the home learning nothing, an aggressive, enterprising editor at the *Chicago American* got through by long-distance telephone. The editor, Harry Reutlinger, learned that there was a ransom note and what it said. Reutlinger's exclusive appeared in the *American* the day after the kidnapping.

"Dear Sir:

"Have $50,000 ready, $25,000 in $20 bills, $15,000 in $10 bills and $10,000 in $5 bills. Have them in two packages.

"Four days we will inform you to redeem the money. We warn you for making anything public, or for notifying the police.

"The child is in gut care. Identification for letters are signatures. Answer three fold. Two rings in blue ink, with center ring of red. A blue ink line of the blue circles on the outer edge of the red. A hole on the outer edge of each dark circle, and one in the center of the red.

"Don't publish this letter."

Murder Most Foul

Kidnappers of Charles Augustus Lindbergh, Jr., twenty-month-old son of Col. and Mrs. Charles A. Lindbergh, demand $50,000 in cash for the return of the boy. This was learned exclusively today by a representative of the *Chicago American*.

A ransom note, left in the nursery crib of the baby when he was stolen from the Lindbergh home here last night, revealed this demand.

The ransom note, written in ink on plain paper, was erratic, with seemingly mysterious directions as to payment of the ransom. But it was specific as to the amount, and the denomination of bills in which the $50,000 was demanded to be paid.

The ransom letter was revealed while Colonel Lindbergh was leading the police in a search for four men and one woman, seen about the borders of the Lindbergh country estate in a densely wooded region near Hopewell yesterday.

That a woman took part in the daring crime was first revealed when footprints of a woman were found, with those of a man, on the grounds of the estate, near the window through which the baby was kidnapped from his second-floor nursery room.

At the time the flying colonel and his wife, Anne Morrow Lindbergh, were in the living room, on the first floor of the residence.

Police had only a scant clue as to the description of the woman, a high police official at the Lindbergh home admitted.

But of the man a more accurate description was given: About thirty to thirty-five years old; 5 feet 9½ inches tall; ruddy complexion; reddish mustache; high cheek bones; medium narrow face; long nose; wearing gray fedora hat and dark blue overcoat.

"This man was seen about one of the entrances to the Lindbergh estate yesterday," the official said.

"At another entrance three other men and one woman were seen during the day. We are after the woman now."

The informer expressed the opinion that the kidnapping was the work of a professional gang. This opinion was shared by Colonel and Mrs. Lindbergh.

The police informant continued:

"It was a clever job. It was not generally known that the baby was here.

"The mere fact that the letter did not state the place where the ransom money was to be left leads us to expect a telephone call or message at any time.

"The entire New Jersey police force and the state militia have been placed at the disposal of Colonel and Mrs. Lindbergh."

Sleepless, Colonel Lindbergh aided the police in their search, which extended over four states. Mrs. Lindbergh was ordered to bed early today by her physician.

It was revealed that the baby had been ill from a cold for several days, and that Mrs. Lindbergh was greatly worried. Colonel Lindbergh, after a fly-drive trip with state police, said upon his return:

"I intend to remain awake until my baby returns home. My wife, Anne, is in bed. I guess the strain was too much for her."

Mrs. Lindbergh, before retiring, said:

"We have been doctoring the baby for several days."

None of the baby's clothing, except the night dress in which it was sleeping, was missing, and this greatly perturbed the mother, who said:

"The poor child has had a cold, and will suffer."

The entire force of New Jersey state police concentrated in the area surrounding the isolated Lindbergh country estate in the belief that the kidnappers might be holding the baby in the surrounding dense woods.

Careful search was made of deserted farmhouses in the region.

Colonel Lindbergh, after a night and part of a day of anxious search, said at 9:00 A.M.:

"We have received several leads, but most of them have fallen down. The police have leads now in Atlantic City, Philadelphia, and Yardley, Pennsylvania. I don't know how important they are, but we are clutching at every straw."

Another tip sent the colonel speeding away to Flagtown, New Jersey, fifteen miles away.

He was accompanied by two state troopers and Oscar Busch, well-known trapper in the region.

Flagtown is in the center of a former "moonshining" area, recently cleared up by federal agents.

The colonel had made several of these auto sorties to various sites on information that later proved of no value.

The only clues for the state troopers to work on were:

The ladder used by the kidnappers in climbing to the upper-story nursery in the Lindbergh house;

Footprints of a man, joined later with those of a woman;

A blue-and-white blanket found sixty feet along the single road leading from the house to the main road;

An abandoned stolen blue sedan found in Hillside, New Jersey.

The ladder, a collapsible affair, found close to the house, contained fingerprints that are being compared with those of notorious kidnappers.

The footprints indicated that the man and the woman removed their shoes or used wrapping about their footwear.

The blanket may have been one used by the kidnappers to wrap the baby. None of his own bed clothing was taken by the gang.

The abandoned sedan answered the description of a machine in which a man and a woman were reported inquiring as to the way to the Lindbergh estate shortly before the kidnapping last night.

Footprints discovered leading to a main road from the isolated Lindbergh home indicated that a man and a woman took part in the kidnapping. This clue was uncovered by Colonel Lindbergh and state troopers working together through the night.

The footprints of the man led from the base of the ladder that was found leaning against a window of the second-floor nursery. The footprints of the woman joined those of the man about halfway down the two-and-a-half-mile stretch of narrow road running from the house.

The two sets of footprints were traced from that point to the main road, where the kidnappers were believed to have parked their car.

Police believed that after the car had been parked at the side of the main road, the woman accompanied the man halfway up the road toward the Lindbergh home. She waited for him while he stole up to the house, mounted the ladder to the nursery, and brought the baby down.

The ladder did not belong on the Lindbergh estate or in the vicinity. It was described as "makeshift" and was believed to have been carried as part of the equipment of the kidnappers.

Everything indicated the kidnappers had carefully prepared the baby-stealing. The isolated nature of the Lindbergh estate contributed to the success of their plans.

The Lindbergh home was built for the famous flying couple while they were on their flight to the Orient last summer. It is a two-and-one-half-story structure standing about half a mile back from the Stoutsburg-Wertsville highway. It is surrounded by dense woodland, and there are no other houses near it.

The baby had been put to bed by Betty Gow, his nurse, and Mrs. Lindbergh, who had given him a good-night kiss at 7:00 P.M. The colonel, the butler, and the butler's wife were the only other occupants of the house.

Colonel and Mrs. Lindbergh were eating a late "snack" at 10:00 P.M. when the disappearance of the baby was discovered.

Mrs. Lindbergh became hysterical, but the colonel retained a grip on his emotions and immediately telephoned state police.

The colonel aided in the search of the grounds dressed in his aviator's leather jacket and without a hat. He would not discuss the kidnapping with newspapermen. He said:

"I'm sure you'll understand how I feel. You will have to excuse me."

Asked about the condition of Mrs. Lindbergh, he added:

"She is bearing up as well as might be expected."

Mrs. Lindbergh has been reported as expecting another child within the next few months.

Immediately after the kidnapping alarm was broadcast by state police, guards were posted along all main roads leading from New Jersey into New York and Pennsylvania.

Police at Princeton, New Jersey were told that men in a black or dark blue sedan, bearing New York license plates, had inquired along a nearby road their way to the Lindbergh home just before the kidnapping. A description of the men and the machine was broadcast throughout New Jersey and adjacent states.

An auto that met the description of the wanted machine later was found abandoned in Hillside, New Jersey.

The abandoned car was a blue Nash sedan with black trimmings. It was found parked without lights near the Newark

City line and gave forth an aroma of perfume. It bore New York license plates.

This car later was identified by a resident of Brooklyn who said it had been stolen from him earlier in the day.

Meanwhile, the Lindberghs had notified Mrs. Evangeline L. Lindbergh, mother of the colonel, and Mrs. Dwight W. Morrow, mother of Mrs. Lindbergh, of the kidnapping.

Mrs. Evangeline Lindbergh was reported ready to start here from Grosse Pointe, a suburb of Detroit. Mrs. Morrow, widow of sen. Dwight W. Morrow, resides in Englewood, New Jersey, where the colonel and his bride formerly lived.

State police began an intensive check on men who have been engaged in construction and renovation work in the Lindbergh home.

A complete list of all persons who have been employed on the estate was obtained from George Hullfish, Lawrenceville, New Jersey, foreman of the Lindbergh home construction job.

The home is of colonial design, built of native stone. It sits on a hillside in the center of an estate of about fifteen acres. There are wings on both ends of the house.

The nursery is in the northwest corner of the house, which was completed last October.

The official alarm that was flashed over the police teletype network was as follows:

"Colonel Lindbergh's baby kidnapped from Lindbergh home at Hopewell between 7:30 and 10:00 P.M. Boy, 20 months, dressed in sleeping suit. Search all cars."

A squad of state troopers scoured the road eighteen miles from here and reported that a bundle "like a doll" had been sighted fourteen miles east of Somerville, New Jersey.

Philadelphia police notified authorities working on the kidnapping that a truck driver had told them of seeing the bundle on the side of the road.

The truckman was driving from Orange, New Jersey to Philadelphia when his headlights picked out the bundle. He said he did not give it any thought at the time, but when he arrived in Philadelphia and read of the Lindbergh kidnapping, he decided he should tell the police.

242

Murder Most Foul

George Jennings, who lives near the Lindbergh estate, said that he had been approached early in the night by a man and woman in a dark sedan who asked to be directed to the Lindbergh home.

State police checked up on the state home for epileptics at Skillman, New Jersey, about four miles from the Lindbergh home, to learn whether any inmates had escaped from the institution.

An examination of the ladder used by the kidnappers in reaching the window of the nursery showed that it was of the type used by house painters. It was in three sections, which could be telescoped so that it might be easily carried on an auto.

Fingerprints were found on the ladder, and experts took photographs of them.

The Lindbergh home was brilliantly lighted throughout the night.

While "official" information from the household was scant, the Lindbergh butler, Ollie Whateley, served coffee to the group of several hundred newspaper reporters and photographers who converged on the estate from many cities.

No sooner had Harry Reutlinger's story hit the street than the *American* and other papers in the Hearst chain received an urgent directive from publisher William Randolph Hearst in New York. Hearst papers, he ordered, were to print absolutely nothing about the case that had not been released by police. Hearst, who didn't know about the *American's* exclusive, wanted at all cost to avoid printing anything that might endanger the kidnapped baby. A fleet of *American* circulation trucks was dispatched to retrieve the papers from newsstands. In the meantime, the opposition papers had lifted the facts and were on the street with the story. When they learned that the *American* was pulling back its papers, they assumed the story was wrong, and sent trucks to pull their papers off the stands. It was impossible to buy a paper in Chicago for several hours. Days later, the Lindbergh family arranged to pay $50,000 ransom after indirect contact with the supposed kidnapper. The bills were marked. Then, on May 12, 1932, a truck driver found the decomposed body of Charles A. Lindbergh, Jr. less than five miles from the family estate. In September, 1934, New York police arrested a thirty-six-year-old German

243

immigrant, Bruno Richard Hauptmann, who had spent one of the marked bills at a filling station. When police searched his home, they found $30,000 more of the marked cash. Hauptmann was convicted by a New Jersey jury in 1934. Two years later he died in the electric chair.

Barbara Mackle buried eighty-three hours, then: "She's here! Over here!"

Barbara Jane Mackle refused all media requests for interviews after her bizarre kidnapping, but did agree to be photographed. Reporter Gene Miller talked to her long enough during a photo session to piece together this detailed account of her ordeal for the *Miami Herald* of December 29, 1968.

"I could hear the footsteps," said Barbara Mackle. "I thought it was the kidnappers coming back for me. I had been there so long I really didn't care."

For eighty-three hours she lay entombed in a wooden, coffin-like box built in Miami with lumber requisitioned at the University of Miami Institute of Marine Science.

Again, she prayed. Again, she listened.

The steps came closer.

"One of the ventilation fans made a zang-zang sound, and I turned it off so I could hear better. I couldn't see. I had no conception of time."

The time was 4:15 P.M. Friday, December 20, and two men in white shirts, neckties, and business suits searched in desperation on the sloping hillside of a Georgia pine forest not ten yards away.

Barbara Mackle, an astonishingly cool-headed young woman of twenty, patiently began to rap on the lid of her coffin.

Neither man heard it.

One kept scuffing through the browned mat of pine needles, kicking. Suddenly he saw fresh red clay. He kicked again.

He began to shout. "Barbara Mackle! Barbara Mackle! This is the FBI!"

He spotted the ventilation tube protruding inches above the

245

Barbara Jane Mackle.

ground. He threw himself on the ground.

"Knock!" he commanded. "Knock!"

"I could hear him," said Barbara Mackle. "I kept rapping."

"Here!" someone else yelled. "She's here! Over here!"

On his knees, an FBI agent frantically dug with his hands in the moist earth. His hands bled. Another agent ripped a limb from a tree to use as a spade.

Still another agent ran up with a rusted and bullet-riddled bucket, once used for target practice, and he fell to his knees and began scooping.

For five, ten, twelve minutes they labored.

"Hold on. We'll have you out in a few minutes," an agent said, his mouth to the tube. "Answer me," he commanded. He heard no response.

The bleeding hands reached screws, painted a marine gray and embedded in the lid perhaps eighteen inches from the surface.

"Get a tire iron!" someone yelled, and a man raced 200 yards to McGee Road, a blacktop the kidnapper of Barbara Mackle failed to mention in his cryptic instructions to the Atlanta FBI office by long-distance telephone three hours earlier.

The tire iron served as a screwdriver.

"When they opened it, there were faces all around, smiling," said Barbara Mackle.

She couldn't walk. Gently, they lifted her.

"How are my parents?" she asked. These were her first words.

The FBI is not an agency easily given to emotion.

"They were all crying," Barbara said.

At this imprecise moment, amid the green honey vines and the tall pines, the critical factor of survival had been established in perhaps the most bizarre kidnapping in the annals of crime in America.

A few moments later a telephone rang by direct line into the home at 4111 San Amaro Street, Coral Gables, and J. Edgar Hoover, the man known as "the director," told Robert Mackle, "We have your daughter. She is safe."

In the years ahead, the Mackle kidnapping is certain to be documented precisely, analyzed, scrutinized. Today, despite the intensity of instant journalism, facts emerge in fragmentation, sometimes out of perspective.

The FBI, which is positive it has its man, is extremely reluctant to prejudice its as yet incompleted case—or provide a handbook of error for the next time.

Witnesses, Barbara Mackle included, are yet to be interrogated thoroughly, completely.

Barbara, a junior at Emory University in the beautiful Druir Hills section near Atlanta, had checked into the nearby Rodeway Inn motel with her mother because she couldn't get into the infirmary.

"The night before I had a temperature of 102. The flu," she said. "I'd missed my econ final the Saturday before. I still had 101 that morning."

No one told her about the man with a beard and the girl in the "foreign station wagon with the Massachusetts plates." Earlier, they had driven through the 560-acre campus asking about her.

After midnight that Tuesday, December 17, one of Barbara's dates, Stewart Hunt Woodward, 21, a bright young man on the dean's list, stopped briefly at the motel and spoke to Barbara and her mother. He drove a white Ford Mustang.

Later, just before 4:00 A.M., Mrs. Mackle answered a knock on the door. A clean-shaven man, wearing a latticed and visored cap lettered "police," said something about an accident involving a young man in a white Ford.

Abruptly, the stranger shoulder-bashed the door of Room 137, ripping the anodized aluminum stripping from the door. He pushed to the face of the mother a cloth reeking of chloroform.

The terrified woman saw another person wearing a ski mask holding what looked like a shotgun. She thought he was a boy about twelve years old.

At 4:00 A.M., Beverly Jenkens, the motel bookkeeper, angrily arose from her bed. Someone was leaning on an auto horn.

The motel is adjacent to a huge Veterans Administration Hospital, and once before, quite literally, men in white coats had retrieved escaped patients from the motel.

Mrs. Jenkens, peeking from her window, telephoned the night clerk, Walter Perkins, 53, a bald-headed gentleman who wears a $279 hearing aid. "Another crackpot is on the loose," she said.

Perkins methodically locked both the front and rear doors of the office and trotted toward Room 137.

"Hey, lady!" he shouted. "Shut up! You'll wake up all the guests!"

Barbara's mother, Jane Braznell Mackle, her bruised and cut legs bound with white cord, a single strip of adhesive tape across her mouth, had hopped to Barbara's parked 350 Firebird, turned around, opened the door with her hands bound behind her back, and backed inside the car, half-leaning, half-sitting on the steering wheel.

The clerk pulled off the adhesive.

" 'They robbed me—and took my daughter.' Those were explicit words," said Perkins. "I thought it was some kind of emotional disturbance between mother and daughter." He departed hurriedly.

"I had to telephone the police myself," said Mrs. Mackle.

She also telephoned her husband in Coral Gables.

As De Kalb County police responded in the 24-degree predawn chill that morning, a blue Swedish-made Volvo with Barbara Mackle inside sped 18.3 miles northeasterly to an open and waiting grave.

She had a blanket over her head.

She had seen distinctly, though, the man's face, a face she could identify.

"I knew the other person was a girl," said Barbara. "She felt my head and said, 'Oh, she's sick!' and later she wanted to leave me nose drops. He wouldn't let her.

"They gave me a shot," she said, indicating her right hip. "They told me it was a tranquilizer." The girl was supposed to give her the shot. She refused. The man did it.

"I was woozy, but I knew what was happening. I tried to talk them out of it."

Perhaps twenty or twenty-five minutes later the car stopped.

She lay sprawled on the damp earth, grass at her head. Her abductor carefully placed a sign lettered "kidnapped" near her—and suddenly yanked off the blanket.

A Polaroid flash camera went off. Again Barbara Mackle saw her kidnappers. This time the man wore the ski mask.

But standing in the headlight beams of the car was the girl. Barbara Mackle caught a good look.

In the first photograph Barbara had her eyes closed. The man took a second one.

They marched her past a junk pile she couldn't see, beyond the rusted shell of an old Kenmore heater, flattened Budweiser cans from someone's picnic.

The man took from her finger a ring, slipped off her watch, and pulled off a buckle and the metal buttons from her red and white flannel nightie. He wanted them for identification.

"The girl gave me a sweater. They told me they'd be back to check on me in two hours," said Barbara.

They never returned.

She heard the screws tightening the lid, then the shovel and the earth thudding over her head, the stomping, packing.

And, finally, the terrible stillness.

For maybe two-and-one-half hours, she had a light that she could turn on and off by herself. "Then it went out."

The blanket and sweater weren't enough. "It was cold and it leaked. It kept dripping from above."

Barbara Mackle never truly panicked. She waited, supremely confident in her own family—and God.

In the monotony of nothingness, Barbara Mackle tried to remember the words of every verse of every song she had sung. Only the week before her alto voice blended with her Delta Delta Delta sorority sisters at a Christmas carolling at an old folks' home in Atlanta.

She kept telling herself today is Wednesday, today is Wednesday, today is Wednesday. She didn't want to know the hours of her entombment.

"You don't know what time it is in the dark," she said.

"I wished I was 5 feet 3," she said, hunching her shoulders. "I couldn't stretch out."

She is, in fact, 5 feet 10 inches, slender, and not too photogenic, much prettier in person. She is a highly intelligent young lady and incredibly stable.

Her kidnappers had stocked the vault with food and water, which she could sip from a tube. "It tasted funny," she said, wrinkling her nose.

She had to be careful not to suck too quickly and blow the water back through the tube.

"I remember eating an apple and some sort of candy," she said. "That's all."

She is mistaken, understandably perhaps. FBI agents, who shipped the casket to the FBI crime laboratory in Washington, found other traces of food.

Perhaps 669 miles from Barbara's pit of captivity, an unlisted telephone rang at 9:10 A.M. that first morning, in the den of the Mackle residence. Barbara's father answered.

Robert Mackle, 56, a graying, subdued image of the affluent corporate executive, perhaps the least aggressive of the three Mackle brothers who established a land-development empire in Florida, listened intently.

A male voice instructed him to dig six inches under a rock at the edge of a cultivated clump of palms in the northeast corner of his backyard. His yard is a punched nine-iron shot off the twelfth green of the Riviera Country Club.

Buried under the rock was a test tube. Inside, the kidnappers of his daughter had left a three-page typewritten ransom note. It wasn't the original copy. It had been made by Xerox or some other reproduction apparatus.

If he was ever to see his daughter again, he must see that $500,000 in $20 bills, none with consecutive serial numbers and none older than the series of 1950, be put in a suitcase with an interior capacity of 4,000 cubic inches.

His daughter, the note declared, was buried in a box underground. Robert Mackle couldn't believe it. He couldn't not believe it either.

When the money was ready for delivery, he was to insert a want ad in the personal columns of the *Miami Herald*, "Loved One—Please come home. We will pay all expenses and meet you anywhere at any time. Your family."

He was to drive alone in his '69 Lincoln, a car he had purchased in October, and deposit the suitcase midway on the 800-foot causeway leading to Fair Island in Biscayne Bay, after waiting for a light to blink three times.

Murder Most Foul

That same Tuesday, as the Mackles flew from Atlanta to Miami by commercial Delta Airlines jet, 85 moneychangers in the board of directors room of the First National Bank of Miami began the first essential task. They counted 25,000 $20 bills, listing the numbers four columns to a page in absolute silence, as if in a deadly poker game.

The bank performed the deed as a business loan, making it at an undisclosed rate (perhaps five per cent, the lowest permitted by federal regulation).

On Wednesday the postman delivered a letter to the Mackle home. It had been postmarked Miami and incorrectly addressed to San Amaro "Dr.," rather than street. It contained Barbara's ring and the Polaroid photo.

Robert Mackle, with the advice and consent of the FBI, made one firm decision: He would obey explicitly the demands.

Even so, the want ad didn't appear immediately. The kidnapper telephoned the Church of the Little Flower in Coral Gables, where the Mackles worshipped, and a stunned, Irish-born priest, Father John Mulcahy, suddenly became an intermediary. Presumably, the kidnapper suspected a wiretap. He was right. At the Mackle household, highly sophisticated electronic equipment could identify almost instantly the human voice.

That night, waiting final instructions from the kidnapper, twenty FBI men, each with a girl borrowed from the stenographic pool, roamed Dade County by car with specific instructions not to interfere.

Finally, the call came, and Robert Mackle delivered his burden to the Fair Island sea wall as instructed. It weighed 100 pounds. He left without seeing a blinking light.

By chance that morning, a hungry sheriff's deputy, Paul Self, left his patrol on Key Biscayne and bought a sack of hamburgers at a Royal Castle nearby on the mainland. Returning, he noticed a car parked where cars seldom park on barricaded Brickell Avenue Extension.

Obviously, something was wrong. Self didn't want to use his radio. He belonged on Key Biscayne. So he returned to the Royal Castle, put a dime in the slot, and telephoned Miami police.

Soon he and Miami police officer William J. Sweeney drove to the scene. When their cars jumped a curb to get there, two startled figures ran in opposite directions, one through a mangrove.

Both officers pursued. Sweeney fired his .38 revolver. The two got away.

The officers returned to the parked car and discovered a "suitcase full of loot," an unfired carbine, and diving gear in an Army duffle bag.

Not wanting anyone to accuse them of sticky fingers, they piled into the car of a third officer and drove hurriedly to headquarters with the money locked in the trunk. This was shortly before dawn.

Capt. Lee Napier suspected what had happened. He telephoned the FBI.

Unaware, Robert Mackle had returned to the sea wall at daybreak with FBI agents to see if the money was gone. Napier's message was relayed.

"My God," he cried, slumping to the sea wall. "They're going to kill my daughter." He wept.

At this juncture, in the opinion of the FBI, the kidnappers already had had it—regardless. Their identity would soon be known.

In an ingeniously contrived crime, though, they had already blundered worse than anyone suspected.

The Volvo station wagon, registered under Massachusetts license P 72-098 to one George C. Deacon, remained at the site with an abundance of pronounced swirl-pattern fingerprints. Also the Polaroid camera.

With a Bonnie and Clyde bravado, Deacon and his girlfriend, Ruth Eisemann-Schier, had taken turns photographing themselves, Deacon in his police cap, his grinning companion—and Barbara Mackle with her eyes closed. It was all on the same roll. The separate photos, numbered consecutively, fit perfectly.

Deacon, it quickly became certain, was Gary Steven Krist, 23, an escaped California convict, aircraft and marine mechanic, electronic technician, a Ping-Pong champion with a small growth on the lobe of his right ear.

Some weeks previously his wife, Carmen, had left their Al-Ril

Trailer Park home in northwest Miami with their two young sons and moved to Redwood City, California.

"He said he just didn't love me anymore. He told me several times the dream he used to have about kidnapping someone and making a lot of money."

The wife described Krist as "highly intelligent." "He could have been anything he wanted, a doctor, even an astronaut."

Krist had told other trailer dwellers he was taking off for Arabia for eight months, that he would park his Volvo on the upper ramp at Miami International Airport, and that they were welcome to use it. Open the hood, pull on a wire, and it will unlock, he instructed them quite accurately.

At the trailer he had discarded lumber sawed from a home-built coffin.

Not far from the Volvo, the FBI had found a 13½-foot Boston Whaler, stolen from the Marine Institute where Krist worked and where his green-eyed lady friend studied as a marine biologist. In the Volvo was her passport.

Rúth Eisemann-Schier, 26, a remarkably athletic girl, conversant in English, Spanish, German, and French, apparently became infatuated with Krist last September on an institute voyage to Bermuda. She often clung to him from the back of his rented motor scooter.

All this, bursting in an investigative geyser, couldn't console Robert Mackle that morning of Thursday, December 19.

"Tell them it was an accident. Tell them not to harm her. Tell them I want to do business."

The distraught man accepted a mild sedative. He slept fitfully. Secretly, the FBI formally charged Krist and Schier under U.S. Code Title 18, the statute enacted after the celebrated Lindbergh kidnapping of 1932.

Would identification put maximum pressure to keep the girl alive—if she wasn't already dead? Or should they give the kidnapper another chance? The FBI vacillated.

Late that day Krist took a taxi to Miami Springs and rented a '69 Ford Fairlane. He drove to the emergency ward of Jackson Memorial Hospital for treatment of cuts the FBI believes he got in the mangrove thicket getaway. He said he had hurt himself in a fall. A physician sewed four stitches in his scrotum. He left without being recognized.

The vigil began again at the Mackle home.

Billy Graham telephoned from Tokyo on his way to Vietnam. He was a friend. He said he was praying.

Peculiarly and inexplicably, two sets of instructions, both from male voices, came within fifteen minutes late Thursday night; one to the priest, one to the home. The priest's was accepted.

Rightly or wrongly, Billy Vessels, a Mackle employee who gained 3,264 yards as an All-American halfback at the University of Oklahoma in 1952, is credited with driving out Tamiami Trail.

Supposedly, at SW 117th Avenue, he checked his speedometer, drove another two miles west, pulled off to his left on a dirt road, stopped near a sign that said, "Private Property, Do Not Enter," and left the suitcase.

At 1:15 P.M. Friday, almost exactly twelve hours from the drop, the kidnapper kept his part of the bargain. From West Palm Beach, he dialed 404-521-3900, the Atlanta office of the FBI.

"I'll give this to you one time," he said hurriedly.

A woman telephone operator, untutored in shorthand, frantically scribbled directions. They weren't too good.

The kidnapper mentioned an intersection in Norcross, Georgia that could have been interpreted as any one of four.

Every available agent took to the woods, searching literally in four directions. The natives took them for raiders in search of a whiskey still.

In West Palm that afternoon, Krist pulled 115 twenties from a paper bag and paid Dix Oliphant for a 16-foot boat. Krist spoke nonchalantly of a trip to Bimini.

Oliphant thought nothing of it initially. "This is a screwy business. People pay you all kinds of ways."

Then he mulled it over. He telephoned the FBI.

Elsewhere that day Krist purchased nautical charts good enough to get him to Mexico along the Gulf Coast.

The FBI office Santa Claus in Miami abruptly took off for Bimini, missing the children's Christmas party. Another agent telephoned Sherrill Prize, the assistant chief of police at Clewiston on Lake Okeechobee.

Prize began asking at fishing camps. "Yessir," said a man named Vancil, identifying a newspaper picture. "That guy filled up and bought two extra five-gallon cans."

Instantly, the FBI agent had his direction: east to west amid the pastoral beauty and the four locks of the Okeechobee Waterway. A radio hook-up of the lock tenders confirmed it. Strangely, the boatman had kept insisting he had lost a routine form at each lock.

It is only slight exaggeration to suggest that the FBI could have had the 101st Airborne Division if need be at this point.

A fixed-wing Coast Guard Albatross made the first sighting off Captiva Pass. From Miami, Tampa, Jacksonville, and Savannah, 250 FBI agents converged in aerial haste, and eventually they made the lazy R. Fish Camp at El Joebean (named for Joel Bean) their command post.

As Krist beached and abandoned his craft, leaving aboard $480,000, a hovering helicopter watched as he dropped what appeared to be a briefcase, hastily retrieved it, then vanished into the primeval foulness of swamp and mangrove that is Hog Island.

An incongruous band of manhunters, some locals with useless bloodhounds oozing in muck to their bellies, some necktied and shoeless FBI agents cradling sub-machineguns, descended upon Hog Island as darkness fell.

The poking searchlights and the parachuted flares, Mark 27s, 2 million-candlepower each, lit the sky.

Dick McLeod, a Charlotte County deputy, and Milt Buffington, a supermarket butcher deputized for the occasion, kept hearing a sloshing, then silence, then sloshing.

A flashlight beam caught the swamp- and sweat-drenched Krist, panting, aching, sitting on a stump.

"Put your hands on your head!" McLeod commanded. Krist complied, unclenching nearly $18,000 of his trophy. In his hip pocket, deputies found a pocket knife. "I'm tired," he said.

Moments later he asked for a drink of water. A deputy motioned toward the brackish swamp water.

"Drink that, you son of a bitch."

The FBI would soon possess all but "two small digits" of the initial six-digit $500,000.

Five days later Krist's accused partner in crime, the missing Miss Schier, would attain the distinction of becoming the first woman ever to make the FBI's "ten most wanted" list, after 273 predecessors.

"I think he killed her," said her landlady, Mrs. Winston F. Harrison, a receptionist at the University of Miami marine lab. "I think she is in a hole somewhere."

The FBI tends to disagree.

At the Mackle home Barbara Mackle, posing for an up-close photograph, said, "Daddy, you're sticking your nose in my eye."

The man Robert Mackle calls "Dick" until Inauguration Day, another good friend, stopped by for a chat and spoke of a book. "It'll be for charity," said Robert Mackle.

Barbara spoke of Gatorade drinks and skimming the hundreds of letters and telegrams to the family, including one wedding proposal.

"Not from George Hamilton," she deadpanned.

"That girl is class, pure class," said an FBI man who also cries.

For several weeks after the kidnapping, Ruth Eisemann-Schier worked as a car hop in Norman, Oklahoma. Her application for a job at a hospital led to her arrest. The hospital required fingerprints, which were identified by Oklahoma authorities. Gary Steven Krist went to trial on May 21, 1969 in Georgia, where kidnapping was punishable by death. Five days later, while the jury was out, a reporter asked him what would be proper punishment for a man who kidnapped for ransom. "Bury the guy in a box for about three months and see how he likes it," Krist replied. The jury found him guilty, but recommended mercy. Krist got off with life and was paroled in May, 1979 on the condition that he return to his home in Alaska. Ms. Schier served three years in prison, then was deported to her native Honduras. In 1971, Barbara Mackle married her college sweetheart, Stewart H. Woodward.

Jailed Frederick Woods dreams of riches from Chowchilla kidnapping

When a schoolbus carrying twenty-six children seemingly vanished from Chowchilla, California on July 15, 1976, there was speculation that it might even be the work of fiends from outer space. Actually, the three perpetrators were average-looking earthlings who had a fantasy about making a movie. They herded the group into vans at gunpoint for a 95-mile ride to a rock quarry near Livermore. There, the children and their driver were imprisoned in a buried, but ventilated, moving van until they scratched their way to freedom seventeen hours later. The abductors, who were arrested and jailed quickly, pleaded guilty to twenty-seven counts of ransom kidnapping. Jail, however, didn't destroy their fantasy, as David Johnston and Robert Kistler reported in the *Los Angeles Times* of August 1, 1977.

From his cell on the tenth floor of the Alameda County Courthouse in downtown Oakland, Frederick N. Woods is still scheming to make a fast buck from the Chowchilla kidnappings.

On sheets of toilet paper confiscated by jailers and obtained by the *Los Angeles Times*, Woods wrote to his fellow kidnappers and jailmates, James and Richard Schoenfeld: "If I make any money for writing a book then it will be split three ways of course."

The scrawled messages refer to plans by Fred and Jim to "tell (the) truth" in a movie about the crime and of how once the evidence against them is entered into court records "we are open for DEALS." The word "deals," written in large capital letters, is underlined.

Not incidentally, it was a fantasy about making a movie that defense attorney Lester Gendron says landed the three behind bars, where they may spend the rest of their lives. It is a fantasy that, the toilet paper notes indicate, still captivates Fred and perhaps his companions as well.

For more than a year, "Chowchilla" has been a code word to many for an unspeakable horror: twenty-six schoolchildren and their bus driver, seized at gunpoint and forced into a hole in the ground with no inkling of what their fate might be.

For some of the captives, the living nightmare that was July 15 and 16, 1976 may never entirely go away. One boy was so emotionally traumatized, the prosecution plans to argue, that he suffered permanent kidney damage.

When the three go on trial soon to determine if they inflicted "bodily harm" on their captives, at least a dozen of the children will be forced to recall from the witness stand the details of those two days, forcing those details through their minds like reruns of an old horror movie.

Should Superior Court Judge Leo Deegan find in the non-jury trial that "bodily harm" was inflicted, it means mandatory life imprisonment without possibility of parole for the kidnappers.

Why, and how, did Fred Woods, 25, and the Schoenfelds—Jim is 25, Richard, 24—conceive of and then carry out the kidnapping of a busload of schoolchildren?

They came from backgrounds that offered them an abundance of the advantages so sought after by modern society. Woods' parents are wealthy (Fred's middle name is Newhall, tying him to a vast California land fortune) and the Schoenfelds' father is a successful podiatrist.

All three went to Woodside High School, academically one of the best in the nation, travelled around the world, and had all the time they wanted to fix up the cars that littered a large field at the Hawthornes, the 100-acre Woods estate on the San Francisco Peninsula.

The Schoenfeld brothers worked part-time, mostly when and how they felt like it. Woods spent his time pretty much as he chose.

Their lives were not even touched by that most common of tragedies among modern families—parental divorce.

Murder Most Foul

Last week the three pleaded guilty to twenty-seven counts of kidnapping for ransom, which carries a maximum sentence of life in prison. Because of those pleas, there will be no trial on the basic issues of the case, no legal vehicle through which to pursue the answers to the haunting question—why Chowchilla?

The keys to understanding Chowchilla are to be found in the minds of the three young men. From extensive interviews by *Times* reporters with close friends and associates of the kidnappers and from writing by Jim and the others, a picture emerges.

It is a picture of three not very bright young men with amorphous goals, few responsibilities, and little understanding of the consequences of their acts. It is a picture of three young men who feared that the easy life-styles they had always known might be coming to an end and that a life with financial uncertainties lay ahead.

And it is a picture of three young men fascinated by television programs and movies that were loaded with action—even if they lacked much of a story line—and who happened to make the acquaintance of a would-be Hollywood scriptwriter from San Jose, California.

To the kidnappers' way of thinking, their friends believe, Chowchilla was not a monstrous crime but a caper, a way to put some adventure into their existence and ensure they would have plenty of money to continue living the good life without having to work for it. Incredibly, the kidnappers apparently thought not of the potential consequences of their actions—of mass violence and death—but only of what in their mind was a nonviolent crime.

As the kidnappers viewed it, they would simply borrow some children for a few hours and, after collecting $5 million from whomever, return the children to their mothers and fathers. The children would be unharmed, at least on the physical level—which apparently was the only one the kidnappers seriously considered.

In their own curious way, the three went to considerable lengths to provide for the physical comfort of their captives. For example, the moving van that they buried in a Livermore rock quarry owned by Fred's father was stocked with the foods that Jim liked best: potato chips, bread, peanut butter, and dry breakfast cereals. That no milk was available for the breakfast cereals came as no surprise to Jim's friends and neighbors. They said he could be seen munching the cereals, dry, from his hand at all hours of the day.

Concern for the physical comfort of the captives is also evident in the mattresses placed inside the van, the makeshift battery-powered ventilation system Jim rigged up to provide outside air. Said a friend of the elder Schoenfeld: "Jim could spend hours lost in planning every detail of that ventilation system, just how it would work, how much air would be needed, what size fans to use, how to wire them, without ever thinking once about what it really meant."

Fred had the same kind of vision, associates said, seeing things but failing to comprehend their larger meaning. David E. Boston, the would-be scriptwriter, recalled travelling to Europe once with Fred. Boston said he hoped to meet people and acquire a feel for the culture of the places they visited. "Fred just wanted to drive through countries, through as many as he could, which was completely boring to me," Boston said. "He just wanted to drive...."

All three kidnappers were naive, unquestioning about the world around them and why and how it worked. That attitude made Rick popular with his bosses at the Stanford Linear Accelerator Center in Palo Alto, California, where he worked part-time as an on-call mailroom attendant. Michele Bondi, a co-worker who had been to dinner with Rick a few times, said, "If I asked him to take out the trash thirty times an hour, he would do it without question."

Jim worked part-time as a clerk for the U.S. Geological Survey in Menlo Park. It was there that he obtained maps used by the trio to choose seventeen California cities as possible kidnapping sites: Atwater, Copperopolis, Denair, Dos Palos, Hollister, LeGrand, Merced, Merced Falls, Panoche Valley, Riverbank, Sacramento, San Jose, Santa Cruz, Santa Rosa, Sonora, Tracy...and Chowchilla.

There is evidence the three scouted the other sites, but rejected them for various reasons, mainly because they offered less security from chance observation during the stopping and hiding of a school bus. Chowchilla, on the other hand, has many flat, little-used roads lined with tall brush. It has easy access to two state highways, 152 and 99, which the kidnappers used to speed their captives to the rock quarry about 100 miles away. Chowchilla was probably picked simply because it was the easiest and most convenient place the kidnappers found.

Even after this careful site selection, the kidnapping almost never occurred. It had been set for the day before it actually happened, but the kidnappers parked their van at the wrong place on the road, and the bus turned off before it reached them.

All three kidnappers lived at home and had pocket money. All, especially the Schoenfeld brothers, went out of their way to endear themselves to adults, particularly their friends' parents.

There were pressures on them to begin careers and become serious about life. "Jim never had a major in college," his best friend said. "He never got around to getting one. I was always bugging him, saying, 'Jim, you've got to get a major and get a career.' His dad was worried. Here he is, twenty-five years old and nothing going for him. And he wasn't too motivated to get something going, either."

Dr. John Schoenfeld and his wife, Merry, talked openly in front of their sons and the sons' friends about selling their four-bedroom home in Atherton. They spoke of moving into a smaller place, one too small for Jim, and perhaps for Rick, to live in.

Fred was under pressure too. He had been married briefly, then divorced. His relations with his father were strained. The father, Frederick Nickerson Woods, had gone to Stanford and was intensely interested in athletics and classic cars, like his 1917 Pierce Arrow. The son spent most of his time fixing up prosaic, worn-out sedans purchased at government auctions.

After Fred's arrest, his father co-operated fully with the police. He also complained to them repeatedly that because of his son he would miss attending the summer Olympics for the first time since 1928.

Fred knew that someday he would come into a lot of money. He had ideas for spending it, like a device for fighting forest fires that he conceived but never worked on seriously. The kidnapping was financed with part of $50,000 that Fred got by arranging to have lunch with an elderly aunt who lives at the Hawthornes and then simply asking her to write out a check for that amount.

None of the three had a large circle of friends. They were so quiet, in fact, that to this day some of their teachers at Woodside High can look at their names in grade books and not recall them.

None of the Schoenfeld brothers' friends cared for Fred—and some distinctly disliked him. But he was tolerated, they said, because they liked Jim and he was Jim's friend. Each of half a dozen young women used the same word to describe Fred to two reporters: "creep." Once, when Jim and Fred were in their early twenties, they stopped by Jim's next-door neighbors', where some fourteen- and fifteen-year-old girls were having a party. Fred, said three sources who were present, literally draped himself over some of the young girls, making them so uncomfortable that an older sister finally went to Jim. "Get that creep out of here," she told Jim.

Even Jim had trouble sorting out his thoughts about Fred. Jim kept a diary, parts of which he wrote in English and parts in a code he made up but told friends was Russian or Persian. Curiously, he sometimes wrote of mundane matters using the code while making incriminating entries in plain English.

Once he made two columns, one headed "With Fred Woods" and the other "Without Fred Woods." Life without Fred, Jim wrote, would be filled with "uncertainties...dull...boring life that one would regret...." Life with Fred, he wrote, had "possibilities ...gold mine... possible arrest for illegal activities...." With Fred he might get rich, he wrote, or he might end up where he is today—in jail.

Jim and Fred liked boyish pranks, even though their ages were beyond boyhood. Once they took two diesel truck cabs to a Mountain View drive-in theater to see a trucking movie, the kind Fred liked. Another time Fred went to a root beer stand and used a public-address system in his car to send electronic feedback through the microphone system the root beer stand had for placing orders. As the car hops scurried about trying to find the source of the eerie noise, Fred laughed. His companion, who told the story, said he was embarrassed and sat quietly.

Jim told detectives after his capture that the crime had its genesis in talks between Fred and Boston, this would-be scriptwriter, about possible movie plots. Police subpoenaed a script by Boston, "The Ransom of San Francisco," which consisted of a collection of disjointed dramatizations seemingly drawn from headlines in Bay Area newspapers in recent years. Police say Boston had no involvement in the crime but only innocently awakened ideas in Fred's mind.

While he was on the run, Fred wrote to Boston that Chowchilla would make "a damn good movie of the week, if not a feature...." Fred said he would co-operate with Boston in return for a percentage of the film's profits but cautioned that the real-life ending "is not exciting enough so you might have to kill some people or something."

Fred and Boston had earlier formed a company, Townhouse Enterprises, Inc. Boston said they planned "to buy cars at auction, fix them up, and raise the money to make a low-budget action film." Fred, Boston said, "liked car chases and figured if we could get enough old cars we could smash them up. Mostly he just liked visual action. He liked mostly action and very little story line."

It was while Boston was using an old railroad car at the Hawthornes to make a surrealistic science-fiction film, "The Red Caboose," for a college class, that Fred's appetite for films was whetted. Boston let Fred hold the lights and even gave him a bit part, with his back to the camera.

The kidnappers went to the movies often, especially to a Redwood City theater that charged only a dollar to see second-, third-, and fourth-run action films. The three, and Boston, were intrigued by "Dirty Harry," a 1971 Clint Eastwood movie about a homicidal maniac in San Francisco. Every major element of the Chowchilla crime can be found in "Dirty Harry," a movie that Jim's friends said he sat through at least five times.

The plot includes a woman who is kidnapped and placed in a hole in the ground after one of her teeth is removed with a pair of pliers and sent to the police, the kidnapping of a school bus full of children, and a demand for ransom from the mayor of San Francisco.

The Chowchilla kidnappers were less brutal than their movie

counterpart. They took trinkets from the children as they forced them into the buried van, and Jim wrote their names down on the back of a white Jack-in-the-Box sack. "Dirty Harry" even ends at a rock quarry. Clint Eastwood, who plays the detective in the title role, saves the children and guns down the kidnapper.

The transition from movie plot to real kidnapping was simple. Jim, who once wrote in his diary that he let Fred talk him too easily into doing what Fred wanted, was asked by detectives how it all began. "Oh, I think Fred mentioned it a year ago, and I told him he was nuts—I just dismissed it," Jim said. "And then when Fred came up with, 'Well, let's do some preliminary stuff.' Well, that just wouldn't hurt—bringing this van and stuff like that."

The mother of the Schoenfeld brothers blames violent and amoral television shows and movies for what her sons did. "The movies portray police as stupid and dumb," she told the *Redwood City Tribune*. "I blame it on that and the crazy morals portrayed."

In the real-life kidnapping, it was not the police, though, who were dumb. Even if bus driver Ed Ray and the children had not dug their way out of their potential tomb, lawmen were hot on the suspects' trail. Defense lawyer Gendron says, "There is no way it would have worked."

Charles Bates, a retired FBI man who worked on Chowchilla, said he was amazed at how easy it was to solve. "I've never seen a case where everything you did fit," he said. "It was just like a TV movie of a crime."

In late 1977, Frederick N. Woods and James and Richard Schoenfeld were sentenced to life in prison without possibility of parole after they were found guilty of causing bodily harm to three of the twenty-six children they admitted kidnapping.

Jesse James.

Chapter IX

OLD WEST

Jesse James gang raids Northfield bank; teller murdered in cold blood

On the morning of September 7, 1876, a band of outlaws composed of Jesse and Frank James, Bill Chadwell, Clell Miller, Charlie Pitts, and Bob, Jim, and Cole Younger rode into quiet Northfield, Minnesota, firing wildly to frighten citizens off the streets. They robbed the town bank, killing a cashier who tried to resist them. The following report from the scene, confusing in its varied eyewitness accounts, appeared in the next day's *Cincinnati Commercial*.

During yesterday forenoon, three common-looking men rode into town and tied their horses in front of a store. They did not appear to have particular business, but sauntered about and chatted with several citizens on ordinary topics.

At two o'clock a party of five more men rode leisurely across the bridge leading to town. No sooner had they crossed the river than they all drew revolvers and, putting their horses into a full gallop, dashed through the street, shouting to the people on the walks to get into the stores, and ornamenting their shouts with the most fiendish curses and imprecations.

While the attention of the citizens was called to the proceedings of these villains, the three who had arrived earlier rushed into the bank and leaped over the counter.

One accosted J. L. Haywood and asked if he was the cashier. He replied that he was not, but they insisted that he should open the safe, which he had closed immediately after banker Taisey had left. The robber brandished a knife and told Haywood that unless

267

Murder Most Foul

he opened the safe, his throat would be cut from ear to ear.

Haywood replied that he would have to cut it then, for he could not open the safe.

Just at this moment, firing was heard outside, and the robbers called to their comrades to "charge out of the bank." The men leaped over the counter, one of them fired at A. E. Bunker, a clerk, wounding him in the shoulder, and another turned and pointed his pistol at Haywood, who stooped beneath the counter as quickly as possible, but not soon enough, as the fatal shot entered his right temple while only the upper portion of his head was visible.

The men rushed from the bank, leaped onto their horses and joined the remainder of the gang.

The outside robbers, after making a dash into town, gathered about the bank, on the steps of which one of them met a merchant. The robber seized this gentleman by the throat and threatened to "blow his head off if he squealed." But the merchant succeeded in getting away and ran into the street crying, "Murder! Robbers!"

Two shots, both harmless, were dispatched after him, and these shots, together with the cries of the man, caused the citizens to know that the invaders were something more than a gang of reckless drunks.

Pistols and guns were quickly secured, and from the second-story window of a building opposite the bank, a young man named Henry Wheeler picked off one of the robbers, shooting him through the heart.

Another shot, thought to be from Wheeler, prostrated another villain, and they found it was time to retreat. It was at this time that the inside men were called out. A third robber was hit, but as his comrades rode off, they picked him up and slung him onto a horse in front of one of them.

Haywood occupied the cashier's seat at a desk at the end of the counter. Bunker and Frank Wilcox occupied seats at the desk, Bunker being nearest the opening at the corner.

"The first thing we knew, the three men were upon or over the counter, with revolvers presented at our heads, one of them exclaiming: 'Throw up your hands, for we intend to rob the bank, and if you halloo, we will blow your brains out,' and we could not do otherwise than comply," Wilcox said.

"They asked which was the cashier, to which Haywood replied: 'He is not in.' They sprang over the counter and demanded the safe to be opened.

"Addressing each in turn, they said, 'You are the cashier,' which each denied. Seeing Haywood seated at the cashier's desk, one of the ruffians went up to him with his long, narrow-barreled pistol and said, 'You are the cashier. Now open the safe.' "

Haywood said, "It is a time lock and cannot be opened now."

One of the men then went into the vault, the door being opened, also the outer door of the safe. Haywood at once sprang forward and closed the door of the vault, shoving the robber in, when another of the men seized Haywood by the collar and dragged him away from the door and released the incarcerated robber.

The man who came out of the vault—a slim, dark-complexioned man with a black mustache—then called to the other to seize the silver, which was lying loose (about fifteen dollars), and put it into the sack.

They did not do this, but seized about twelve dollars in script and put it into a two-bushel flour sack that they had with them.

The dark-complexioned man, who appeared to be the leader, then attacked Haywood again, insisting upon his opening the safe, threatening to cut his throat if he did not, and actually drawing a big knife across his throat.

The heroic and faithful teller, however, was not to be deterred from his duties, and would rather sacrifice his life than betray his trust. Some few moments—it seemed ages to the bewildered and terror-stricken lookers-on—were spent in Haywood's struggling to break from the murderous villain and gain his liberty.

At length he broke away, and, regaining his feet, ran toward the door, crying "Murder!"

The man at once struck him with a pistol and knocked him down, and, dragging him to the safe door, commanded him to open it. But the intrepid clerk stolidly refused, when the villain shot at him but did not hit him. Evidently, the shot was intended to intimidate rather than to injure, but the scoundrel had reckoned without his host, for the effect was lost upon Haywood. But upon the discharge of the pistol, Bunker made a start for the back door and ran for dear life, one of the robbers pursuing and firing, the shot taking effect in the shoulder.

Bunker reached the street and ran into Dr. Coombs' office.

A statement of G. E. Bates, who witnessed that part of the affair that occurred in the streets, is interesting. Bates said that about eleven o'clock, his attention was called to four men who came from over the river. They came over the bridge, and were mounted on four splendid horses. The men were well-dressed, and Bates says four nobler-looking fellows he never saw; but there was a reckless, bold swagger about them that seemed to indicate that they would be rough and dangerous to handle. Altogether, he did not like the looks of them.

Again, about 2:00 in the afternoon, as he was standing at the entrance to the store, talking to C. C. Waldo, commercial traveller from Council Bluffs, he saw the same men ride past—three came up the street from Mill Square and one down the street, moving within thirty feet of the bank.

They dismounted and tied their horses to the hitching posts, and two, he thought, went into the bank and two came down to the staircase leading to the upper story of Lee & Hitchcock's building, and there they stood against the bannisters, talking.

Commenting on their fine physiques and their unusually good mounts, Bates and Waldo withdrew to the far end of the store to look over some sample trusses. They had not long been so occupied when they heard several shots fired in rapid succession, and the thought flashed upon the mind of Bates at once that the bank was in danger, Waldo stating that he cried out, "Them men are going for the town; they mean to rob the bank," although Bates does not recollect saying anything, he became so excited.

He remembers, however, rushing to the door, and seeing some men riding up from the bank. They came riding toward him with long pistols in their hands and called out, "Get in there."

Bates at once seized a shotgun and ran back to the door, but the gun would not go off. He then put down the gun and seized a seven-shooter, which was not loaded, and as the men came down again (they were riding to and fro, evidently intent upon keeping people from going toward the bank), he called out, "Now I've got you," and pointed the empty pistol as if drawing a bead on them.

Old West

They turned their horses suddenly and fired at Bates, the ball crashing through the plate glass. This ruse he practiced over and over again with the same effect. There were other men at the bank firing down the street. The next he saw was J. S. Allen running down the street from the bank, and two shots were fired at him.

Manning of Mill Square, whose store is in the same block as the bank, next came upon the scene. He ran out of his store with a Remington repeating rifle, and took a deliberate aim and fired from the corner, Bates calling out, "Jump back now or they'll get you."

Next J. B. Hide came up with a double-barrelled shotgun and discharged the two barrels and retired to reload.

The Reverend Phillips also took a turn at the scoundrels. Bates next heard a report over his head, and saw one of the desperadoes fall from his horse. The horse made a faltering plunge forward and then suddenly stopped, and the man pitched over on his face to the ground, and in a few moments was dead.

This shot was fired by Wheeler from one of the windows of the Dampier House, from the very room in which this report is written.

Manning was still firing, and as he crept to the corner to fire, Waldo called, "Take good aim before you fire." Immediately after the shot, one of the horses started up the street, and the rider began to reel and sway to and fro, and suddenly fell to the ground, just opposite Eldridge's store.

Another horseman immediately rode up, dismounted, and spoke to the prostrate man, who was stretched out at full length, supporting himself on his outstretched arms, when he rolled over on his back. Then the other man took from him his cartridge belt and two pistols and, remounting, rode off.

Another horseman, finding Manning's fire too hot, dismounted and got on the opposite side of his horse for protection, when an unerring ball from the Remington brought the horse down, the man running behind some boxes that were piled beneath the staircase before mentioned, and now ensued a lively fusillade between this fellow and Manning, the scoundrel keeping himself well under cover.

But a ball from Wheeler's musket struck the fellow on the leg,

271

halfway above the knee. He at once changed his pistol to the left hand and grasped the wounded limb with the right, still trying to get Manning. Finding himself getting weak, he turned and limped off up the street, but, seeing Bates with a pistol in his hand, he sent a ball whizzing toward that gentleman, grazing the side of his cheek and the bridge of his nose, and burying itself in a collar box in the store.

The man cried out to his retreating companions, "My God, boys, you're not going to leave me; I am shot."

One of the party, riding a sorrel horse with white tail and mane, turned and took up the wounded man behind him.

The bandits killed in Northfield were Charlie Pitts and Bill Chadwell. The other six headed southwest, pursued by almost every able-bodied man in Northfield. The governor offered a $1,000 reward for each of the six, dead or alive. Jesse and Frank James split off from the other four and escaped unscratched. A week after the robbery, the posse caught up with the Youngers and Clell Miller. In a brief gun battle—150 men against 4—Miller was killed and the Youngers were badly wounded. They were tried and convicted but, thanks to able counsel, escaped hanging. Bob Younger died in prison of tuberculosis in 1889. Cole and Jim Younger were paroled in 1901 after serving twenty-five years. Jim, failing as a travelling salesman, subsequently committed suicide. Cole went on the lecture circuit, earning a comfortable income until shortly before his death in 1916.

Pat Garrett's bullet takes Billy the Kid in his stocking feet

The life of Billy the Kid is our greatest legend of the Old West. Dozens of songs, books, and movies and at least one ballet have been written about him, portraying him variously as a Robin Hood and as a cold-blooded killer. In truth, he was neither of those. It is untrue that he killed twenty men and vowed to make Sheriff Pat Garrett the twenty-first, giving Billy a notch on his gun for every year of his life. Only four killings are documented. He was fast with a gun, not especially bright, was attractive to many women, and intensely loyal to his friends. Garrett caught up with the Kid in July, 1881 at Fort Sumner, New Mexico, and the *Las Vegas* (New Mexico) *Daily Optic* of July 18, 1881 published the following "particulars of the affair as poured into the ears of eager reporters."

Pat Garrett, the terror of all evildoers in this lower country, planted a ball with his unerring deadly aim in the heart of "Billy the Kid" Thursday about midnight.

Pat had come up to Fort Sumner on account of so many rumors reaching him that the Kid was lurking in that place or vicinity. About the hour mentioned, Pat rode up near the town and, in company with John W. Poe and T. M. McKinney, started on an exploring expedition. Pat went into Pete Maxwell's room to get what news he could of the Kid, and he had not been there two minutes before the Kid, in his stocking feet, entered the room and walked up to the bed (on the edge of which Pat was sitting talking to Maxwell), with a pistol (self-cocker) in one hand and a big butcher knife in the other.

Pat reached behind him for his pistol, and, at the action, the Kid dropped his pistol on him and asked in Spanish, "¿Quien es?"

"Billy the Kid."

Sheriff Pat Garrett.
(Courtesy Newberry Library, Chicago)

This delay in firing on the Kid's part gave Pat all the time he needed, and the words were barely uttered before Pat's dauntless courage had driven a ball through the center of the Kid's heart. He died in a moment, almost without a groan.

The belief is that the Kid received intelligence of Pat's presence and was searching for him at the time, or that he had gone to murder Maxwell in his bed.

An inquest was held on his body today, and the verdict of the jury was "justifiable homicide, and that Pat Garrett ought to receive the thanks of the whole community for his indomitable courage and energy in ridding the country of this desperado, and that he is truly worthy of a handsome reward."

* * *

George Miller, colored sergeant, Company G, 9th Cavalry, enroute from Fort Stanton to Santa Fe, arrived in Las Vegas last evening and confirms the death of the young desperado. On Thursday night, July 14, Miller stopped at the hotel in Fort Sumner, and about 12:30 A.M. his peaceful slumber was disturbed by two pistol shots fired in rapid succession. The sounds proceeded from the house of Pete Maxwell, distant about twenty-five yards, and soon the startling information, "Billy the Kid is killed," was the theme of every tongue.

The wild inquiry, "Who killed him?" was answered by the facts that soon became known to all. Pat Garrett had done it with his trusty revolver, backed up by cool judgment and undaunted courage. It appears that Sheriff Pat Garrett had ascertained from a sheepherder that Billy was prowling around in the vicinity of Fort Sumner, and, acting upon this intelligence, he concluded to visit that place and see if he could effect the arrest of the desperado.

In company with two plucky men, Garrett rode into Sumner about midnight and ascertained that Billy was stopping at the house of a Mexican named Juan Chavez. Not deeming it best to swoop down upon him as he was undoubtedly on the alert for danger, the sheriff and his two followers proceeded to Maxwell's house, the two latter remaining outside, and made inquiries in regard to the whereabouts of the Kid.

Billy's presence was confirmed by Maxwell, and, as the words escaped from his lips, a man in his stocking feet, with a Bowie knife in one hand, a drawn revolver in the other, and a silk handerchief around his neck, entered the room, in which there was no light, and asked for some meat.

Almost in the same breath, he inquired in Spanish who the men were outside. Not receiving an immediate reply, he made the inquiry in English. His voice was recognized by Garrett, who was standing in a rear part of the room, and, in the least possible time imaginable, almost, the fatal bullet from Garrett's revolver had entered the Kid's heart. Another shot was fired in quick order, but it missed its mark, the form of the desperado having fallen in the icy embrace of death. On Friday morning, a coroner's inquest was held, and, in the afternoon, his mortal remains were interred in the cemetery at Fort Sumner.

****

Sheriff Pat Garrett, Lincoln County, arrived in the city today in company with Pete Maxwell, at whose house Billy the Kid was shot, and, soon after, he was corralled by an *Optic* reporter.

Pat, as is well known, has no desire to parade his experiences before the public. Consequently, he had very little to say about the affair of which he is the hero. However, he stated to eager listeners that the first definite information he received that the Kid was at Fort Sumner was contained in a letter written to him by Mr. Brazil.

Immediately upon receiving the news, he set out for that place, taking with him John Poe and Kit McKinney. Arriving in town, they went to Maxwell's house, where Pat advanced and entered, leaving his companions at the door, and, in a low tone of voice, asked Pete if Billy the Kid were on his premises.

Pat was told that he was not, but not far off. The conversation between the two men had not lasted two minutes when a man in his stocking feet, heavily armed and with a stealthy step, pushed the open door noiselessly aside and entered. Maxwell took in the situation at a glance and whispered in scarcely audible tones,

Death warrant of "Billy the Kid."
(Courtesy Newberry Library, Chicago)

county, and there, between the hours of
ten o'clock, A.M., and three o'clock,
P.M., of said day, you hang the
said William Bonny, alias Kid, alias
William Antrim by the neck until
he is dead. And make due return of your acts hereunder.

Done at Santa Fe' in
the Territory of New
Mexico, this 30th day
of April, A.D. 1881.
Witness my hand and
the great seal of the
Territory.

By the Governor
W. G. Ritch
Secretary
N.M.

Lew Wallace,
Governor New Mexico.

"That's him."

Pat knew what that meant, but had not time to prepare himself for action until the outlaw approached the bed on which Maxwell was reclining and near which sat Garrett, and, seeing a third party in the room, demanded of him, "Who are you?" Again the question was asked, aimed at a man the Kid little thought was Garrett. The latter, who had taken advantage of the dim, uncertain light to get his weapon ready for use, brought it to bear upon the Kid, shooting him through the heart at the first pull of the trigger.

The Kid died in two minutes without uttering a word. A second shot was fired without effect.

As will be seen from the above thoroughly reliable sources, Billy the Kid, the terror not only of Lincoln County but of the whole territory, a young desperado who has long been noted as a bold thief, a cold-blooded murderer, having perhaps killed more men than any other man of his age in the world, has at last received his just dues.

All mankind rejoices and the newspapers will now have something else to talk about. It is now in order for Pat Garrett to be well rewarded for his services in ridding the territory of this desperado. He is in very moderate circumstances, but has spent many dollars in his pursuit of the Kid.

Already, we understand, a subscription paper is circulating for this purpose. It should be signed by all. Other counties, who alike breathe easier because the Kid is dead, should join in and make substantial showing of their appreciation of the cool, brave conduct of Pat Garrett.

The next day, the *Optic* told its readers: "The revolver that killed Billy the Kid was from Haughton's establishment. This is not an advertisement, but an interesting fact." The Kid was buried in a cheap pine box, and the *Optic* of July 20 commented: "The doctors of Las Vegas are anxious to procure the 'stiff' that was once the animated person of Billy the Kid. If Billy has any friends who hallow his name, they had better keep close watch on that stiff." A public subscription campaign raised several hundred dollars to reward Garrett, Poe, and McKinney.

Gunfight at OK Corral: the Earps and Holliday send three to eternity

This account of the legendary gunfight at OK Corral is from the *Tombstone* (Arizona) *Daily Epitaph* of Thursday, October 27, 1881.

Stormy as were the early days of Tombstone, nothing ever occurred equal to the event of yesterday. Since the retirement of Ben Sippy as marshal and the appointment of Virgil Earp to fill the vacancy, the town has been noted for its quietness and good order. The fractious and formerly much-dreaded cowboys were upon their good behavior, and no unseemly brawls were indulged in.

It seems that this quiet state of affairs was but the calm that precedes the storm that burst in all its fury yesterday.

Since the arrest of Frank Stilwell and Pete Spence for the robbery of the Bisbee stage, there have been oft-repeated threats conveyed to the Earp brothers—Virgil, Morgan, and Wyatt—that the friends of the accused would get even with them. The active part the Earps have always taken in going after stage robbers has made them exceedingly obnoxious with the bad element of this country and put their lives in jeopardy every month.

Sometime Tuesday, Ike Clanton came into town and had some little talk with Doc Holliday and Virgil Earp, but it was nothing to cause either to suspect that he was thirsting for blood. Shortly after this occurred, someone came to the marshal and told him that Frank and Tom McLowry had been seen a short time before, just below town. Marshal Earp, not knowing what might happen and feeling his responsibility for the preservation of the peace and order of the city, stayed on duty all night and added to the police force his brother Morgan and Holliday.

281

The night passed without disturbance, and at sunrise he went home and retired to sleep. A short time afterward, one of his brothers came to his home and told him that Clanton was hunting him, with threats of shooting him on sight. He discredited the report and did not get out of bed.

It was not long before another of his brothers came down and told him the same thing, whereupon he got up, dressed, and went with his brother Morgan up town. They walked up Allen Street to Fifth, crossed over to Fremont and down to Fourth, where they came upon Clanton, who had a Winchester rifle in his hand and a revolver on his hip.

The marshal walked up to Clanton, grabbed the rifle and hit him at the same time with a blow on the head, stunning him so that he was able to disarm him without further trouble. He marched Clanton off to the police court, where he entered a complaint against him for carrying deadly weapons. The court fined Clanton $25 and costs, making $27.50 altogether.

Close upon the heels of this came the finale, which is best told in the words of R. F. Coleman, who was an eyewitness from the beginning to the end. Coleman says:

"I was in the OK Corral at 2:30 P.M. when I saw the two Clantons (Ike and Bill) and the two McLowry boys (Frank and Tom) in earnest conversation across the street in Dunbar's Corral. I went up the street and notified Sheriff (Johnny) Behan, and told him it was my opinion they meant trouble. I told him they had gone to the West End Corral.

"I then went and saw Marshal Earp, and notified him to the same effect. I then met Billy Allen, and we walked through the OK Corral, about fifty yards behind the sheriff.

"On reaching Fremont Street, I saw Virgil Earp, Wyatt Earp, Morgan Earp, and Doc Holliday, in the center of the street, all armed. I had reached Bauer's meat market and Behan had just left the cowboys, after having a conversation with them. I went along to Fly's photograph gallery, when I heard Virgil Earp say, 'Give up your arms, or throw up your arms.'

"There was some reply by Frank McLowry, but at the same moment there were two shots fired simultaneously by Doc Holliday and Frank McLowry. When the firing became general, over thirty shots were fired.

"Tom McLowry fell first, but raised and fired again before he died. Bill Clanton fell next, and raised to fire again when Mr. Fly took his revolver from him. Frank McLowry ran a few rods and fell. Morgan Earp was shot through and fell. Doc Holliday was hit in the left hip, but kept on firing. Virgil Earp was hit in the third or fourth fire in the leg, which staggered him, but he kept up his effective work.

"Wyatt Earp stood up and fired in rapid succession, as cool as a cucumber, and was not hit. Doc Holliday was as calm as if at target practice, and fired rapidly.

"After the firing was over Sheriff Behan went up to Wyatt Earp and said, 'I'll have to arrest you.' Wyatt replied, 'I won't be arrested today. I am right here and am not going away. You have deceived me. You told me those men were disarmed. I went to disarm them.' "

Coleman's story, in the most essential particulars, has been confirmed by others.

Marshal Earp says that he and his party met the Clantons and McLowrys in the alley by the McDonald place; he called to them to throw up their hands, that he had come to disarm them. Instantaneously, Bill Clanton and one of the McLowrys fired, and then it became general.

Marshal Earp says that it was the first shot from Frank McLowry that hit him. In other particulars his statement does not materially differ from Coleman's statement.

The two McLowrys and Bill Clanton all died within a few minutes after being shot. The marshal was shot through the calf of the right leg, the ball going clear through. His brother Morgan was shot through the shoulders, the ball entering the point of the right shoulder blade, following across the back, shattering off a piece of one of the vertebrae, and passing out the left shoulder in about the same position that it entered the right. This wound is dangerous but not necessarily fatal, and Virgil's is far more painful than dangerous. Doc Holliday was hit upon the scabbard of his pistol, the leather breaking the force of the ball so that no material damage was done other than to make him limp a little.

The feeling among the best class of our citizens is that the marshal was entirely justified in his efforts to disarm these men, and that being fired upon they had to defend themselves, which they did most bravely. So long as our peace officers make an effort to preserve the peace and put down highway robbery—which the Earp brothers have done—they will have the support of all good citizens.

If the present lesson is not sufficient to teach the cowboy element that they cannot come into the streets of Tombstone in broad daylight, armed with six-shooters and rifles to hunt down their victims, then the citizens most assuredly will take such steps to preserve the peace as will be forever a bar to further raids.

Virgil Earp was crippled for life from the wound described in the *Epitaph* story. Morgan Earp recovered, but was murdered March 17, 1882 by ambushers thought to include Frank Stilwell and Pete Spence. Doc Holliday died of tuberculosis four years after the gunfight. Wyatt Earp tracked down and killed the men he believed ambushed Morgan, and then retired to a quiet life in California, where he died in 1929 at age eighty.

Robert Ford shoots Jesse James in back; outlaw dies instantly

The legend of Jesse James is second only to that of Billy the Kid. James was shot in the back the morning of April 3, 1882 in St. Joseph, Missouri by a young man he trusted, Robert Ford. This story is reprinted from the St. Joseph Evening News of that day.

Between eight and nine o'clock this morning Jesse James, the Missouri outlaw, before whom the deeds of Frank Diavolo, Dick Turpin, and Schinderhannes dwindled into insignificance, was instantly killed at his temporary residence on the corner of 13th and Lafayette streets, in this city, by a boy, twenty years old, named Robert Ford.

In the light of all moral reasoning the shooting was unjustifiable; but the law is vindicated, and the $10,000 reward offered by the state for the body of the brigand will doubtless go to the man who had the courage to draw a revolver on the notorious outlaw even when his back was turned, as in this case.

There is little doubt that the killing was the result of a premeditated plan formed by Robert and Charles Ford several months ago. Charles had been an accomplice of Jesse James since November 3 and entirely possessed his confidence. Robert Ford, his brother, joined Jesse near the home of Mrs. Samuel (the mother of the James boys) last Friday and accompanied Jesse and Charles to this city Sunday, March 23.

Jesse, his wife, and two children removed from Kansas—where they had lived several months, until they feared their whereabouts would be suspected—to this city, arriving here November 8, 1881, coming in a wagon and accompanied by Charles Ford. They rented a house on the corner of Lafayette and 21st streets, where they stayed two months, when they secured the house No. 1381 on

Murder Most Foul

Lafayette Street, formerly the property of Councilman Aylesbury, paying fourteen dollars a month for it, and giving the name of Thomas Howard.

The house is a one-story cottage, painted white, with green shutters, and is romantically situated on the brow of a lofty eminence east of the city, commanding a fine view of the principal portion of the city, river, and railroads, and adapted by nature for the perilous and desperate calling of Jesse James. Just east of the house is a deep, gulch-like ravine, and beyond that a broad expanse of open country backed by a belt of timber. The house, except from the west side, can be seen for several miles. There is a large yard attached to the cottage and a stable where Jesse had been keeping two horses, which were found there this morning.

Charles and Robert Ford had been occupying one of the rooms in the rear of the dwelling, and have secretly had an understanding to kill Jesse ever since last fall. Ever since the boys have been with Jesse, they have watched for an opportunity to shoot him, but he was always so heavily armed that it was impossible to draw a weapon without James seeing it. They declared they had no idea of taking him alive, considering the undertaking suicidal.

The opportunity they had long wished for came this morning. Breakfast was over. Charlie Ford and Jesse James had been in the stable currying their horses preparatory to their night ride. On returning to the room where Robert Ford was, Jesse said:

"It's an awfully hot day."

He pulled off his coat and vest and tossed them on the bed. Then he said:

"I guess I'll take off my pistols, for fear somebody will see them if I walk in the yard."

He unbuckled his belt, in which he carried two .45-caliber revolvers, one a Smith & Wesson and the other a Colt, and laid them on the bed with his coat and vest. He then picked up a dusting brush with the intention of dusting some pictures that hung on the wall. To do this he got on a chair. His back was now turned to the brothers, who silently stepped between Jesse and his revolvers.

At a motion from Charlie, both drew their guns. Robert was the quicker of the two, and in one motion he had the long weapon to a level with his eye, and with the muzzle not more than four feet from the back of the outlaw's head.

Even in that motion, quick as a thought, there was something that did not escape the acute ears of the hunted man. He made a motion as if to turn his head to ascertain the cause of that suspicious sound, but too late. A nervous pressure on the trigger, a quick flash, a sharp report, and the well-directed ball crashed through the outlaw's skull.

There was no outcry, just a swaying of the body, and it fell heavily backward upon the carpet of the floor. The shot had been fatal, and all the bullets in the chambers of Charlie's revolver, still directed at Jesse's head, could not more effectually have decided the fate of the greatest bandit and freebooter that ever figured in the pages of a country's history.

The ball had entered the base of the skull and made its way out through the forehead, over the left eye. It had been fired out of a Colt .45, improved-pattern, silver-mounted, and pearl-handled pistol, presented by the dead man to his slayer only a few days ago.

Mrs. James was in the kitchen when the shooting was done, separated from the room in which the bloody tragedy occurred by the dining room. She heard the shot and, dropping her household duties, ran into the front room. She saw her husband lying extended on his back, his slayers, each holding his revolver in his hand, making for the fence in the rear of the house. Robert had reached the enclosure and was in the act of scaling it when she stepped to the door and called to him:

"Robert, you have done this! Come back!"

Robert answered, "I swear to God I didn't!"

They then returned to where she stood. Mrs. James ran to the side of her husband and lifted up his head. Life was not yet extinct, and when she asked him if he was hurt, it seemed to her that he wanted to say something but could not. She tried to wash the blood away that was coursing over his face from the hole in his forehead, but it seemed to her that the blood would come faster than she could wipe it away, and in her hands Jesse James died.

Charlie explained to Mrs. James that "a pistol had accidentally

gone off." "Yes," said Mrs. James, "I guess it went off on
purpose." Meanwhile, Charlie had gone back into the house and
brought out two hats, and the two boys left the house. They went
to the telegraph office, sent a message to Sheriff Timberlake of
Clay County, to Police Commissioner Craig of Kansas City, to
Governor Crittenden, and other officers, and then surrendered
themselves to Marshal Craig.

When the Ford boys appeared at the police station, they were
told by an officer that Marshal Craig and a posse of officers had
gone in the direction of the James residence, and they started
after them and accompanied the officers to the house and returned
in custody of the police to the marshal's headquarters, where they
were furnished with dinner, and about 3:00 P.M. were removed to
the old circuit courtroom, where the inquest was held in the
presence of an immense crowd.

Jesse was buried April 6, 1882 in Kearney, Missouri, and the *St.
Joseph Daily Gazette* commented: "The name of Jesse James
will have no grave while Missouri's history is remembered, but
under four feet of the loam of old clay his body now is sleeping. It
is the only peace his troubled life could find."

Gunfight in El Paso leaves Buck Linn dead and Will Raynor dying

Among gunfighters of the Old West, Will Raynor and Buck Linn were hardly major figures. But the *El Paso Daily Times'* brief account of their demise is fascinating for its irreverent, light style. It was published April 15, 1885 under the general headline "Municipal Matters" and a smaller headline: "El Paso Indulges in a Little Pistol Practice."

Last night when the clock struck twelve, as we were returning from the Pierson Hotel, six or seven shots cried out in rapid succession, startling the slumber hour. We hurried down the street and found a large crowd collected and much excited around a streetcar in front of the theater.

We wedged our way in as far as possible, and after a long time we gathered that Will Raynor was in the car and had been shot twice or three times.

It seems that Raynor was drinking tonight, something quite unusual in him to our knowledge, and became aggressive and provocative, and in a crowd there will always be found someone actuated either by malice or some other cause, who is willing to prove himself a bad man, and thus the row began in which Raynor was shot, probably fatally, we cannot say.

The party with him was one of the guards at the jail, known as Buck Linn, a former ranger, a very quiet man when not under the influence of liquor, but who when drinking was considered a crazy man. He was partially in this fix tonight, if not wholly so, and was with Raynor when the first shooting commenced. He went out of the house shooting off his pistol, and went in the direction of the jail.

Having been gone some three-quarters of an hour or so, he

returned, and it is said ordered one of the dealers to throw up his hands, but, instead of this, the dealer pulled down on him and commenced firing with fatal effect. Linn was shot through the heart and died almost instantly in the theater. Dr. Justice was summoned but pronounced him dead when he arrived.

It is understood that the attending doctor thinks Raynor mortally wounded. We could not get anything straight tonight. It is too near going to press. We learn that the last party who did the killing was named Robert Cahill and that four shots were fired which we heard distinctly in our office as we were writing up the first casualty.

Raynor died. Cahill was arrested for murder but was released on ten-dollar bond after a coroner's inquest. He never came to trial.

There's talk of escape as Tom Horn awaits execution at Cheyenne

Missouri-born Tom Horn was almost seven feet tall and had served with honor in the Spanish-American War and earlier in the U.S. Cavalry campaign against the Apaches. Horn personally had persuaded Geronimo to surrender in 1886. At the turn of the century, no frontier remaining, Horn became a hired gun for Wyoming cattle barons, desperately resisting the onslaught of home-steaders—and sheep. On July 18, 1901, Willie Nickell, the fourteen-year-old son of a particularly strong-willed sheepman, was found slain near Iron Mountain, Wyoming. Horn was arrested and charged with murder. He escaped once from the Cheyenne jail, but was recaptured because he couldn't figure out how to shoot a new kind of pistol he took from the sheriff. At his trial after the escape, he was convicted and sentenced to hang, despite high-powered counsel imported by the cattle interests. As the day of execution approached, Horn's friends gathered in Cheyenne, prompting talk of another escape attempt, as this story by John Craig Hammond explained in the *Denver Post* of November 17, 1903.

Two hundred feet from the cell occupied by Tom Horn and his deathwatch, the mournful tolling of the funeral bell in St. Mary's Cathedral brought the man who has four days to live to his feet this morning, nervous and excited.

Out of the little Catholic cathedral of Cheyenne, a black casket was carried on its last journey to the cemetery.

Horn could not see the funeral procession, but the bell ringing clear in the frosty morning air filled the jail corridor and cells with its message of death.

"Funeral?" questioned Horn.

Two of his deathwatch nodded and then tilted their chairs and went on with the long task of watching every movement of the condemned man.

It was like hours to the nerve-wracked man; the wailing of the bell, each dong of the clapper sent a shudder through his bent form. As a matter of fact, the tolling bell did not last five minutes, but when it died away Horn was on the verge of nervous collapse.

Even the crunching of the carriage wheels on the crisp snow filtered in through the bars.

Outside, Kels P. Nickell, father of the murdered boy, stood looking at the brick jail. He too had heard the tolling of the bell, and it brought back anew how he had followed his son to the grave.

To the father who has followed Tom Horn day and night, watching with more care than the attorneys every new phase of the case, a stronger and firmer determination was taken to see that Tom Horn paid the penalty for his crime.

If Horn is released from jail through the overpowering of the guards by his friends, he will have to take into consideration Kels Nickell. Nickell will have the strength of a dozen men, and he will slay and slay until he falls or Tom Horn is again locked in his cell.

There are hundreds of persons in Cheyenne who have worked themselves into a fever of excitement and they openly declare that they know an attempt will be made to free Horn. Actually, it is doubtful such an attempt will be made. It is true there are at least a hundred men in the city who would lead the attack. But the Colt rapid-firing guns, the extra guards, and the efforts being made by the local officers against any such effort stand as a stone wall.

Talk with those who are not suffering from such pent-up excitement and they will tell you that a stronger effort will be made to let Horn take his own life. He has told friends he wants to do this if all other efforts fail. And they have failed, it would appear.

Deputy Sheriff Dick Proctor declared there is not the slightest chance to give Horn a weapon or poison to kill himself.

Sheriff Smalley today declared he will keep the names of the deathwatch a secret until the day of execution. The men have been picked with the greatest care. Their bravery cannot be questioned, and their honesty is known. Still, to keep all temptation out of their way, their names will be kept from the public.

Proctor said that he has no fear that the guards would take bribes, but they might meet with foul play or be threatened by friends of Horn if they did not join the scheme to let him cheat the gallows.

The hour of execution has been agreed upon. Officials have let it out that the drop will be sprung between the hours of 9:00 in the morning and 3:00 in the afternoon. No one is to know the exact time. No more than thirty-five will be present. Six of these will be visiting sheriffs, some eight newspapermen, the doctors, guards, and six friends of Horn.

An example of the great care being taken by the sheriff is shown in the fact that each person will be searched before being allowed to enter the jail corridor.

Revolvers and knives will be taken from every person who bears an invitation. The guards on the platform, however, will wear their huge revolvers.

Horn has decided upon the six friends he will ask to have present. He is guarding their names with care and will not turn them over to the sheriff until Thursday evening.

Today a little black box was delivered to the sheriff's office. When it was opened, it was found to contain the little black cap, the last thing that will be added on the gallows before the trap goes bounding downward.

It was a gruesome sight, this bit of black goods, cheap in material. Nearly a yard of common black dress goods was used in making the cap, which is more like a black paper bag.

This was barely stowed away in the sheriff's desk when a small boy came in with another box. It contained four long straps, two for the arms and two for the legs. The straps were made to order and under the direction of Deputy Sheriff Proctor. The buckles are so adjusted they will slip into place without tugging. The straps were well-oiled and made as flexible as possible.

Proctor is trying to escape from having the least hitch in the scene upon the gallows.

The rope has been ordered and will arrive tomorrow. It has not been decided who will make the noose, but a number of persons are in the city who can make the noose that will rest behind Horn's left ear.

Maybe these are gruesome details, but they are not a marker for the stories being told on the street corners at all hours of the day and night. Not the slightest scrap of information is escaping those who are interested in the case. Laramie County has not had a hanging for a number of years, and it was discovered that some of the timber used in the scaffold was missing. The order was given for the lumber to make the platform while extra braces also had to be ordered.

When Horn was arrested, he was a powerful man, weighing 206 pounds. Today he weighs between 175 and 180 pounds. While this still makes him a large man, he is described as being "a skeleton of his former self."

Owing to his weight, the gallows will be given extra tests. The bags of sand will be brought into play, some of them weighing 200 pounds. The ropes will be tied around the bags, and the trap will be sprung again and again.

To those who have witnessed a hanging, one of the harrowing details is the banging of the trap door as it flies downward and backward. Horn will have to listen to the thud of the sandbags and the crash of the trap many times before he steps onto the gallows.

As Horn is led from his cell on the march to his death, he will be met by his six friends. He will be given a chance to shake hands with them and to say goodbye.

One man at a time will pass by Horn, and he will be able to give him his farewell message. It is said that Horn will make a speech on the gallows. He will, it is claimed, call on vengeance upon a number of persons. All hopes of his making a confession have been given up by a number of persons. He has been asked to die game, and he has sent out word that "I will swing without preaching."

Horn has not asked for a minister or priest. In fact, he is a man without a religion. He refuses to talk about it, but it is expected by persons near him that he will call for a spiritual as the time draws nearer. Still he has never been a member of a church or had any interest in religion even in his childhood days. He is a man of the day, free from such thoughts.

While the public knows of the daring attempt Horn made to escape from jail, it has never been made public that he attempted to escape a score of times. There has not a week gone by since Horn was arrested that something wasn't found in his cell that he was trying to use to force his way out of the prison.

Horn has a wonderful brain in many ways. He is constantly planning, thinking, acting. While the chances of his escape have been reduced a thousandfold, he is still up to his old tricks.

Proctor has an interesting collection of wires, bones, pieces of glass, case knives, pieces of wood, and wire that Horn has used in the past weeks.

While it is not an elegant expression, the so-called "Shirttail Wireless Telegraph System" shows that Horn is a man of brains. Only a few weeks ago Proctor found a ball of red string in Horn's cell. Incidentally, he found a number of messages.

Horn was on the second tier of cells. He wanted to send a message to a prisoner who was on the first floor and on the other side of the jail. He tore a piece of his blanket about the size of a man's hand, rolled it into a ball after he had placed his message inside. He stood at his cell door, gave the ball a snap of his fingers, and it fell to the first floor.

A prisoner managed to rake it in front of his cell, and, after placing it in just the right position, he gave it a snap with his finger and it went to the next cell. This was kept up until the ball with the message reached the cell of a prisoner who was to be given liberty the next day. The string was then untied, and Horn pulled it back for further use.

When the string was found and taken away from him, Horn did not give up. He wanted to send a second message, so he took his shirt and carefully tore off the tails. Then he made strips of these until he had a long cord. He repeated the operation as above, using three shirts in the operation. Horn has been on the constant lookout for pieces of wire. Through the aid of prisoners who have the liberty of the corridor, he secured half a dozen different supplies.

A long stove pipe was suspended from the ceiling by some four feet of wire. Different men would climb on the cells, cut off a piece of wire and, under the direction of Horn, tie up the pipe again. This has been kept up so often that the pipe is now only a few inches from the ceiling.

When this area of securing wire was stopped, Horn turned to the jail brooms. He was wise enough not to take off the outside wire but would part the broom cane and unwrap the wire. Proctor found half a dozen such pieces, but it took him weeks to discover how Horn was getting the wire.

One day Horn was served with a soup bone. He managed to keep a piece of the bone about five inches long. With the utmost care he filed away at the bone for days and days until he had made a key to throw his bolt. He was busy at work when discovered, and the bone key was taken away from him.

Just a thirty-second part of an inch and he would have fashioned a bone key to throw the bolt. He secured a feather duster one day and managed to cut off a piece of the wood between the feathers.

He used matches to burn away the wood until he had fashioned a key. The burnt end of his matches he used to write his messages. Horn also managed to collect a number of pieces of glass, which he used to make a number of cell keys. He was skilled in bending wire into a score of shapes and was high on the way in making a key out of five pieces of wire when he was discovered.

These are but a few of the many schemes resorted to by the clever prisoner. He managed to send out a number of messages but was detected, and now this avenue of sending messages to his friends has been cut off.

In the midst of the snowstorm that swept in from the north last night, a number of strange men came to Cheyenne. Who they are is not known at this time.

"I tell you thousands of people will come to Cheyenne for the hanging," said a local lawyer in the Inter-Ocean Hotel. "We will have a day second only to Frontier Day if the weather is anyway near fine."

The weather is to play a strong part in any attempt that may be made to "rush" the jail. If the weather is good, then hundreds of persons will come and Horn's friends will mingle among the crowds. An effort is being made by the local police at this time to account for every stranger that comes to the city. The police declare they can pick out the average Westerner from the average traveler, and it is the former who will be watched and in many instances will be asked to give an account of themselves. This has been done in a number of incidents during the past few days. A few persons have been warned to get out of town.

Tom Horn refused this morning to see the local preacher who came to talk to him about the hereafter. A man and two women then called on him. They pleaded for half an hour and in the end Horn gave in.

Tonight at seven o'clock the three will be admitted to the jail, and they will pray with Horn.

"It won't do any harm and not do much good for you to come," he said. "If it will make your happiness greater, then come ahead, that is if Dick Proctor will let you."

Proctor said he would be glad to have Horn consult with someone on the question of religion.

Ira D. Williams; his wife, Mary, and Sister Butler, all of Bay City, Michigan, have travelled a long way to pray with him.

"We hope to help this poor man," said Williams, who has been spending the last few years saving souls.

"He is the very kind that can be saved," his wife added. "We will pray and talk to him for just half an hour tonight and again tomorrow, if the sheriff will let us and Horn will listen. My husband, I pray, will be at his side when he goes to the other world."

Mr. and Mrs. Williams and Sister Butler said they will open a mission in Cheyenne if they can get Horn to his death a believer.

Horn went to his death on schedule and was buried by friends at Boulder, Colorado. His autobiography, published a year after the hanging, contended that he was framed.

Chapter X

ASSASSINATION

"Hang him! Hang him!" the crowd exclaims as Lincoln's killer escapes

Abraham Lincoln, sixteenth president of the United States, was shot at 10:15 P.M. on April 14, 1865, but still clung to life when this report was published the next morning in the *National Intelligencer* of Washington, D.C.

President Lincoln and wife, together with other friends, last evening visited Ford's Theatre, for the purpose of witnessing the performance of the "American Cousin." It was announced in the newspapers that General Grant would also be present, but that gentleman, instead, took the late train of cars for New Jersey. The theatre was densely crowded, and everybody seemed delighted with the scene before them.

During the third act, and while there was a temporary pause for one of the actors to enter, a sharp report of a pistol was heard, which merely attracted attention, but suggested nothing serious, until a man rushed to the front of the president's box, waving a long dagger in his right hand, and exclaiming, *"Sic Semper Tyrannis,"* and immediately leaped from the box, which was of the second tier, to the stage beneath, and ran across to the opposite side, thus making his escape, amid the bewilderment of the audience, from the rear of the theatre, and, mounting a horse, fled.

The screams of Mrs. Lincoln first disclosed the fact to the audience that the president had been shot, when all present rose to their feet, rushing toward the stage, many exclaiming, "Hang him! Hang him!"

John Wilkes Booth in 1864.
(Courtesy Newberry Library, Chicago)

The excitement was of the wildest possible character, and, of course, there was an abrupt termination of the theatrical performance.

There was a rush toward the president's box, when cries were heard, "Stand back!" "Give him air!" "Has anyone stimulants?"

On a hasty examination it was found that the president had been shot through the head, above and below the temporal bone, and that some of the brain was oozing out. He was removed to the private residence of Mr. Ulke, opposite the theatre, and the surgeon general of the Army and other surgeons sent for to attend to his condition.

On examination of the private box, blood was discovered on the back of the rocking chair in which the president had been sitting, on the partition, and on the floor. A common single-barrelled pocket pistol was found on the carpet.

A military guard was placed in front of the private residence to which the president had been conveyed. An immense crowd was in front of it, all deeply anxious to learn the condition of the president. It had been previously announced that the wound was mortal, but all hoped otherwise.

The shock to the community was terrible.

At midnight the cabinet, with Messrs. Sumner, Colfax, and Farnsworth, Judge Cartter, Governor Oglesby, General Meigs, Major Hay, and a few personal friends, with Surgeon General Barnes and the medical associates, arrived at his bedside. The president was in a state of syncope, totally insensible, and breathing slowly, the blood oozing from the wound at the back of his head. The surgeons were exhausting every possible effort of medical skill, but all hope was gone.

The parting of his family with the dying president is too sad for description.

The President and Mrs. Lincoln did not start to the theatre till eight. Speaker Colfax was at the White House at the time, and the president stated to him that he was going, although Mrs. Lincoln had not been well, because the papers had advertised that General Grant and themselves were to be present, and, as General Grant had gone North, he did not wish the audience to be disappointed. He went with apparent reluctance, and urged Colfax to go with him, but that gentleman had made other engagements and, with Mr. Ashmun of Massachusetts, bid him goodbye.

When the excitement at the theatre was at the wildest height, reports were circulated that Secretary William H. Seward had also been assassinated.

On reaching this gentleman's residence, a crowd and a military guard were found at the door; and on entering it was ascertained that the reports were based upon truth.

Everybody was so much excited that scarcely an intelligible account could be gathered; but the facts are substantially as follows: About ten o'clock a man rang the bell, and the call having been answered by a colored servant, he said he had come from Dr. Verdi, Secretary Seward's family physician, with a prescription, at the same time holding in his hand a small piece of folded paper, and saying, in answer to a refusal, that he must see the secretary, as he was entrusted with particular directions concerning the medicine. He still insisted on going up, although repeatedly told that no one could enter the chamber. The man pushed the servant aside, and walked heavily toward the secretary's room, and was there met by Frederick W. Seward, of whom he demanded to see the secretary, making the same representation that he did to the servant. What further passed in the way of colloquy is not known; but the man struck him on the head with a billy, severely injuring the skull, and felling him almost senseless.

The assassin then rushed into the chamber and attacked Major Seward, U.S. Army paymaster, and Mr. Hansell, a messenger of the State Department, and two male nurses, disabling them all. He then rushed upon the secretary, who was lying in bed in the same room, and inflicted three stabs in his neck, but severing, it is thought and hoped, no arteries, though the secretary bled profusely.

The assassin then rushed downstairs, mounted his horse at the door, and rode off before an alarm could be given, and in the same manner as the assassin of the president.

It is believed that the injuries of the secretary are not mortal, nor those of either of the others, although both the secretary and the assistant secretary are seriously injured.

Secretaries Stanton and Welles, and other prominent officers of the government, called at Secretary Seward's house to inquire into his condition, and, learning there of the assassination of the president, proceeded to the house where he was lying, exhibiting, of course, intense anxiety and solicitude.

An immense crowd was gathered in front of the president's house, and a strong guard also stationed there, many persons evidently supposing that he would be brought to his home.

The entire city last night presented a scene of wild excitement, accompanied by violent expressions of indignation and the profoundest sorrow. Many persons shed tears.

The military authorities have dispatched mounted patrols in every direction, in order, if possible, to arrest the assassin, while the metropolitan police are alike vigilant for the same purpose. The attacks, both at the theatre and at Secretary Seward's, took place about the same hour—ten o'clock—this showing a preconcerted plan to assassinate these gentlemen.

Some evidence of the guilt of the party who attacked the president is in possession of the police.

Vice President Johnson is in the city, and his hotel quarters are guarded by troops.

EPILOG

SATURDAY MORNING, 2½ O'CLOCK—The president is still alive, but is growing weaker. The ball is lodged in his brain, three inches from where it entered the skull. He remains insensible, and his condition is utterly hopeless.

The vice president has been to see him, but all company, except the cabinet, his family, and a few friends, is rigidly excluded.

Large crowds still continue in the street, as near to the house as the line of guards allows.

President Abraham Lincoln died at 7:20 A.M. on April 15 in a roominghouse across the street from Ford's Theatre. The assassin, John Wilkes Booth, suffered a broken leg in his leap from the president's box to the stage. He eluded capture until April 26, when federal troops surrounded him in a barn near Fredericksburg, Virginia. When he refused to surrender, the barn was set on fire and Booth was shot, perhaps by his own hand.

*Dr. Patrick Henry Cronin in an 1889 engraving.
(Courtesy Chicago Historical Society)*

Murder most foul: Dr. Cronin's stripped body found in sewer

To the modern reader it might seem at first that the assassination of Dr. Patrick Henry Cronin was just another tale of mystery and horror, Chicago-style. But, internationally, it was one of the most celebrated crimes of the nineteenth century. A native of Ireland and graduate of St. Louis Medical College, Dr. Cronin was America's leading advocate of Irish home rule. So prominent was he that Irish-Americans had been divided into "Cronin" and "anti-Cronin" factions. He was an officer in the Chicago chapter of Clan-na-Gael, a secret society founded in 1869 to raise money for Irish revolutionaries. In 1888, he accused three other leaders of embezzling the society's funds. They retaliated with rumors that Cronin was a British spy. Shortly before his disappearance, Cronin threatened to publish what he knew in the *Celto-American*, a controversial Irish-American weekly he edited. The search for the forty-three-year-old bachelor physician—and speculation that he had been slain—dominated the headlines for nearly three weeks before the mutilated body was found. This story appeared in the *Chicago Times* of May 23, 1889, under the headline "Murder Most Foul."

Dr. P. H. Cronin was murdered! His body was found yesterday afternoon stark naked with the head a mass of horrible wounds, any one of which might produce death. At least fifty of his friends have seen and identified the body. The identification is undoubtedly complete, and there now remains no doubt of the fate that befell him.

The body was found in a catch basin at the southeast corner of Evanston Road and 59th Street, Lake View, where it had been hidden by the murderers or their accomplices. The discovery was made accidentally by a gang of ditch cleaners—Henry Rosch, John Feningar, and William Nichols.

About 4:00 P.M. they arrived at the corner of 59th Street and Evanston Road. Rosch crossed over from the north to the south side of the street and began shovelling out the sand in the ditch near the catch basin.

When within a few feet of the basin, he detected the odor of a dead body and called out to his assistants, "I guess there's a dead dog here." He got down on his knees and looked into the catch basin through the iron bars at the side. What he saw made him recoil with horror.

There, wedged into the narrow catch basin, was the body of a man partly screened from view by a lot of cotton batting that had been thrown over it. Rosch called his two assistants, who merely glanced at the body and retreated.

Rosch told the men to stay there and at once ran to Argyle Park station, nearly a mile away, where he telephoned the Lake View police station with a hasty account of his discovery. It was 4:25 P.M. when the telephone summons was received at the station.

The patrol wagon with Captain Wing himself in charge hastened to the spot. There the officers removed the top of the catch basin. The body was then clearly brought to view. It was floating, face downward, in two feet of water. The body was doubled up like a partly open jackknife. It was immediately taken from the hole, wrapped in a blanket, and taken to the Lake View station.

"We had been working on the north side of the street for half an hour," Rosch said. "When I crossed the street I observed an odor. The catch basin has a number of iron rods on the side. The bottom of the rods is about even with the ditch. To see in, I had to get down on my knees. There is about two feet of water in the basin. The body was floating on the water. The catch basin is really a well six feet deep and about four feet across. On the top of the basin is a wooden frame about two feet square. This is covered with a wooden lid, which we had to pry open with a pick. Everything shows plainly that the lid was taken off the basin with some tool or pry. The body was then put in head first, and the cotton thrown in afterward. The cotton was next to the grating and may have been crowded in from the outside after the body was hidden there. I tell you I was scared. I ran to the Argyle Park station and telephoned to the police, who came with a wagon."

The body was taken to the little morgue connected with the Lake View police station and laid on one of the zinc slabs. When the blanket in which the officers had strapped the body was removed, nearly all the mustache and a large portion of the hair on the head adhered to it. This accident made the identification more difficult.

Word was sent at once to city authorities and friends of Dr. Cronin.

The news of the discovery soon spread all over Lake View, and the station was filled with a curious crowd of morbid sightseers.

The body was naked with the exception of a blood-soaked towel that had been twisted around the throat. An Agnus Dei was suspended from the neck by a leather string. Decomposition had begun but had not progressed to such a stage that recognition was impossible.

The most hideous and ghastly portion of the body was the head. Here the heavy bruises and great gaping wounds bore overpowering evidence of horrible murder and desperate assassination. All the long mustache worn by Dr. Cronin was gone, save a tuft at the left corner of the mouth. The bruised and broken forehead was hairless nearly to the crown of the head.

There were seven horrible wounds on the head, apparently inflicted with a hatchet or similar weapon. Dr. J. P. Brandt of the county hospital made a careful examination of the wounds.

The skull was crushed at the outer corner of the left eye; there was a big dent in the forehead; a cut nearly two inches long on the top of the head; a cut more than two inches long midway between the left ear and the top of the head; another cut joining this at the lower end and extending toward the left temple for two inches; a huge cut nearly four inches long on the back of the head, extending nearly from ear to ear, and a gash under the chin.

The little morgue was crowded when Dr. Brandt made the examination. The water on the floor was nearly an inch deep. A long, perforated pipe extended the length of the slab, and tiny streams ran over the body and down to the floor. The dropping of the water was the only sound heard in the room.

"These cuts," said Dr. Brandt, "were made with a hatchet, I believe. They did not break the skull, but cut to it. Any one of them would knock a man insensible and might result in death. The wound near the left eye would cause death almost at once, for the temple is crushed. None of these wounds, so far as I can now judge, was made after death. The man must have made a noble fight."

No mere pen-picture can convey an adequate idea of the trembling, agitated, intense silence—the silence of overwrought suspense—that was preserved while Dr. Brandt made his examination and gave his opinion. It was something like the silence that might follow the engulfing of half a city by an earthquake before those who escaped realized the awfulness of the calamity. There were white and set faces there, and muscles stood out on men's jaws as teeth were clenched with emotion.

John P. Scanlan was sent for and soon arrived. He walked into the morgue and stood looking at the body of his murdered friend. He did not say a word, but a set look was seen about his jaws. For fifteen minutes he surveyed the corpse, but did not speak. The body's right hand was picked up from its position at the side of the body and laid across the swollen breast. The right hand was the only portion of the body that preserved a perfectly lifelike appearance. The silence was not broken by the spectators, but all waited for Scanlan to conclude his scrutiny. Finally, he raised his blanched face, and in a trembling voice said:

"It is Dr. Cronin's body. The hand I will swear to. The doctor was a very hairy man, especially about the wrists; so was this man. The goatee on the lower lip does more than resemble Dr. Cronin's; it is exactly like it. The long hair of this mustache is like his; so is the long hair left on the head. The size and shape of the body are his. The forehead is his; the teeth are his; the nose, after I raise the nostrils thus with a lead pencil, is his. The body is that of Dr. Cronin. He was taken into a room, stable, or ice house and there killed. The Agnus Dei is the one he had around his neck."

Dr. Parker of Lake View said the body was that of a man who had been dead between two and three weeks.

By that time the news of the identification of the body had reached the street, and the crowd outside steadily increased. The officer at the head of the stairs took off his coat and fought the crowd back. Everybody wanted to rush in and see the body. Captain Wing gave orders to admit no one except intimate friends of Dr. Cronin.

While the crowd was the thickest, Mr. Conklin, a close friend of Dr. Cronin, arrived. He looked at the Agnus Dei and said: "That is the one Dr. Cronin wore, or a facsimile of it, string and all."

Mr. Conklin identified other features as those of Dr. Cronin. As he turned to the door he said: "There is no longer any doubt. That is Dr. Cronin's body, and he was murdered."

Dr. Rutherford, who was associated with Dr. Cronin when the latter was a member of the staff at the county hospital, did not hesitate in deciding the body was that of the missing doctor. Mr. McCary, who knew the doctor well, and Captain O'Connor, his friend, added their positive identifications.

Two of the visitors whose opinions were considered of great importance were Frank Scanlan, the last of Dr. Cronin's friends to see him alive, and Hal Buck, the barber at 472 North Clark. Scanlan identified the body, but went further. "Dr. Cronin had peculiar teeth," he said. "I think two were missing. His heavy mustache came over his mouth and completely hid his teeth, but I have seen them. His upper teeth were large, nearly as wide as long, and had a space between them. The teeth on the under jaw were small, crowded in tight, and stained black around the edges." A careful examination of the teeth showed that Scanlan had described them perfectly.

Buck, the barber, said: "The goatee is Cronin's; the hair is Cronin's; the mustache is Cronin's, and the body is Cronin's. It is not generally known that Dr. Cronin had his mustache dyed. I have shaved him daily a long time and used to dye his mustache. The tuft of hair left of his mustache still shows the dye. There is no mistake about it—the body is poor Dr. Cronin's."

The Catholic charm still around the body's neck may be an important link in the identification. The Agnus Dei is attached to a leather thong and can be described by Dr. Cronin's sister and by several intimate friends.

Of all who came to the morgue who knew Dr. Cronin in life, there was not one who failed to identify the body. Therefore, there can remain no doubt that the body is that of Dr. Cronin.

Everything around the place where the body was found suggests quiet. The nearest house to the catch basin is 100 yards north, and Argyle Park village is close to the lake, or about one mile southeast from Evanston and 59th.

Evanston Road is smoothly graded, while the cross streets are in bad shape, being sandy and having the appearance of roads newly built. The lots in the immediate vicinity are vacant and covered with long weeds. A section of the ground at the northeast corner of Evanston and 59th is used as a small market garden; otherwise, there is no evidence of civilization.

The ditch in which the workmen were engaged is a narrow and shallow affair, through which the water flowed sluggishly. Except in case of rain, the flow of water could not reach the catch basins at that point, and men were sent out to dig deeper ditches. At the foot of the basins are iron gratings, each having five rods, and it was not until Rosch and his two assistants had dug their way to one of these that the strange stench was noticed. The basins are substantially built of masonry and are capped with boards. On the top there is a square opening or manhole. The lids are hinged and are quite heavy. Inside the basin everything is extremely forbidding—blackness, dampness, and dirty, ill-smelling water being the main features.

Nobody would think for a moment of lifting the lid and exploring the damp recesses of such a clammy dugout, and, had it not been that the road repairers thought they had discovered a dead dog, they would have been satisfied with cleaning the basin by poking through the iron grating.

A dozen bunches of cotton batting that had been removed from the basin were scattered about the neighborhood and were regarded with considerable awe by passers-by. Half a dozen curiously inclined folks made excursions into the bush and fields hoping to run across other evidences of a tragedy, but their searches were fruitless.

Lonesome and unfrequented and almost surrounded with cemeteries was the place in which was stowed the body of Dr.

Cronin. No better spot could have been found unless possibly the middle of the lake, but the person or persons who had a hand in the cowardly occurrence did not take into consideration the fact that even manholes and catch basins and sewers are sometimes pried into and their contents turned over.

The Cronin conspiracy remains a mystery. Although it apparently involved a raft of principals and accessories, including several Chicago policemen, only six indictments were returned. The evidence was mostly circumstantial, and the defense called a swarm of alibi witnesses. One defendant was extradited to Kansas as a horse thief, midway through the trial. Another was acquitted, and a third was sentenced to only three years. The other three drew life, but won a new trial four years later. Two of them died in prison before the second trial. The third man was acquitted.

The archduke and wife.

The shots that started World War I: archduke and wife assassinated

Franz Ferdinand, archduke of Austria and heir apparent to the throne, and his wife, Bohemian countess Sophie Chotek, who became duchess of Hohenberg, were the targets of two assassination attempts on June 28, 1914 at Sarajevo, Bosnia. The second attempt succeeded—touching off World War I, which began a month later. The following report is from the Vienna newspaper *Arbeiter-Zeitung* of June 29, 1914, and was translated from the German for this book by Armand Petrecca.

The first attempt: Before noon today, as the Archduke Franz Ferdinand, accompanied by his consort, the duchess of Hohenberg, was proceeding to a reception at the Town Hall, a bomb was thrown at their auto, but the archduke pushed it away with his arm. The bomb exploded after the archduke's car already had moved ahead. Count Boos-Waldeck and the aide de camp of the provincial military governor, Lieutenant Colonel Merizzi, both of whom followed in the next car, were slightly injured. Among the onlookers, six persons were more or less seriously wounded. The perpetrator is a typesetter from Trebinje, named Nedeljko Cabrinowitsch. He was immediately apprehended.

The second attempt: After the stately reception in the Town Hall, the archduke and his spouse continued on their tour. It was then that an eighth-year preparatory school student named Gavrilo Princip, from Grahovo (Bosnia), fired a number of shots from a Browning pistol at the archduke's auto.

The archduke was wounded in the face, and the duchess of Hohenberg was wounded by a shot into her abdomen. The couple were conveyed to the Konak (a government palace used to house visiting dignitaries) and there died of their wounds. The second assailant was also captured. The infuriated crowd came close to lynching the two assailants.

How the assassination occurred: After the first assassination attempt, during which the aide de camp, Lieutenant Colonel Merizzi, was wounded in the neck, the archduke ordered his car to stop. After that, having found out what had happened, he entered the Town Hall. Awaiting him inside were the members of the municipal government with the mayor at their head. The mayor wished to make a speech. As he prepared to do so, the archduke said to him sharply:

"Mr. Mayor! We come to Sarajevo to pay a visit and a bomb is thrown! This is revolting!"

And then, after a pause: "Very well, now you may speak!"

The mayor then made his speech to the archduke, who replied to him in turn. The townspeople, who in the meantime had learned of the assassination attempt, rallied on behalf of the archduke with spirited cries.

After his inspection of the Town Hall, which had lasted half an hour, the archduke desired to go to the military hospital to visit his wounded aide. When the archduke had just reached the corner of Franz Josef and Rudolf streets, two revolver shots were fired by an individual named Princip.

The first shot, which drilled through the auto, pierced the abdomen of the duchess on her right side.

The second shot struck the archduke in the neck and pierced his carotid artery.

The duchess lost consciousness immediately and fell over into the lap of the archduke.

The archduke himself lost consciousness after a few seconds.

The auto proceeded to the Konak. Also in the auto were the provincial military governor and Count Harrach, who was driving; the chief of staff to the archduke, Colonel Bardolff, who hastened to give aid, and Major Erich Huttenbrenner, attaché to the military staff.

There, Surgeon-Major Wolfgang and Regimental Medical Officer Payer, who had been at the scene of the first assassination attempt, gave first aid.

However, the archduke and the duchess of Hohenberg no longer showed any signs of life.

The commandant of the hospital, Surgeon-Major Arnstein, then pronounced them dead. Thereupon, the facts of the matter were recorded by the civilian and military authorities.

The assassin fired in a narrow street and at close range. The deed was carried out with lightning speed; many of the people closest to the scene did not hear the shots at all.

Some women had noticed the suspicious appearance of Princip, who was standing at the street corner with his hand in his pocket. The assassin was seized by security guards.

After the attack, the archducal auto proceeded without delay to the Konak. All medical attention proved futile. The military chaplain recited prayers for the dead. For the time being, both bodies are lying in state in the Konak.

After the assassination, a huge excitement swept over the crowd; many people wept. The sorrow in the city is beyond description. Black banners of mourning are everywhere. At the scenes of both tragic events, large groups of people assembled all day long to discuss the assassinations.

Regarding the first attempt, it is reported that the bomb was a so-called "bottle-bomb," filled with nails and small pieces of lead. When the bomb exploded, the iron shutters were torn through in several places at one of the nearby business establishments.

About twenty persons were injured, most only slightly. Among the injured were a forestry commissioner and his wife, an apprentice attorney, and several women and children. One official named Reich, of the provincial government, suffered serious injuries from the bomb fragments.

After the first assassination attempt, the archduke gave the order for his auto to continue to the Town Hall, even though he was asked by the chief of police to return to the Konak. General Potiorek, the provincial military governor, also requested that the archduke forgo the drive to the Town Hall.

Despite these entreaties, however, the archduke stood firm in his determination to see the scheduled program carried out. Then, too, before the archduke departed from the Town Hall, the chief of police reported to him once again, and in words of unmistakable urgency he asked the archduke to return to the Konak by the shortest route. This request was seconded by General Potiorek, and the duchess of Hohenberg was also in favor of turning back to the Konak without delay.

The archduke made clear, however, that first of all he wished to visit Lieutenant Colonel Merizzi in the military hospital. The duchess agreed to accompany him. On the strength of their insistence, the vehicle proceeded along the route of the Appeals Court Quay.

At the corner of the quay and Franz Josef Street, a young man, who until then had been standing quietly in the first row of the assembled onlookers, suddenly rushed toward the auto. The young man discharged two shots from his revolver in rapid succession.

Several officers and policemen, as well as people from the cordon of spectators, flung themselves immediately upon the assailant, who was injured by saber slashes and by the pounding fists of the people. Meanwhile, the archducal auto drove off rapidly to the Konak, which is barely two minutes from the scene of the attack. There the archduke and his consort were borne by persons of their entourage into their chambers at the Konak. While the medical pronouncement of death was being made over the archduke, the duchess lay in a deep coma. Then, a few minutes later, she too died.

The assassin, Gavrilo Princip, is nineteen and a native of Grahovo in the Livno District of southern Bosnia. He was a student in Belgrade for quite some time. Upon interrogation, he confessed that it had long been his ambition to kill some high-ranking personage out of nationalistic motives. Today he waited at the Appeals Court Quay for the archduke to pass by, and when the auto was compelled to slow down to turn into Franz Josef Street, he carried out his machination. For a brief moment he wavered, because the duchess of Hohenberg was also in the car, but then he very quickly fired two shots. He denies having had any accomplices.

The twenty-one-year-old typesetter, Nedeljko Cabrinowitsch, whose bomb attack miscarried, declared that he had obtained the bomb from an anarchist in Belgrade. He, too, denies having had any accomplices. He had been captured after the assassination attempt at the Mijacka River, only to escape. This time, however, security guards and civilians pounced on him and made him prisoner.

A few steps from the scene of the second attack, the discovery was made of a bomb that had remained inoperative. It must have been discarded by yet a third assailant after he had observed the success of Princip's attempt.

Austro-Hungarian Foreign Minister Leopold von Berchtold sent an ultimatum to Serbia on July 23, 1914, and declared war five days later—exactly a month after the double assassination. Gavrilo Princip and Nedeljko Cabrinowitsch were executed.

Trotsky breathes his last after a savage axe attack by a "disciple" in Mexico

Leon Trotsky was born Lev Davidovich Bronstein in 1879 in the southern Ukraine. Despite restrictions on education for Jews, he was sent to school at Odessa and Nikolayev, where a well-educated gardner interested him in socialism. Trotsky organized a radical group at Nikolayev in 1897—an activity that led to his arrest the next year. He was exiled to Siberia, where he wrote prolifically and became a dedicated revolutionary. He escaped in 1902 to London, where he joined Vladimir Ilyich Lenin. After the overthrow of the czar by Russian moderates in 1917, Trotsky made his way to Petrograd, where he played a role hardly less important than Lenin's in organizing the Bolshevik revolution. He became the people's commissar for foreign affairs and later commissar of war in the new Soviet government headed by Lenin. When Lenin died in 1924, it was widely assumed that Trotsky would be the successor. But that assumption underestimated Joseph Stalin, who portrayed Trotsky as a Judas-Fagin-Shylock and toppled him from his posts. Trotsky was banished four years after Stalin became premier. He lived in Turkey and Norway, where he wrote of Stalin: "He seeks to strike not at the ideas of his opponent but at his skull." In 1937, Trotsky settled near Mexico City. At his home there on August 20, 1940, a supposed Stalinist agent struck at Trotsky's skull with a pickaxe. He died a day later. This story, from *Mexico City Novedades* of August 22, 1940, was translated for this book by Armand Petrecca.

At 7:25 P.M. yesterday, Leon Trotsky ceased to breathe. The efforts of his physicians to prevent the fatal outcome proved useless. No fewer than ten vials of chemical substances had been administered to him, some of them directly into the heart and

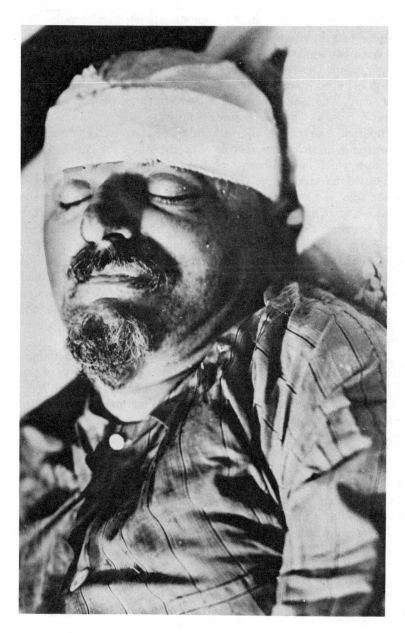

Leon Trotsky after death.

others into his system, in the hope of causing him to rally, but only served to ease the pain.

Death came abruptly. There was no death rattle, nor even a single moan. Dr. Lenero, who had been taking Trotsky's pulse, shook his head; and Dr. Mass, who stood beside him, listened to the heart. The looked at each other, but there was no need for them to speak. The few persons who were present in the room understood everything, and without a word the doctors departed, after removing from the nostrils of their patient the rubber tubes through which he had been breathing warm oxygen.

The woman who is now Trotsky's widow had been napping on a green sofa, next to the bed of the dying man. It seems that she guessed what had just occurred. With great composure she rose from her seat, then fell to her knees and silently placed kisses on the brow of him who had been her companion in life for so many years. She sobbed for a while and then spoke with two of Trotsky's guards and his private secretary. A woman who had been standing in the room began to cry, and Mme. Natalya gestured to her to be quiet. The secretaries hurried to the telephones in the hallway. They made a number of calls, all of them to say simply: "Mr. Trotsky is dead."

From that moment, the phones were busy without interruption. Everyone was eager to know with whom the last moments of the Red leader had been shared. Whether they had spoken with him. Whether they had gesticulated in this or that manner. In short, everyone was anxious to find out something, something that might slake his curiosity.

The secretaries asked Gen. José Manuel Núñez and Col. Leandro Sánchez Salazar for permission to enter the room where Leon Trotsky had died, where he still appeared to be sleeping, just as he had slept yesterday, and to speak with his widow. The two high-ranking officers then entered the death room. The widow, still very downcast, asked that they please leave her alone with her husband for a few more minutes before allowing outsiders to break in upon her immense grief.

The general granted her wish and ordered that no one was to enter the room. Moments later there also assembled Joseph Hansen, who had been the private secretary of the deceased, the bodyguards Jackie Cooper and Otto Schuessler, and Harold Robbins.

News of the death spread through the city with dizzying speed. In the streets rose the rumor of what had befallen the man who at one time had been the strong man of Russia, Leon Trotsky.

Additional policemen were called in and security was redoubled. We journalists and photographers already on the scene were forced back from the entrance. General Núñez emerged onto the street, running. Now and then the uniformed guards would become excessively forceful; and at times they would approach the various little groups of "the fourth estate" to listen in on the most disparate accounts that each newsman might give according to his fancy and in the words that best pleased him. The foreign correspondents would run to the telephones, and at the telephone switchboard we witnessed the most amusing scenes, as if they had been made for the movies. There was one reporter who went so far as to yank out the wire to prevent a rival from calling in the news first.

We tried a thousand times to enter the emergency room. Our only thought was to give our readers the best picture of what was going on inside; but all our efforts failed. And today too our strategy proved a failure. We gained nothing from having so many friends within the praiseworthy Green Cross. They wanted to help us get information, but the police held them back.

Several times, all of us shouting as one, we attempted to protest vigorously, but nobody listened to us. We asked, we begged, we demanded the right to enter. Some even gave their opinions regarding the most correct manner in which to enter. Always we ran up against the old phrase: "We have orders not to admit anyone."

Then, suddenly, the rumor:

"They're going to take out the body through the back door."

Some returned to the street, searching for that door. But nothing came of it. It was only a false rumor, spread in the heat of impatience fired by the long wait. Then the roof of the Central Emergency Station began to be invaded by policemen who looked down on us apprehensively, as if fearful of an armed attack.

Two young men in blue uniforms with sparkling buttons

suddenly arrived carrying a basket on their shoulders. Some American reporters were convinced that it contained the corpse and took countless shots of it. But, just as quickly, the basket was ordered back into the street to make way for the gold-plated casket with a plush lining of white satin. Some of the more curious opened it. We saw a costly white tapestry, a soft pillow, and a kind of thin mattress of the same whiteness, with fringes of silver braid.

It contained not a single religious artifact.

Then the door leading to the first-aid room was opened. Passing through it we saw our friend, Dr. Carlos Zuloaga. We knew that yesterday he was in attendance and that, therefore, he was bound to know something about the death of Trotsky. We approached him and, after cornering him in the physicians' room, we got him to speak.

Indeed, he was among those who saw Trotsky die. He told us that "as early as 5:00 P.M., when Dr. Mass realized that there was flooding of the cerebral ventricles, he recommended that we not leave the patient, even for a moment. It was then that we began to inject Coramine directly into the heart. Plus adrenaline and many other substances, but the patient was already feverish and that was proof that blood poisoning had already set in.

"We did not leave the patient's side for a moment. His wife was constantly asking us to inform her of her husband's condition. As is only understandable, we gave her words of consolation.

"Dr. Lenero arrived and Dr. Mass returned to the sickroom. Dr. Roberto Méndez also arrived and took charge of administering the anesthesia during surgery. Gradually the minutes slipped by, and the patient's heart ceased to beat.

"The medical efforts were intensified, but without result. At 7:25 P.M. sharp, he was gone. Those present were the persons I have already mentioned, as well as Trotsky's wife, who was napping on a green sofa, three of their attendants, and a woman who was not known to me. The death occurred peacefully. There was no death rattle, no painful moaning, absolutely nothing. Now you will see the body, and you will realize that I am telling the truth. He looks as if he's sleeping."

Finally, at 9:30 P.M., two long hours after Trotsky died, we were told that we would be permitted to view his body. We milled about at the door. We all wanted to be the first to go in. Once again we were halted and had to wait more than three-quarters of an hour while Ignacio Asúnsulo fashioned the death mask.

Then the wait was over. General Núñez guided us to where the body of Trotsky lay. Socorrito Zapata, head nurse of the Green Cross, was at work cleaning the face, to which bits of plaster still clung.

It was as though Trotsky slept. His face was pallid; his gray beard and mustache were neatly trimmed. A bandage had been fastened around his head to conceal the wound, and through it a stray drop of blood oozed. His body was clad in gray pajamas with dark stripes.

A number of chairs had been placed at the head of the bed. Two of them were occupied by the widow and by Joseph Hansen, who held her in his arms, trying to assuage her intense inner pain. The woman's face was free from any grimace of grief. Her gaze, fixed upon her husband's body, seemed to yearn for kinder days, when they did not have to suffer persecutions. In her clasped hands she held a handkerchief. Another chair was occupied by a girl who looked American, quite shockingly dressed, with her legs crossed and wearing bobby sox that clashed with the solemnity of the occasion. Two police officers and two of Trotsky's bodyguards rounded out the complement of persons in this room, which measured less than five square meters.

We turned back to speak with Trotsky's widow, but we did not stop. We understood that she was both very close to and very far from the scene. Her grief was intense, but, as an educated woman and one accustomed to such grief, she did not show it in the way that other women would.

General Núñez indicated that many others were awaiting our departure so that they in turn could enter the room.

A stenographer was busy transcribing some statements earlier dictated by Hansen, who had been Trotsky's private secretary. Now and then she wept. She wore a small black hat with a red feather that reminds us of her ideology.

We returned to the street, where there were hundreds of people, all anxious to enter the death chamber. All of them tried to question us, but the atmosphere of deep mourning had rendered us almost gruff. We left those curious people and hurried to the car waiting to take us back to *Novedades*.

Just last night the funeral parlor was made ready in one of the leading undertaking establishments in Tacuba. To the embalming room of that establishment will proceed the team of medical examiners. Even in its final moments of repose among the living, the body of Leon Trotsky will not be required to lie alongside those unfortunates who lacked influence or the money to pay the doctors who performed their autopsies.

The first visit to the bier was made by his secretaries, who in turn were followed in this order: his servants, the adjutants of the president of Mexico, General Núñez and high-ranking police chiefs, all of the commandants of the police force, and those sympathizers and friends of Leon Trotsky.

The president of Mexico, General Lázaro Cárdenas, is following very closely the case of the Russian refugee, Leon Trotsky, victim of this terrible assassination.

Leon Trotsky's body was cremated and his ashes "given to the sea." The assassin, whose real name was never established, was arrested immediately. The man, whom Trotsky had accepted as a disciple, gave a statement to police saying he had asked Trotsky to read an article. As the old man began to read, the assassin said, "I took the axe out of my raincoat, took it in my fist, and, closing my eyes, I gave him a tremendous blow....The man screamed in such a way." First identified as Frank Jackson, alias Jacques Vandendreischd, he was put on trial and sentenced to twenty years in prison under the name Jacques Mornard. He claimed to be a Belgian and to have entered Mexico on a forged Canadian passport. The generally accepted theory is that he was a Spanish communist named Ramon Mercader del Rio. When his prison term ended in 1960, he was whisked away by Czech officials and reunited with his girlfriend, Rogelia Mendoza. Mercader died of cancer in 1978 in Havana.

Kennedy assassination: "We have suffered a loss that cannot be weighed"

Merriman Smith, veteran White House reporter for United Press International, was foresighted to sit beside the telephone in the front seat of the wire-service car behind the presidential car in the November 22, 1963 motorcade through Dallas. This enabled him to beat Associated Press reporter Jack Bell with the initial bulletins on the assassination. Smith won a Pulitzer Prize for his coverage. The following story by Smith appeared in newspapers throughout the world on November 24.

It was a balmy, sunny noon as we motored through downtown Dallas behind President Kennedy. The procession cleared the center of the business district and turned into a handsome highway that wound through what appeared to be a park.

I was riding in the so-called White House press "pool" car, a telephone-company vehicle equipped with a mobile radio-telephone. I was in the front seat between a driver from the telephone company and Malcolm Kilduff, acting White House press secretary for the president's Texas tour. Three other pool reporters were wedged in the back seat.

Suddenly we heard three loud—almost painfully loud—cracks. The first sounded as if it might have been a large firecracker. But the second and third blasts were unmistakable. Gunfire.

The president's car, possibly as much as 150 or 200 yards ahead, seemed to falter briefly. We saw a flurry of activity in the Secret Service follow-up car behind the chief executive's bubble-top limousine.

Next in line was the car bearing Vice President Lyndon B. Johnson. Behind that, another follow-up car bearing agents assigned to the vice president's protection. We were behind that car.

Our car stood still for probably only a few seconds, but it seemed like a lifetime. One sees history explode before one's eyes, and, for even the most trained observer, there is a limit to what one can comprehend.

I looked ahead at the president's car but could not see him or his companion, Gov. John B. Connally of Texas. Both men had been riding on the right side of the bubble-top limousine from Washington. I thought I saw a flash of pink that would have been Mrs. Jacqueline Kennedy.

Everybody in our car began shouting at the driver to pull up closer to the president's car. But at this moment, we saw the big bubble-top and a motorcycle escort roar away at high speed.

We screamed at our driver, "Get going, get going." We careened around the Johnson car and its escort and set out down the highway, barely able to keep in sight of the president's car and the accompanying Secret Service follow-up car.

They vanished around a curve. When we cleared the same curve, we could see where we were heading—Parkland Hospital, a large brick structure to the left of the arterial highway. We skidded around a sharp left turn and spilled out of the pool car as it entered the hospital driveway.

I ran to the side of the bubble-top.

The president was face down on the back seat. Mrs. Kennedy made a cradle of her arms around the president's head and bent over him as if she were whispering to him.

Governor Connally was on his back on the floor of the car, his head and shoulders resting in the arms of his wife, Nellie, who kept shaking her head and shaking with dry sobs. Blood oozed from the front of the governor's suit. I could not see the president's wound. But I could see blood spattered around the interior of the rear seat and a dark stain spreading down the right side of the president's dark gray suit.

From the telephone car, I had radioed the Dallas bureau of UPI that three shots had been fired at the Kennedy motorcade. Seeing the bloody scene in the rear of the car at the hospital entrance, I knew I had to get to a telephone immediately.

Clint Hill, the Secret Service agent in charge of the detail assigned to Mrs. Kennedy, was leaning over into the rear of the car.

"How badly was he hit, Clint?" I asked.

"He's dead," Hill replied curtly.

I have no further clear memory of the scene in the driveway. I recall a babble of anxious voices, tense voices—"Where in hell are the stretchers?...Get a doctor out here....He's on the way....Come on, easy there." And from somewhere, nervous sobbing.

I raced down a short stretch of sidewalk into a hospital corridor. The first thing I spotted was a small clerical office, more of a booth than an office. Inside, a bespectacled man stood shuffling what appeared to be hospital forms. At a wicket much like a bank teller's cage, I spotted a telephone on the shelf.

"How do you get outside?" I gasped. "The president has been hurt, and this is an emergency call."

"Dial nine," he said, shoving the phone toward me.

It took two tries before I successfully dialed the Dallas UPI number. Quickly I dictated a bulletin saying the president had been seriously, perhaps fatally, injured by an assassin's bullets while driving through the streets of Dallas.

Litters bearing the president and the governor rolled by me as I dictated, but my back was to the hallway, and I didn't see them until they were at the entrance of the emergency room about seventy-five or a hundred feet away.

I knew they had passed, however, from the horrified expression that suddenly spread over the face of the man behind the wicket.

As I stood in the drab buff hallway leading into the emergency ward trying to reconstruct the shooting for the UPI man on the other end of the telephone and still keep track of what was happening outside the door of the emergency room, I watched a swift and confused panorama sweep before me.

Kilduff of the White House press staff raced up and down the hall. Police captains barked at each other, "Clear this area." Two priests hurried in behind a Secret Service agent, their narrow purple stoles rolled up tightly in their hands. A police lieutenant ran down the hall with a large carton of blood for transfusions. A doctor came in and said he was responding to a call for "all neurosurgeons."

Murder Most Foul

The priests came out and said the president had received the last sacrament of the Roman Catholic Church. They said he was still alive, but not conscious. Members of the Kennedy staff began arriving. They had been behind us in the motorcade, but hopelessly bogged for a time in confused traffic.

Telephones were at a premium in the hospital, and I clung to mine for dear life. I was afraid to stray from the wicket lest I lose contact with the outside world.

My decision was made for me, however, when Kilduff and Wayne Hawks of the White House staff ran by me, shouting that Kilduff would make a statement shortly in the so-called nurses room a floor above and at the far end of the hospital.

I threw down the phone and sped after them. We reached the door of the conference room, and there were loud cries of "Quiet!" Fighting to keep his emotions under control, Kilduff said, "President John Fitzgerald Kennedy died at approximately one o'clock."

I raced into a nearby office. The telephone switchboard at the hospital was hopelessly jammed. I spotted Virginia Payette, wife of UPI's Southwestern division manager and a veteran reporter in her own right. I told her to try getting through on pay phones on the floor above.

Frustrated by the inability to get through the hospital switchboard, I appealed to a nurse. She led me through a maze of corridors and back stairways to another floor and a lone pay booth. I got the Dallas office. Virginia had gotten through before me.

Whereupon I ran back through the hospital to the conference room. There Jiggs Fauver of the White House transportation staff grabbed me and said Kilduff wanted a pool of three men immediately to fly back to Washington on Air Force One, the presidential aircraft.

"He wants you downstairs, and he wants you right now," Fauver said.

Down the stairs I ran and into the driveway, only to discover Kilduff had just pulled out in our telephone car.

Charles Roberts of *Newsweek* magazine, Sid Davis of Westinghouse Broadcasting, and I implored a police officer to take us to the airport in his squad car. The Secret Service had requested that no sirens be used in the vicinity of the airport, but the Dallas officer did a masterful job of getting us through some of the worst traffic I've ever seen.

As we piled out of the car on the edge of the runway about 200 yards from the presidential aircraft, Kilduff spotted us and motioned for us to hurry. We trotted to him, and he said the plane could take two pool men to Washington, that Johnson was about to take the oath of office aboard the plane and would take off immediately thereafter.

I saw a bank of telephone booths beside the runway and asked if I had time to advise my news service. He said, "But for God's sake, hurry."

Then began another telephone nightmare. The Dallas office rang busy. I tried calling Washington. All circuits were busy. Then I called the New York bureau of UPI and told them about the impending installation of a new president aboard the airplane.

Kilduff came out of the plane and motioned wildly toward my booth. I slammed down the phone and jogged across the runway. A detective stopped me and said, "You dropped your pocket comb."

Aboard Air Force One, on which I had made so many trips as a press association reporter covering President Kennedy, all the shades of the larger main cabin were drawn and the interior was hot and dimly lighted.

Kilduff propelled us to the president's suite two-thirds of the way back in the plane. The room is used normally as a combination conference and sitting room and could accommodate eight to ten persons seated.

I wedged inside the door and began counting. There were twenty-seven people in this compartment. Johnson stood in the center with his wife, Lady Bird. U.S. District Judge Sarah T. Hughes, 67, a kindly faced woman, stood with a small black Bible in her hands, waiting to give the oath.

The compartment became hotter and hotter. Johnson was worried that some of the Kennedy staff might not be able to get inside. He urged people to press forward, but a Signal Corps photographer, Capt. Cecil Stoughton, standing in the corner on a chair, said if Johnson moved any closer, it would be virtually impossible to make a truly historic photograph.

It developed that Johnson was waiting for Mrs. Kennedy, who was composing herself in a small bedroom in the rear of the plane. She appeared alone, dressed in the same pink wool suit she had worn in the morning when she appeared so happy shaking hands with airport crowds at the side of her husband.

She was white-faced but dry-eyed. Friendly hands stretched toward her as she stumbled slightly. Johnson took both of her hands in his and motioned her to his left side. Lady Bird stood on his right, a fixed half-smile showing the tension.

Johnson nodded to Judge Hughes, an old friend of his family and a Kennedy appointee.

"Hold up your right hand and repeat after me," the woman jurist said to Johnson.

Outside a jet could be heard droning into a landing.

Judge Hughes held out the Bible, and Johnson covered it with his large left hand. His right arm went slowly into the air, and the jurist began to intone the constitutional oath, "I do solemnly swear I will faithfully execute the office of president of the United States...."

The brief ceremony ended when Johnson, in a deep, firm voice, repeated after the judge, "...and so help me God."

Johnson turned first to his wife, hugged her about the shoulders, and kissed her on the cheek. Then he turned to Kennedy's widow, put his left arm around her, and kissed her cheek.

As others in the group—some Texas Democratic House members, members of the Johnson and Kennedy staffs—moved toward the new president, he seemed to back away from any expression of felicitation.

The two-minute ceremony concluded at 3:38 P.M. Eastern Standard Time, and seconds later, the president said firmly, "Now, let's get airborne."

Col. James Swindal, pilot of the plane, a big gleaming silver and blue fan-jet, cut on the starboard engines immediately. Several persons, including Sid Davis of Westinghouse, left the plane at that time. The White House had room for only two pool reporters on the return flight, and these posts were filled by Roberts and me, although at the moment we could find no empty seats.

At 3:47 P.M. EST, the wheels of Air Force One cleared the runway. Swindal roared the big ship up to an unusually high cruising altitude of 41,000 feet, where at 625 miles an hour, ground speed, the jet hurtled toward Andrews Air Force Base outside Washington.

When the president's plane reached operating altitude, Mrs. Kennedy left her bedchamber and walked to the rear compartment of the plane. This was the so-called family living room, a private area where she and Kennedy, family, and friends had spent many happy airborne hours chatting and dining.

Kennedy's casket had been placed in this compartment, carried aboard by a group of Secret Service agents.

Mrs. Kennedy went into the rear lounge and took a chair beside the coffin. There she remained throughout the flight. Her vigil was shared at times by four staff members close to the slain chief executive—David Powers, his buddy and personal assistant; Kenneth P. O'Donnell, appointments secretary and key political adviser; Lawrence O'Brien, chief Kennedy liaison man with Congress, and Brig. Gen. Godfrey McHugh, Kennedy's Air Force aide.

Kennedy's military aide, Maj. Gen. Chester V. Clifton, was busy most of the trip in the forward areas of the plane, sending messages and making arrangements for arrival ceremonies and movement of the body to Bethesda Naval Hospital.

As the flight progressed, Johnson walked back into the main compartment. My portable typewriter was lost somewhere around the hospital, and I was writing on an oversized electric typewriter that Kennedy's personal secretary, Mrs. Evelyn Lincoln, had used to type his speech texts.

Johnson came up to the table where Roberts and I were trying to record the history we had just witnessed.

"I'm going to make a short statement in a few minutes and give you copies of it," he said. "Then when I get on the ground, I'll do it over again."

It was the first public utterance of the new chief executive, brief and moving:

"This is a sad time for all people. We have suffered a loss that cannot be weighed. For me it is a deep personal tragedy. I know the world shares the sorrow that Mrs. Kennedy and her family bear. I will do my best. That is all I can do. I ask for your help—and God's."

When the plane was about forty-five minutes from Washington, the new president got on a special radio-telephone and placed a call to Mrs. Rose Kennedy, the late president's mother.

"I wish to God there was something I could do," he told her. "I just wanted you to know that."

Then Mrs. Johnson wanted to talk to the elder Mrs. Kennedy.

"We feel like the heart has been cut out of us," Mrs. Johnson said. She broke down for a moment and began to sob. Recovering in a few seconds, she added, "Our love and our prayers are with you."

Thirty minutes out of Washington, Johnson put in a call for Nellie Connally, wife of the seriously wounded Texas governor.

The new president said to the governor's wife:

"We are praying for you, darling, and I know that everything is going to be all right, isn't it? Give him a hug and a kiss for me."

It was dark when Air Force One began to skim over the lights of the Washington area, lining up for a landing at Andrews Air Force Base. The plane touched down at 5:59 P.M.

I thanked the stewards for rigging up the typewriter for me, pulled on my raincoat, and started down the forward ramp. Roberts and I stood under a wing and watched the casket being lowered from the rear of the plane and borne by a complement of armed forces body-bearers into a waiting hearse. We watched Mrs. Kennedy and the president's brother, Atty. Gen. Robert F. Kennedy, climb into the hearse beside the coffin.

The new president repeated his first public statement for broadcast and newsreel microphones, shook hands with some of the government and diplomatic leaders who turned out to meet the plane, and headed for his helicopter.

Roberts and I were given seats on another 'copter bound for the White House lawn. In the compartment next to ours in one of the large chairs beside a window sat Theodore C. Sorensen, one of

Kennedy's closest associates with the title of special counsel to the president. He had not gone to Texas with his chief but had come to the air base for his return.

Sorensen sat wilted in the large chair, crying softly. The dignity of his deep grief seemed to sum up all the tragedy and sadness of the previous six hours.

As our helicopter circled in the balmy darkness for a landing on the White House south lawn, it seemed incredible that only six hours before, John Fitzgerald Kennedy had been a vibrant, smiling, waving, and active man.

Lee Harvey Oswald was arrested swiftly and identified as the assassin. Two days later, as police were moving him to the county jail for more protection, nightclub owner Jack Ruby fatally shot him—the first nationally televised murder. Ruby was convicted and sentenced to death, but died of cancer before his appeals were exhausted.

White sniper cuts down Dr. Martin Luther King on Memphis hotel balcony

James Earl Ray reportedly told a fellow inmate at the Missouri Penitentiary in 1964 that there was a bounty on Dr. Martin Luther King, Jr. and said, as if talking directly to the civil-rights leader, "You are my big one, and one day I will collect all that money on your ass, nigger, for you are my retirement plan." The other inmate, Raymond Curtis, related the story to George McMillan, who recorded it in the book on Ray, *The Making of an Assassin* (Little, Brown, 1976). On April 23, 1967, Ray, who had been serving a sentence for petty theft, escaped from the penitentiary and, according to McMillan, told his brothers the next day in Chicago, "I'm gonna kill that nigger King." Almost a year later, on April 4, 1968, Dr. King was slain in Memphis. John Means wrote the following account of the assassination for the *Memphis Commercial Appeal* of April 5.

A sniper shot and killed Dr. Martin Luther King, Jr. Thursday night as he stood on the balcony of a downtown hotel.

The most intensive manhunt in the city's history was touched off minutes after the shooting.

Violence broke out in Memphis, Nashville, Birmingham, Miami, Raleigh, Washington, New York, and other cities as news of the assassination swept the nation.

National leaders, including President Lyndon B. Johnson, and aides close to the slain thirty-nine-year-old Nobel Peace Prize winner urged the nation to stand calm and avoid violence.

The entire nation was tense.

All 11,000 Tennessee National Guardsmen were on alert early Friday.

Mayor Henry Loeb placed Memphis under a tight curfew until

5:00 A.M. All schools were closed Friday. Parents were urged to keep their children at home.

A rifle bullet slammed into Dr. King's jaw and neck at 6:01 P.M. Thursday. He died in the emergency room at St. Joseph Hospital at 7:05 P.M.

Dr. King, the foremost American civil-rights leader, was alone on the second-floor walk of the Lorraine Hotel, 406 Mulberry, when the bullet struck.

A young white man was believed to have fired the fatal shot from a nearby building.

Looters and vandals roamed the streets despite the curfew. Shooting was widespread. National Guardsmen were rushed to the North Memphis area of Springdale and Howell after bullets blasted the windshield from a police car near there.

Police, estimated at more than 150, descended on the South Memphis hotel, sealed off the area, and almost immediately broadcast a description of the sniper—a white male, 30 to 32 years old, 5 feet 10 inches tall, about 165 pounds, dark to sandy hair, medium build, ruddy complexion as if he worked outside, wearing a black suit and white shirt.

Dr. King returned to Memphis Wednesday morning to map plans for another downtown march, scheduled for Monday, in support of the city's striking sanitation workers.

He had spent part of the day Thursday awaiting reports from his attorneys, who were in federal court asking that a temporary restraining order against the proposed march be lifted.

The injunction was obtained by the city after Dr. King's first march last week broke into violence downtown, brought the National Guard to the city in strength, and seriously damaged the Negro leader's reputation for nonviolence. For the first time in his career, he had been present during violence, and it was this picture he was planning to dispel with the march Monday.

Mayor Loeb declared Friday, Saturday, and Sunday days of mourning, and said all flags in the city would be lowered "with appropriate observances."

All ministers, priests, and rabbis in the Memphis area were asked to meet at 10:00 A.M. Friday at St. Mary's Cathedral (Episcopal).

Murder Most Foul

Frank Holloman, fire and police director, who took personal command of the murder investigation minutes after the shooting, said "every resource" of city, county, state, and federal law enforcement agencies "is committed and dedicated to identifying and apprehending the person or persons responsible."

Mayor Loeb ordered a curfew, much stricter than the one imposed after last week's rioting. "All movement is restricted except for health or emergency reasons," the order said.

A few minutes after the shooting, police reported a high-speed chase in which a blue Pontiac was being pursued by a white Mustang out the Austin Peay Highway. Shots were reported fired between the two cars. A white Mustang, seen near the scene of the slaying, was still being sought by police early Friday.

Officials of Dr. King's Southern Christian Leadership Conference (SCLC), some of whom were standing near him on the narrow balcony of the hotel when he was shot, continued to urge his nonviolent teachings. His chief lieutenant, Dr. Ralph D. Abernathy, went to the Mason Temple Thursday night to address a gathering of Dr. King's followers.

"Let us live for what he died for," Dr. Abernathy told the mourning group. "If we respect his leadership, if we appreciate the service that he rendered, then we must do all in our power to carry forth the work that is incomplete.

"If a riot or violence would erupt in Memphis tonight, Dr. King in heaven would not be pleased."

A few had other ideas. "He died for us, and we're going to die for him," a young man shouted.

Early Friday morning, Holloman said police believed the murder weapon was a .30-caliber, pump-action Remington rifle equipped with a telescope sight. Such a weapon was among those stolen Tuesday night from Dowdle Sporting Goods Company, 2896 Walnut Grove Road.

"The distance the bullet traveled before it struck Dr. King was 205 feet, 3 inches, at a down angle," Holloman said.

He also detailed other evidence that may help identify the assassin: The shot was fired from the window of a common bathroom at the end of the hall on the east side of the building at 420 South Main. The suspect checked into the boarding house between 3:00 and 3:30 P.M. His room was close to the bathroom.

"We do know he bought a pair of binoculars Thursday afternoon in Memphis....The man was seen to run from the 420 South Main building and discard the gun and a suitcase at 424 South Main. He simply faded. Nobody saw him get into the car, but a white Mustang was seen fleeing the area.

"The evidence we now have indicates that only one man was physically in the area (the bathroom)."

Holloman would not reveal where the binoculars had been purchased and said he did not know if the name used by the sniper is his real one.

The rifle found at the Main Street address was turned over to the FBI for ballistics tests. Holloman said his office is "working closely with the FBI" on other aspects of the investigation.

He added that the investigation was "impaired by the riot situation that developed almost immediately."

Holloman said he had assigned about forty officers to protect Dr. King, though none of the SCLC officials had asked for protection for their leader. Some of these officers had been nearby ever since Dr. King returned to Memphis, and some were "within a few yards of him" when he was shot.

The Rev. Jesse L. Jackson, who was with Dr. King in the hotel room, said Dr. King had walked out of the room, ahead of several friends, onto the balcony that led to exit stairs. He was on his way to a dinner engagement.

"The bullet knocked him off his feet," said Mr. Jackson, an executive staff member of SCLC. "It sounded like a stick of dynamite, or a big firecracker."

Mr. Jackson said police "came from everywhere" after the shooting. He estimated there were 150 officers on the scene within seconds, but "it was similar to the Kennedy incident (the assassination of President Kennedy). The police were all around, but there is no military protection against an ambush, and he (Dr. King) was ambushed."

Dr. King's last words were in reply to his chauffeur, Solomon Jones, Jr., on the street below.

"I went out to start the car," Jones said. "Dr. King was on the porch. I yelled up at him it was cool out, you better put your topcoat on. Dr. King said, 'O.K., I will.' He smiled, and then I heard the shot.

"He just fell back. I turned around and saw a man jump out of the thicket across the street. He ran toward Main. We all scattered.

"I got to the fire escape and climbed up to Dr. King's balcony. There was a white man there. I don't know who he was, but they said he lived at the hotel. Dr. King looked dead. The white man covered his face with a cloth."

Moments before, Dr. King had been talking to Ben Branch, a singer and bandleader who was to appear with him at the Mason Temple rally.

"I want you to sing for me tonight," the world's youngest Nobel Peace Prize winner said. "I want you to do that song for me, 'Precious Lord.' Sing it real pretty."

The slain leader's wife, Coretta, remained in Atlanta Thursday night. Told by telephone that her husband had been shot, she was awaiting a plane to Memphis when she was notified that the wound had been fatal.

Dr. King was bleeding profusely from a huge wound in the jaw and neck area as he lay face down on the concrete walkway of the hotel.

About forty Negro men and women heard the announcement from the emergency room shortly after 7:00 P.M. The women began to cry, and the men began exclaiming:

"Dr. King is dead. He'll have to be buried. We gotta do something about it. Do you hear?"

Two men inside the Canipe Amusement Company, 424 South Main, said they saw a man racing from the scene in a white Mustang. Bernell Finley and Julius Graham said they heard "a thump" outside and looked out.

David Wood, 25, of 3639 Townes, was drinking beer at Jim's Grill next door to the amusement company. He saw the Mustang parked in front of the cafe.

"The car had no front tag and no inspection sticker, so it must have been from out of state," said Wood.

Six others corroborated Wood's account. They had been drinking beer in the grill for an hour.

Lloyd Jowers, owner of the grill, said the Mustang was parked in front of his white Cadillac. He also said he felt he would have known if anyone had rented a room in the last few days at 418½ South Main, over the cafe. He identified the owner of the rooming area as C. L. Short and the manager as Charles Stevens. The rooms were blocked off by police.

Ironically, Dr. King had chosen the hotel where he was shot because it was operated by Negroes, spurning the more secluded Holiday Inn-Rivermont, where he was quartered last week.

He had reported threats on his life after last week's march, but "these reports did not bother him," said the Rev. Andrew Young, executive director of SCLC. Dr. King often joked with newsmen that his schedule depended on whether he lived long enough to fill it.

Beaten several times, he was stabbed in 1958 by a Negro woman in a Harlem bookstore, and almost died. His home was once booby-trapped with a dynamite bomb, and another house where he was staying was sprayed with rifle bullets.

He came to Memphis in 1965 for another march, the completion of the one begun by James Meredith, who was gunned down by a Memphian near Hernando, Mississippi as he walked down U.S. 51 on his way to Jackson. Meredith was not seriously hurt.

The man who made "We Shall Overcome" a national anthem to millions of Negroes now joins a growing list of their martyrs, including Medgar Evers and Vernon Dahmer, civil-rights leaders who died violently. Evers, too, was the victim of a sniper's bullet, and Dahmer was burned to death in his fire-bombed home in Hattiesburg, Mississippi.

Dr. King's nonviolent-protest policy earned him numerous comparisons to Mohandas (Mahatma) Gandhi, the Indian religious leader who used nonviolence to break the back of the British Empire in India. Gandhi, too, was the victim of an assassin, in 1948.

In Washington, the leaders of the union whose attempts to organize Memphis' sanitation workers brought Dr. King here said the union will march Monday in his honor.

Jerry Wurf, president, and Joseph L. Ames, secretary-treasurer of the American Federation of State, County and

Murder Most Foul

Municipal Employees, called on Mayor Loeb "to provide conditions of safety for the men and women who march in this tribute to our martyred leader."

Ray was arrested at London's Heathrow Airport on June 8, 1968, returned to the United States, and promptly pleaded guilty to the murder. Although authorities contend that Ray acted alone, there are widespread doubts that he could have assassinated Dr. King without help. In the fourteen months between his escape from the Missouri Penitentiary and his capture, Ray travelled widely — from Acapulco to Montreal, from London to Lisbon. Where did he get the money? And how could he, a small-time thief, have acquired phony identification, including passports, under credible aliases? A 1976 Harris Poll showed that sixty per cent of the population believed that the assassination must have been a conspiracy. However, author McMillan, who spent seven years researching *The Making of an Assassin,* concluded that Ray could have acted alone. Ray, according to McMillan, was given $4,700 by his brothers in Chicago the day after his escape and later was given another $1,500 by one of the brothers. Ray earned another $500 as a laborer. It was enough, in all, to finance the travels, and McMillan points out that Ray committed a holdup in England just before his arrest—leading to the conclusion that no one was financing him then. The motive of a lone killer then may simply have been racism. McMillan quotes Walter Rife, a frequent drinking companion of Ray, as saying, "He was unreasonable in his hatred for niggers. He hated to see them breathe."

Index

Index

343

Index

Index

Index